THE WORLD OF ARCHAEOLOGY
General Editor: GLYN DANIEL

Barrow, Pyramid and Tomb

LESLIE V. GRINSELL

Barrow, Pyramid and Tomb

Ancient burial customs in Egypt, the Mediterranean and the British Isles

with 150 illustrations

 THAMES AND HUDSON · LONDON

Printed and bound in Great Britain
by Jarrold and Sons Ltd, Norwich

ISBN 0 500 78004 8 Hardcover
ISBN 0 500 79004 3 Paperback

Contents

Preface

This work has resulted from some forty-five years' study of the funerary archaeology of Egypt, the Mediterranean, parts of the European continent, and the British Isles, both at first hand and through the literature.

Part One is devoted to showing the prevalence in space and time of most of the topics treated: the concept of the tomb as a house for the dead; the varying methods of disposing of the body; human and animal sacrifice; the offering of food and other objects (and their substitutes) to the dead; the ceremonial 'killing' of grave-goods; the character of the funerary ritual; beliefs concerning the journey to the after-life; the later use of the tombs of the great as places of assembly; and methods of coping with the tomb robber. If there had been space to deal with an even larger area, the universality of these concepts would be even clearer.

During the last few decades one of the chief 'models' in European archaeology has been to try to 'derive' everything from some supposed place of origin usually farther east or southeast. It was difficult to consider a British megalithic tomb without discussing whether the type originated in France or the Iberian peninsula or the western Mediterranean; and it was not easy to report a boat-shaped dug-out coffin from Bronze Age Britain without bringing in the solar boats of Ancient Egypt. This hypothesis has been the subject of much criticism during the last twenty years. Much of the subject matter of funerary archaeology shows that similar necessities have given rise to similar inventions. Any reader hoping to find out when and where they originated is unlikely to find the answers in this book. Instead, it is hoped that the reader specializing in the tombs of one period or region may here find useful comparative material.

With regard to chronology, the writer has expressed dates before 1000 BC (other than those from Egypt and the eastern Mediterranean which follow their accepted chronology) approximately as bristle-cone pine calibrated C14 dates given to the nearest century. These dates are given to provide chronological perspective and not to support diffusionist or other theories (Renfrew 1973).

Part Two is concerned with the author's favourite tomb-groups – the Egyptian pyramids; the royal tombs in the Valley of the Kings at Thebes; the Mycenaean tholos tombs; the great necropolis at Salamis in Cyprus; the Etruscan cemeteries at Tarquinia and Cerveteri; the rock-cut tombs and Giants' Tombs of Sardinia and the megalithic tombs of Corsica; the sepulchral caves and navetas of the Balearic Islands; the megalithic tombs of the Channel Islands; the Severn-Cotswold chamber tombs of southwestern Britain; the Wessex round barrows and the cairns and stone rows of Dartmoor; the cruciform passage-graves of the British Isles; and the cairns of the Kilmartin area. Everything described in detail has been seen by the author with the exception of the Treasury of Minyas at Orchomenos and tomb 80 at Salamis.

Some tomb groups which the author knows have had to be excluded for various reasons. The Egyptian private tombs were omitted (with great regret) to avoid giving a disproportionate amount of space to Egypt for which there is already abundant literature; Sicily, because the author has seen the great cemetery at Pantalica only on a casual visit and knows little about the other tombs; Malta, as there is scarcely enough material for a chapter; the Netherlands and Denmark, on account of lack of space.

Areas omitted because the author has not yet visited them include the all-important megalithic areas of the Iberian peninsula and France, but these are covered by other accessible literature. Nearly all the sites described were visited by the author between 1958 and 1973 and (with the exception of those in the United Kingdom) on package-tours which to some extent determined the areas visited. The author's preference for Mediterranean islands is evident in the choice made and the tours were nearly all done as archaeological holidays.

Acknowledgments

For criticism of sections in draft the author is grateful to Dr Jonathan Musgrave (treatment of the body), Mr Martin R. Davies (Valley of the Kings), Dr Warwick Bray and Mrs M. Guido (Sardinia), Dr J.J. Renouf (Jersey), and Dr Michael Herity (Irish passage-graves). The author was accompanied by Mr Roger Howell (Athens) in Messenia; Prof. G. Peretti (Sartène) in Corsica; J. Mascaró Pasarius (Palma) and the late Sta. M.L. Serra (Mahon) in Marjorca and Minorca, the last three of whom also provided transport to sites often difficult of access. Assistance in matters of detail was kindly given by Prof. Richard Atkinson (Cardiff), Dr Keith Branigan (Bristol), Miss Frances Lynch (Bangor), Dr J. Malek (Griffith Institute, Oxford), Dr Kenneth Oakley (Oxford), and Lady Frederica Rose (Ajaccio). For the errors remaining the author is alone responsible. The research was mostly done in Bristol University Library, the London Library, the Society of Antiquaries, London, and the Ashmolean at Oxford; during field trips use was made of libraries in Cairo, Luxor, Nicosia, Athens, Mahon, and Palma, to the staff of which the author offers his best thanks. He is grateful to Prof. Glyn Daniel for the invitation to prepare this work, and to the staff of Thames and Hudson Ltd for their help in seeing it through the press.

Photographic Acknowledgments

Photographs not listed were kindly supplied by the author or are from originals in Thames and Hudson archives. Those used for the undermentioned illustrations are reproduced courtesy of: the Royal Scottish Museum (photo Tom Scott), 1, 28; Sopraintendenza Antichità, Florence, 3; Landesmuseum für Vorgeschichte, Halle/Saale, 4; Museum of Western Pomerania, Szczecin, 5; Archeologické rozhledy, 6; Pigorini Museum, Rome, 7; Mårten Stenberger, 9; Biological-Archaeological Institute, University of Groningen, 12; Binger Mörner Collection (photo Limmé), 13; National Museum, Copenhagen, 15; National Archaeological Museum, Athens, 16, 26; Gregorian Etruscan Museum, the Vatican (photo Alinari), 17; *Illustrated London News*, 18; British Museum, 19, 45; Egypt Exploration Society, 20; Lord Taylour, 21; Vassos Karageorghis, 23; Netherlands Institute for the Near East (photo W. B. Emery), 25; Metropolitan Museum of Art, New York, 29; Department of Antiquities, Ashmolean Museum, Oxford, 30, 137; Archaeological Museum, Florence (photo H. Hencken) 31; Archaeological Museum, Florence, 33; Villa Giulia Museum, Rome (photo H. Hencken), 34; Lavigerie Museum, 32; National Archaeological Museum, Madrid, 35; City and County Museum, Lincoln (photo H. N. Hawley), 36; Barbican House Museum, Sussex Archaeological Society (photo Edward Reeves), 37; Museum of Fine Arts, Boston, 38; Hirmer Fotoarchiv, 39, 46, 53, 90–1; Keller, 40; Archaeological Museum, Heraklion (photo Josephine Powell), 41; Archaeological Museum, Heraklion (photo Peter Clayton), 42–4; Statens Historiska Museum, Stockholm, 47, 50; Antivarisk-Topgrafiska Arkivei, Stockholm, 48–9; Department of Antiquities, Cairo, 51; Deutsches Archäologisches Institut, Athens, 54; Gaby, 56; Martin Davies, 61; J. Raftery, 62; Peter Clayton, 73, 143; J. R. Freeman, 74; A. F. Kersting, 76; Mansell Collection, 98–9; Villa Giulia Museum, Rome, 100; A. Akerstrom, 107; C. Zervos, 113; Dr Glyn Daniel, 126; Société Jersiaise, 127; Prof. J. K. St Joseph, 135; West Air Photography (photo John White), 139; James Dyer, 147.

PART ONE ANALYTICAL

Chapter One

The house for the dead

When the winter snow melted round the copings, her house fell down and killed old Lysidicĕ. Villagers who were her neighbours made as her sepulchre not a tomb of dug earth but the house itself. Antipater of Thessalonica, translated by A.S.F. Gow and, Sir D.L. Page. *The Greek Anthology* 1968, I, 53.

Occasions where a house was converted into a tomb for reasons such as that quoted above would have been most unusual. Careful excavation of certain tombs, especially later prehistoric barrows in western Europe, now and then reveals post-holes and other features which sometimes suggest conversion of a hut or house into a tomb. Such conversions may well have followed a death from an infectious disease and the consequent desertion of the hut by the rest of the family. The purpose of this chapter, however, is to demonstrate the extent to which the resting place of the dead has been modelled on the house of the living.

As early as the Mesolithic period, for which details of both hut foundations and graves are now available from several regions, the graves appear to reproduce the form of the huts (Piggott 1965, 29–35). Only a little later the 'Proto Lepenski Vir' levels at Lepenski Vir in the Danube valley (*c.* 6500 BC) include a ceremonial burial of a skeleton in a trapezoidal grave identical with the form of the houses of Lepenski Vir I (Srejović 1972, 118 and pl. 56).

Egypt

In Predynastic times, the change from circular huts to rectangular houses is reflected in the change in tomb plan from the circular to the rectangular pit (Brunton 1946, 201). From the Early Dynastic period the royal tomb was known as *per djet*, the house of eternity. The tomb of the first pharaoh of Dynasty I, Hor-aha, included a model estate. Several royal tombs of Dynasty II included a lavatory near the burial chamber. The 'palace façade' panelling of the enclosures of the Step Pyramids of Zoser and Sekhemkhet at Sakkara is most likely a reproduction of the façade of the royal residence. Some of the wooden coffins and stone sarcophagi of the Early Dynastic period and Old Kingdom are in the shape of a house with similar panelled exterior decoration. It has been noted that houses of this type survive in present-day Nubia (Badawy 1954*b*, 164 and fig. 107: 3). At Giza the sarcophagus of the builder of the Third Pyramid, Mycerinus, was carved with 'palace façade' decoration, and the tomb chambers of the pyramids of late Dynasty V and Dynasty VI, containing Pyramid Texts, have a panelled decoration finely executed on the alabaster-lined north, west, and south walls

9

surrounding the royal sarcophagus, perhaps reproducing a palace interior.

Most of the Old Kingdom mastaba tombs at Giza and Sakkara are built on the general principle of a superstructure containing a chapel whose walls are adorned with scenes of daily life, and a substructure containing the coffin or sarcophagus in a tomb chamber. The tomb chapels at Sakkara, including such well-known examples as those of Ty, Mereruka, and the joint tomb of Ptah-hotep and Akhet-hotep, provide a most comprehensive series of illustrations of the scenes of agriculture and pasture, handicrafts, and the market-place, as well as defaulters being brought to justice. Indeed these reliefs depict most of the environment which had been experienced during life, or at least those parts of it which one would wish to enjoy in the hereafter. The false doors of these mastabas have door drums (usually inscribed with the name of the dead) which imitate the rolled-up reed matting of the doors of the real house to exclude the glare from the sun.

1 Soul-house from a tomb at Rifa, Egypt. First Intermediate Period–Early Middle Kingdom. Dynasty XI. The practice of placing pottery soul-houses in tombs was common in Middle Egypt during this period

During the Middle Kingdom the rectangular wooden coffins are sometimes painted to represent a house with door and other details. Pottery soul-houses, often placed on top of tombs in Middle Egypt, usually have façades similar to those of contemporary tombs in their vicinity, as at Beni Hasan, where some have elaborate wrestling scenes which doubtless reflect the interests of their owners and seem to express the hope that such pleasures might continue in the after-life.

During the New Kingdom most of the royal tombs in the Valley of the Kings have their walls adorned with religious and funerary scenes and inscriptions. It is to the private tombs, especially those at Thebes, that we have to turn to study in their tomb chapels the abundant portrayals of scenes of daily life. Perhaps the widest range of activities is shown on the walls of the tomb of Rekhmire at Thebes.

The pyramid is exceptional in that it is *not* a reproduction of a house. In its earlier stepped form it probably symbolized a stairway to the sky, and in its final form it is believed to have symbolized the sun's rays.

Palestine

2 House-tomb sarcophagus with dog at the door, from Side, southern Turkey. (After Bean)

At Eynan, near the southern border of Lebanon, a large circular pit nearly 5 m in diameter, bordered by a circle of stones, 6·4 m in diameter, contained human burials including two complete skeletons. This structure, which was covered by stone slabs, is of the Natufian period (*c.* 8000–7000 B C) and resembles the circular hut-bases of the same period from the same locality (Perrot 1960; 1968).

In the Copper Age there are numerous deposits of human bones in pottery house-urns at Hederah, Azor, and elsewhere (Perrot 1961, 1–83). From Middle Bronze Age tombs at Jericho, where wooden furnishings were preserved by the presence of hydrocarbon gases, remains of beds, stools, and three-legged tables have survived, some showing Egyptian influence (Kenyon 1960, 463).

Cyprus

Of about eleven tombs excavated by J. R. B. Stewart in the Bronze Age cemetery at Karmi/Paleolona in 1962, two or three have panelled façades suggesting the exterior of a house.

Minoan Crete

It has been suggested that the circular tombs of the Mesara (*c.* 2800–1700 B C) may have been representations of circular dwellings, but no such dwellings of this date have yet been found in Crete, and the only evidence is provided by a lamp in the shape of a circular hut with windows from Lebena (Branigan 1970, 84). Foundations of a slightly earlier round house have, however, been identified at Phaestos (Hood 1971, 32, 153 note 9). In eastern Crete there are at this period both houses and tombs of rectangular plan.

Asia Minor

In the vicinity of Termessus, southern Turkey, some Hellenistic tombs are built in the form of wooden houses. In the necropolis at Side, southern Turkey, a sarcophagus in the form of a house with a double door has one door ajar with a dog looking out – 'the faithful guardian of the tomb as he formerly was of the house' (Bean 1968, 99, 133–5).

Villanovan and Etruscan Italy

The cremated bones of the richer pre-Etruscan Villanovans (early first millennium B C) were often placed in house-urns or hut-urns which show a roughly rectangular house with slightly overhanging

3 Villanovan hut-urn,
containing human cremation

gabled roof having a smoke-hole at each end. On one side is an opening often with a pottery door and the external walls are decorated schematically with windows (usually unpierced) and wall designs. The study of these hut-urns, many of which have come from the Vetulonia region, has contributed materially to our knowledge of contemporary domestic architecture.

The chamber tombs at Tarquinia have walls decorated with various scenes of daily life, including banqueting, music, and dancing; boxing, wrestling, running, disc-throwing, and chariot-racing; these and other scenes attempt to provide for the dead the permanent enjoyment in the hereafter of the pleasures which he had experienced during his lifetime. Only occasionally are funerary scenes included, mostly towards the end of the Etruscan period.

In some instances, as at Cerveteri, the cemeteries were laid out in imitation of a town plan, with streets, and other features, just as the tombs within them were copies of the houses inhabited by the living.

The many Etruscan tombs at Cerveteri, and rock tombs as at San Giuliano, Norchia and elsewhere in central Etruria, which reproduce either the exteriors or the interiors of houses, almost invariably simulate domestic architecture in wood. It is even possible to classify house-types from those copied in the tombs and Rosi (1927) has grouped them as follows:

(i)   houses with flat roof, characteristic of regions where snow seldom or never occurs, and where rapid changes of weather are rare

(ii) houses with gabled roof to facilitate the sliding of snow from the roof

(iii) the circular tumulus possibly reproducing the round house or hut which must have been common in many regions

Differences in the house-types of aristocracy and the lower classes, evidenced by both archaeological and literary sources, are reflected in tomb architecture. Thus the tomb of the Volumni at Perugia reproduces a Later Etruscan palace, while several tombs with flat ceilings at Cerveteri are copies of the houses of noble families of the sixth and fifth centuries BC (Boethius and Ward-Perkins 1970, 63–4, 71, 75). Tombs reproducing the houses of the lower classes occur often between the larger tombs.

The reproduction in stone of house interiors with their furnishings, which occurs only occasionally in the tombs at Tarquinia, becomes standard practice in many of those at Cerveteri. Among the best examples are the Tomb of the Alcove; the Tomb of the Ship; the Tomb of the Shields and Chairs; the Tomb of the Capitals; the Tomb of the Hut with the Thatched Roof; the Tomb of the Funerary Beds; and especially the Tomb of Painted Reliefs, in which an extensive range of utensils, weapons, armour, implements and other objects hanging on the walls and pillars are reproduced in the carvings. At Canosa di Puglia, in southern Italy, three tombs of the fourth century BC, known as the *Ipogei Lagasta*, have their interiors designed in house form, with ceilings cut to imitate wooden beams (Guido 1972, 100).

Some of the cemeteries on the Alban Hills and in and near Rome have yielded numerous hut-urns (*c.* 800–700 BC) the study of which has helped the interpretation of house foundations discovered fairly recently on the Palatine in Rome (Bloch 1960, 69–70; Trump 1966, 168). Hut-urns of special types are a feature of the Chiusi area.

Germany, Russia and northern Europe

The decoration on the wall of a megalithic gallery grave from Göhlitzsch, Merseburg, simulates that of textile hangings on the wall of a house (Clark 1952, 236 and fig. 129). Similar megalithic tombs at Halle (Saale) and Lohne have wall-slabs decorated apparently to reproduce 'house-decoration' (Powell 1960, 186–7). Several cist-slabs from a remarkable group of Late Neolithic or bell-beaker tombs at Petit-Chasseur, Sion (Switzerland) are

4 Decorated wall-slab from a tomb at Göhlitzsch, Germany. It simulates the wall of a house hung with patterned textiles and with the bow, arrows and axe of the dead

5 Hut-urn from Obliwice, Gdansk, Poland. Hallstatt D, c. 450 BC

decorated apparently to simulate wall-hangings (Gallay 1972).

The Russian Copper Age provides numerous instances of burials in house-like structures beneath barrows (kurgans). Among the most typical are the Kurgan house-graves of north Caucasia, where the burials are in 'houses' of timber or stone slabs or both, some having their walls decorated with incised or painted scenes (Gimbutas 1956, 56–7).

In the Lausitz (Lusatian) culture of Poland and its derivatives, many interments are within the remains of hut-like structures, or are placed in hut-urns (Jazdzewski 1965, 128; Malinowski 1963). Cremation urns in the form of houses occur frequently in the pre-Roman Iron Age, especially in central, northern, and eastern Germany. They occur in great variety, including pottery reproductions of earth-domed huts, tent-shaped huts, rectangular houses, and pile-dwellings (Behn 1924). There are also house-shaped sarcophagi. Behn has also described house-urns from Holland, Denmark, and Sweden, all probably belonging to the Iron Age except a few in Sweden which date from the end of the Bronze Age. Among the latter is an oval example from a barrow at Stora Hammar, Scania, showing a hut with a slightly conical thatched roof and a removable door in the side; another door is painted in black and yellow on each long side. Stenberger (1962, 106–7) suggests that the idea of house-urns spread from the Villanovan cultures of Italy via the Hallstatt regions of central Europe to Sweden.

Sardinia and the Balearic Islands

In Sardinia, the doorways of some of the Early Bronze Age tombs at Anghelu Ruju and elsewhere are carved apparently to simulate the wooden door-frames of houses. It is possible that the carvings of bulls' horns on their walls may represent the trophies customarily hung on the walls of the houses. Among the most convincing reproductions of houses are the tombs, probably Copper Age or Early Bronze Age, at Sant Andria Priu, where three of the tombs are hewn in the rock and their interiors reproduce those of timber-built houses (Guido 1963, 53–5).

In the Balearic Islands there are, probably from *c.* 1500 BC onwards, the *navetas* (tombs shaped like an upturned boat) and the *navetiform houses*. Nearly all the known navetas are in Minorca but many of the navetiform house foundations are in Majorca. This odd feature in their distribution may be due to the incompleteness of the surviving record and it is uncertain whether the navetas are earlier (as existing evidence seems to suggest) or later than the navetiforms. If the whole of the evidence were available one would surely expect the naveta to be a tomb modelled on a house form. In addition there are the *micro-navetas* in the cemetery of Son Real in the Bay of Alcudia; these are probably later than the Minorcan navetas (Pericot 1972, 61–7, 75–80).

The British Isles

There is more than a suggestion that the Neolithic long barrow, whether chambered or unchambered, is derived from a contemporary house type. It is true tht this cannot yet be proved because scarcely any Neolithic house foundations have yet been discovered in Britain, but rectangular house foundations of this period are already known at Clegyr Boia (Pembrokeshire), Haldon Hill (Devon), and near Lough Gur (Co. Limerick), as well as from the Netherlands and elsewhere in northwestern Europe. It is also possible, on the analogy of the orientation of the long houses of this period in the Netherlands (SE/NW with the entrance at SE), that there may be a relationship between the orientation of the British long barrows (strong tendency to E/W with entrance or 'business end' at E) and that of the contemporary houses.

More than fifty years ago, Addy (1918–20) assembled much evidence which could be interpreted as indicating that some of the Early Bronze Age round barrows of Britain might have been built over circular house or hut foundations. This problem has recently been reconsidered by Ashbee (1960) and Simpson (1971) in the light of evidence from later and more scientific excavations. In Shetland the remains of many stone-built oval houses are similar to contemporary heel-shaped cairns. A site known as Benie Hoose was apparently an oval house later converted into either a temple or a tomb. Timber circles beneath round barrows are of two main types – *external* circles which may have been to assist in containing the material of the mound or cairn; and *internal* circles placed well within the circumference. The latter are considered by Ashbee to have been most probably mortuary huts or houses.

In the New Forest two rectangular 'mortuary houses' were found beneath round barrows assumed to have been Early Bronze Age. Similar square or rectangular timber 'mortuary houses' have been found beneath barrows of Corded Ware culture (*c.* 2400–2000 BC) in Germany and Switzerland.

A class of Viking hog's back tombstone in northern Britain, made in the form of a house, has been the subject of studies by Walton (1954) and Schmidt (1970), the latter with James Lang's distribution map, showing that they occur mostly in and around Northumbria. The interlaced pattern on the walls of some of these tombstones probably reproduces the wattle walling of the cruck-built long house, while the top of the slab shows in detail how these buildings were roofed.

Conclusion

The main point of this chapter is to show that when excavation in tombs reveals structures or features which cannot readily be explained in terms of funerary ritual, it is worth while considering whether they are intended to provide the dead with something connected with his domestic life. It also carries the implication that a knowledge of settlements and contemporary house architecture is an excellent background for the archaeologist intending to excavate a tomb of the period with which he is familiar.

Chapter Two

The treatment of the body

Men have been most phantasticall in the singular contrivances of their corporall dissolution; whilest the sobrest Nations have rested in two wayes, of simple inhumation and burning. Sir Thomas Browne. *Urne Buriall* 1658. Chapter I.

Inhumation of the unburnt body

THE CONTRACTED POSTURE, also called the crouched or flexed posture, usually involves placing the body on the right or left side. Two British writers (Childe 1957, 353; Ashbee 1960, 69) have distinguished between *contracted* (90 degrees or less between thighs and spinal column) and *flexed* (more than 90 degrees between thighs and spinal column), but this distinction cannot normally be applied to the earlier literature and is seldom adopted by continental writers. It seems preferable to state the angle between thighs and spinal column whichever term is used. Adoption of the contracted posture could have been (*a*) because it is the natural attitude of sleep (Howell 1970, 130); (*b*) because it involves less grave-digging than the extended posture; (*c*) because, being the pre-natal posture, it might have been hoped to facilitate rebirth into a future life; but James (1957, 29) questioned whether such a philosophic idea would have been held by Palaeolithic man. The earliest known burials (Mousterian) are in this posture, and include those at La Ferrassie, La Chapelle-aux-Saints, and Le Moustier itself (Clark 1969, 45). They have come from numerous Upper Palaeolithic sites in France and from Dolní Věstonice in Czechoslovakia. They were often laid on the ground rather than placed in dug graves. In the Mesolithic they have been found in the cemeteries on the islands of Téviec and Hoëdic off Quiberon Bay (Péquart 1937; 1954), and in a 'half-sitting' posture at Durrenberg near Merseburg in eastern Germany (Jazdzewski 1965, 54). Ten of the Natufian burials from the Skhul cave, Mount Carmel, were also contracted (Garrod 1937).

In Egypt the contracted posture was universal in the Neolithic and Predynastic, and continued into the Early Dynastic and the Old Kingdom (Petrie 1937, 2, 17), and even later for the poor. At Tarkhan (Dynasties II, III) contracted interments were tightly bandaged and at Nuerat near Beni Hasan (Dynasty III–IV) some of the limb bones were separately wrapped in linen (Garstang 1907, 30).

During the Neolithic period the contracted posture was normal over most of Europe (Tringham 1971, 87–8). In the Mediterranean it was the rite at Khirokitia in Cyprus (Dikaios 1953), in the

Cyclades, and is known from Minoan Crete (Charles 1965, frontispiece; Branigan 1970, 87). At Mycenae some of the burials in Grave Circles A and B were contracted (Taylour 1964, 75).

The sequence of contracted burials in Czechoslovakia is of unusual interest. At the Corded Ware cemetery of Vikletiče (Bohemia) men were laid on their right side and women on their left side. The Beaker period cemetery at Mochov (Bohemia) had the men laid on their left side and the women on their right side. At the Únětice period cemetery of Holesov (Moravia) the men were placed on their right and the women on their left side (Filip 1966, 98–100, 107, 121). The contracted posture was frequent over much of Europe during the Copper and Early Bronze Ages.

In the British Isles contracted interments occur in both chambered and unchambered Neolithic long barrows, and burials of the Beaker, Copper and Early Bronze Ages are usually in this posture.

From several regions, including Byblos (Jidejian 1968, 11) and Lipari (Brea 1957, 124–5, 143), have come contracted burials in jars or pithoi, known accordingly as jar- or pithos-burials, mostly dated 3500–2000 B C.

Interment in the contracted posture was resumed in various areas including the British Isles (e.g. the barrow-cemeteries in Yorkshire) during the Iron Age.

There is evidence from several periods and areas that some of the contracted bodies had been tightly bound, possibly to fit into a small grave, but perhaps to prevent the dead from returning as 'revenants' to molest the living. From Britain a possible instance comes from Crichel Down in Dorset, barrow 5, probably Early Bronze Age (Piggott 1944, 68–9).

THE EXTENDED POSTURE usually involves laying the body on its back. The earliest known extended burials include one of the Chatelperron culture from Le Roc de Combe Capelle in Dordogne

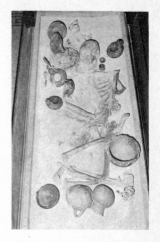

6 (*Opposite*) Contracted interment of the Bell-Beaker period from Bohdalice, Moravia. Bones of a lamb in one of the vases show that the burial was made in early spring

7 (*Above*) Contracted burial of a woman with grave-goods including pottery and objects of personal adornment. Picene culture, Iron Age

8 Pithos burial from the Copper Age necropolis at Byblos

9 Extended burials in a Late Neolithic grave in Skuttunge parish, Uppland, Sweden. In the foreground bones of around twenty individuals have been displaced to make way for the two final interments

(Oakley 1969, 156, 315) and the 'Red Lady of Paviland' (actually a man) from a cave in south Wales, which yielded Aurignacian implements. The Early Neolithic burials at Ertebølle are normally in this posture as are those from Lepenski Vir. A Late Neolithic extended interment at the Grotta Fabrizi near Rome had a trepanned skull (Tringham 1971, 59–60). Many of the Russian Neolithic burials are extended, especially those of the Dnieper-Donetz culture (Sulimirski 1970, 114–15, 117).

In Egypt, from the Old Kingdom onwards, the introduction of the wooden coffin and stone sarcophagus and the development of mummification led to the adoption of the extended posture which best fitted into the container. The interment of Queen Shub-ad at Ur was also extended (Woolley 1934, pl. 36).

The extended posture was the normal rite in the Late Neolithic burials of the Funnel Beaker culture of northern Europe (Piggott 1962*b*). The Early Bronze Age cemetery at Cernavoda (Romania) contained more than four hundred interments, all extended (Berciu 1967, 54; Tringham 1971, 154). In other areas extended interment was often limited to princely burials as in the Unetice culture of central Europe, and 'chieftain' burials in the British Isles, such as Bush Barrow in Wiltshire, and several others, perhaps including Rillaton in Cornwall and Hove in Sussex (Piggott 1962*b*; Grinsell 1959, 50). Many of the burials in wooden coffins are likely to have been in this posture. These occur in Britain (Ashbee 1960, 87, map) and are even more frequent in Scandinavia and north Germany. Extended burials are also usual in the Tumulus Bronze Age culture of Germany. Some of the burials in Grave Circles A and B at Mycenae, and the final burial in the unplundered tholos tomb at Pylos, were extended (Taylour 1964, 75, 80). During the later Bronze Age cremation was the rule; but a Late Bronze Age cemetery at Toscanella in Italy contained rows of extended skeletons without grave-goods (Trump 1966, 131).

During the Iron Age extended burial was usual over most of Europe among those who inhumed (Childe 1945, 14); it was the rite followed alike in the Scythian royal tombs and in the lowly *fossa*-graves of northern and central Italy (Bloch 1960, 86, 162). In Czechoslovakia, extended burials were usually with head to south in Slovakia, and with head to north in Moravia (Filip 1962, 180). In the Roman period the introduction of the carved sarcophagus in the reign of Hadrian (AD 117–38) led gradually to the adoption of extended inhumation which had become almost universal in the Roman Empire by *c*. AD 250 (Toynbee 1971, 40). During the Anglo-Saxon period the Jutes and Saxons normally buried their dead extended or loosely flexed (Meaney 1964, 17). This is, incidentally, a timely reminder that the difference between contracted and extended posture is sometimes one of degree and that intermediate postures do occur.

Variations of the extended posture include the *Yamnaya posture* of the Russian Steppes – an extended posture but with the knees drawn nearly upright (Sulimirski 1970, 127–33). The *standing posture* was adopted for some richly furnished burials of the Russian Karelian culture at Olenii Ostrov near Lake Onega (Sulimirski 1970, 139). At Lepenski Vir burials occasionally have the knees extended.

10 The Yamnaya posture. (After Sulimirski)

The occasional practice of weighting the corpse or placing heavy slabs over it, evidently to discourage the dead from return - as 'revenants', should be mentioned in this context. In the Russian Late Neolithic, a female adult at Karavaikha (Kargopol culture) had been buried face downwards, pressed down by three large stones, the largest on its head (Sulimirski 1970, 138). From Wessex, a contracted skeleton with a beaker in barrow Bulford 71a (Wiltshire) was covered by an immense sarsen stone (Grinsell 1957*a*, 164). The Romanian Iron Age includes a skeleton from tumulus 17 at Balta Verde which had a stone slab weighing 60 kg placed on its chest, and a boar's tusk had been plunged into the chest of another (Berciu 1967, 124). Instances from France were assembled by Forrer (1922), and extensive ethnographical parallels were cited by Frazer (1933–6). Mutilation of a body before burial may also have served to discourage the dead from returning. Cleft skulls claimed from British long barrows (Daniel 1950, 102) could be interpreted in this context, and also certain burials from Wessex round barrows, including barrow Litton Cheney 3 in Dorset

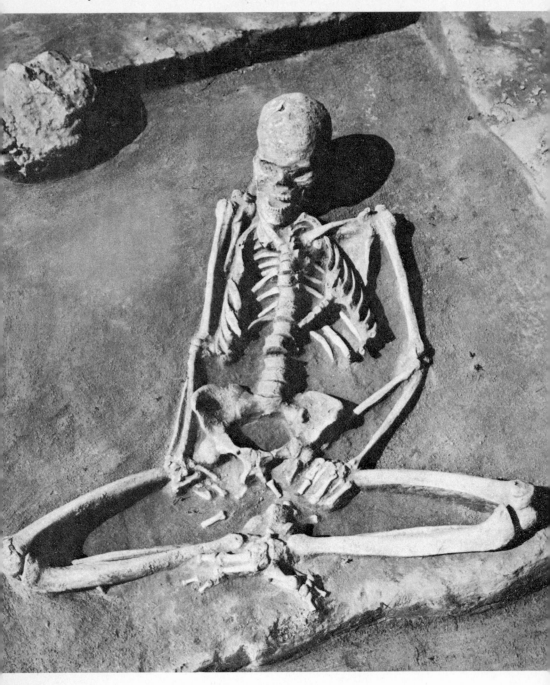

11   Early 'Lepenski Vir' posture in a trapezoidal grave at Lepenski Vir, *c.* 5500 B C

12 Soil-mark of a body in a
posture intermediate between
contracted and extended. From
barrow 2, Elp, Netherlands.
Late Neolithic

in which a burial had both hands severed and buried first (Grinsell 1959), and barrow Tyneham 18 in the same county, in which the head of one of seven inhumations (date unknown) had been severed from the body (Grinsell 1959, 138).

SELECTIVE INHUMATION. The cult of skulls was frequently practised in Palaeolithic and Mesolithic times (Clark 1969, 36–9,

13 Plastered skull with eyes of shell, from Jericho. Pre-Pottery Neolithic, *c.* 7000–6500 BC

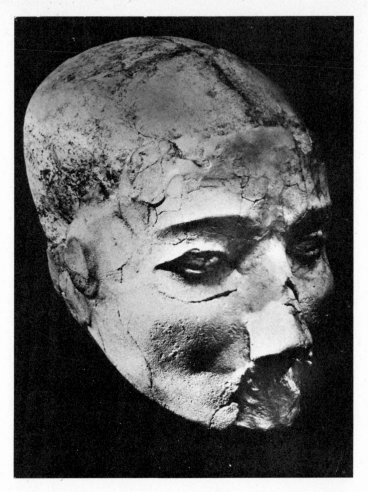

45). From beneath the floors of Pre-Pottery Neolithic houses at Jericho (*c.* 7000–6000 BC) came nine skulls, all of which had their facial parts modelled in gypsum and their eyes marked with shells, in one instance cowrie. Near by were about forty skeletons, mostly headless. The care with which the facial parts had been moulded suggests that they were the skulls of venerated ancestors and not those of enemies (Kenyon 1957, 60–5).

In Predynastic Egypt the head of a Badarian skeleton was found replaced by a pot and the head of an Amratian skeleton by an ostrich egg (Murray 1956, 87, 90). A skull cult was still being practised until recently in parts of West Africa (Petrie 1914, 117).

In many, perhaps most, instances until the Pre-Pottery Neolithic of Jericho, the skull may have been entered through the *foramen magnum* (which had been enlarged for this purpose) to extract the brain for food (Henschen 1965, 49; Oakley 1955). Ethnographical parallels suggest that the reason was to partake of a tasty and nourishing morsel rather than to acquire the virtues of the dead.

There is little evidence of any skull cult in Neolithic and Bronze Age Britain. However, round barrow Winterslow 20 (Wiltshire)

contained a primary deposit of a human skull only, with a phallus-shaped chipped flint. As the site adjoins a group of flint mines of the same period this may have been a ritual burial to ensure a good supply of workable flint (Stone 1934).

Representation of the dead by the head alone among the Celts has been studied by Lambrechts (1954). From the Anglo-Saxon cemetery at Bidford (Warwickshire) came an interment of the skull of a woman with a bronze pin, hair-ring and pot, placed in an area defined by three stone slabs (Meaney 1964, 17, 258). Various instances of special treatment of the human skull in historical times have been assembled by Henschen (1965).

OTHER SELECTIVE AND PARTIAL INHUMATIONS. The term *two-stage burial* is used for the deposit of a selection of bones, frequently including skulls and long bones, after the body has been exposed until the flesh has decayed. It is preferable to the term *secondary burial* (used in this context in the USA) as this is used in western Europe for those burials later than the primary interment. At Lepenski Vir, during the earlier period (*c*. 6000 B C), the dead are believed to have been exposed on trees to birds of prey and insects, but above the reach of animals, until the flesh had been removed when the bones were collected and deposited in holes dug in or near the settlements (Srejović 1972, 117).

In Egyptian mythology, the body of the god Osiris was dismembered by his enemies and afterwards reassembled by his son Horus to become a God of the Dead. The latter part of this process is thus described in the *Pyramid Texts* (§1684):

'I am Horus. I have come for you that I may cleanse you and purify you, that I may bring you to life and collect your bones for you, that I may gather you together and collect your soft parts for you and collect your dismembered parts for you.'

Many burials of the Predynastic Amratian and Gerzean cultures show evidence of having been dismembered, possibly in accordance with this myth (Petrie 1937, 8; Murray 1956).

In Palestine two-stage burial was practised during the Proto-Urban period (*c*. 3200–3000 B C) roughly contemporary with the end of Predynastic Egypt. The Pottery and Bead type of burial in the Early–Middle Bronze Age (the Intermediate Early–Middle Bronze Age of Kenyon) at Jericho (*c*. 2600–2300 B C) contains interments of collections of bones probably deposited in a cloth bag or on a rush mat. Similar deposits occur at Tell el-Ajjul and probably also at Megiddo (Kenyon 1957, chapter 8; 1960, 86, 141–50).

The Neolithic (Michelsburg) culture cemeteries at Spiennes and Furfooz in Belgium contained skeletons from which the flesh had been removed with flint knives, which had frequently cut into the bone (De Laet 1958, 80).

In the British Neolithic, evidence for two-stage burial in chamber tombs has been discussed by Daniel (1950, 109–10), and Piggott (1962a, 65–8), and the tomb at Millin Bay (Northern Ireland) seems to provide proof of the custom (E. E. Evans 1966,

103–6). With most of the chamber tombs, however, evidence is difficult to assess as a result of the ease with which they could be entered. More reliable evidence is found in the unchambered long barrows which suggests that the custom was sometimes followed (Ashbee 1970, 63–5). It would be proved if it were certain that 'long mortuary enclosures' such as that on Normanton Down (Wiltshire) were for temporary exposure of the dead before final deposit in the long barrow.

Gresham (1972) has suggested that selected bones of a dead relative may have been removed temporarily from chamber tombs and carried in a bag to be venerated at religious ceremonies, or to take part in some special event, and afterwards returned to the tomb. This practice is followed by some ethnographical groups today (James 1957, 119–22).

From burials of the Funnel Beaker culture at Las Stocki (Poland) there is evidence that bodily extremities were removed and placed in the mouth of, or beneath, the dead (Jazdzewski 1965, 91–2).

THE APPLICATION OF RED OCHRE TO INHUMATIONS is common throughout the Upper Palaeolithic, the 'Red Lady of Paviland' (south Wales) being a well-known example. It occurs also at numerous Mesolithic sites, including Ofnet and Mas d'Azil, and in the Natufian burials of Palestine (Garrod 1937; Perrot 1960; 1968). From Neolithic contexts we can deduce that Romania has its 'Ochre Grave' culture centred north and west of the Black Sea (Berciu 1967, 64–5), while ochre-covered Combed Ware burials in pit-graves extend from Finland to east Prussia (Kivikoski 1967, 37–8), and there are numerous other areas in Europe where Neolithic burials are covered with this substance (Tringham 1971, 87–8; De Laet 1958, 70). Copper Age burials covered with red ochre occur in the Tiszapolgar culture of eastern Europe (Tringham 1971, 189–91); in the Conca d'Oro culture of Sicily (Brea 1957, 88); in Italy a tomb at Sgurgola south of Rome contained an interment with red ochre smeared on the face (Trump 1966, 75). In Malta many of the burials in the hypogeum of Hal Saflieni were covered with red ochre; indeed, when in 1901–2 a workman hit upon a water-logged burial at this site, he reported having found a human skeleton lying in 'fresh blood' (J.D. Evans 1959, 135). In all these instances the considerable quantity of ochre used suggests that its purpose was to restore life to the dead by providing what was visually the best substitute for blood.

In Britain one or more lumps of red ochre may be deposited in Neolithic round barrows – Liff's Low in Derbyshire and Broom Ridge in Northumberland (Grinsell 1953a, 225, 249). There are at least four instances of small deposits in Copper or Early Bronze Age round barrows in Yorkshire – Greenwell's barrows CXVIII and CXXI (Goodmanham) and Mortimer's 40 and C53 (Garton Slack). In these instances the small quantity of ochre suggests deposit for cosmetic purposes only.

ORIENTATION. There is a tendency for the bodies to be placed E–W at La Ferrassie (Dordogne), Spi (Belgium), Kiik-Koba (Poland), and Solutré (Saône-et-Loire) (Howell 1970, 130).

During the Mesolithic there seems to have been no fixed rule concerning orientation of the body. In Egypt, Predynastic bodies were usually placed s(head)–N, and as they are nearly all near the Nile the intention was probably for them to occupy the 'upstream' position. The head normally faces w, possibly suggesting a belief that the land of the dead was in the direction of the setting sun. From Dynasty I to XVII the body was normally laid N(head)–s, facing E, presumably implying a belief that rebirth was connected with the rising sun. During Dynasties XVIII–XX the pharaohs in the tombs in the Valley of the Kings were placed w–E, as shown by the orientation of the royal sarcophagi. The only undisturbed royal burial, that of Tutankhamun, had the head towards w. In the private tombs the body was usually placed w–E but the head could be at either end (Brunton 1946, 231). Among the Mycenaeans there was no regard for orientation of the burials (Mylonas 1966, 112). The evidence from Minoan Crete is indecisive, but a 'tholos' tomb at Vorou contained several skeletons placed E–w with the head 'facing west' and therefore presumably at the E end (Branigan 1970, 88). The Únětice culture inhumations in Czechoslovakia are usually placed s(head)–N, but in Moravia they are often placed w(head)–E. In his review of the Únětice cemetery of eighty-eight burials at Dolní Počernice near Prague, Hasek (1959, 33) observed, 'perhaps the dead were placed so as to "look" in the direction of the sunrise. As, in the course of the year, this point changes its position on the horizon, the orientations of the burials vary with the seasons.'

In the British Isles little study seems to have been devoted to the orientation of prehistoric burials. The evidence from chamber tombs is unsatisfactory because of periodical disturbance. In Wiltshire, of twenty-nine excavated Copper and Bronze Age round barrows adequately published up to about 1950, nineteen had the head to N, NW, or NE; five had the head to s, sw, or SE; and five had it to w or E (Grinsell 1957a, 227–31). No fixed rule was followed for the orientation of the Iron Age inhumations of Yorkshire or of those of the same period in France. The same applies to pagan Saxon inhumations, but at the cemetery at Abingdon (Berkshire) most of the skeletons had their heads to w, NW, or sw (Leeds and Harden 1936, 29). After the introduction of Christianity there gradually developed the practice of interment with feet to E pointing towards Jerusalem. During the Viking period, orientation of the body was sometimes with the head to s or sw, the supposed direction of Valhalla.

Thus the factors determining orientation vary. Among many peoples, however, orientation denotes 'the route which the dead must take on leaving the body, whether it be towards the final destination of the soul or away from its earthly abode and the dwellings of the living' (James 1957. 134).

Partially burned inhumations: fumigation and ritual

At several Upper Palaeolithic sites bodies were laid out on the family hearth while it was still burning and were therefore partly burned (Breuil and Lantier 1965, 248). In the Spanish Neolithic, some of the megalithic tombs in Almeria contained human bones partly burned, probably by fumigation or ritual fires (James 1957, 76). The funerary chambers of Minoan and Mycenaean tholos and chamber tombs were fumigated probably before each burial was made after the primary interment (Mylonas 1966, 113–14, 180; Branigan 1970, 86, 108–9). In Brittany a burnt area in the chamber of the megalithic tomb of Mané Seule near Crach (Morbihan) may have resulted from fumigation (L'Helgouach 1965, 88).

In the British Isles some of the bones from chamber tombs, including Tinkinswood (Daniel 1950, 99) and West Kennet (Piggott 1962a, 24), were burned after the flesh had decomposed. It is uncertain whether this was a ritual to ensure that the soul had departed from the body (Onians 1954, 254f., 543) or the result of fumigation which must have been essential when re-using tombs of this type. Earthen long barrows in Yorkshire provide evidence of the charring of disarticulated human bones in a mortuary enclosure within the barrow resulting from the burning of the enclosure itself; the unequal burning of the bones as a result is quite different from cremation proper (Ashbee 1970, 65–7).

Cremation

There are two practical aspects of ancient cremation to be considered here. As it is almost impossible to pick out all the bones from the pyre, the quantity normally selected for interment is often no more than about half the total, and is sometimes very much less. Burnt bones were usually reduced in size by crushing to enable them to fit more easily into their container. This is indeed the practice in modern cremation (Gejvall 1969).

True cremation first appears in the Neolithic period. It was sometimes practised by the Danubian I people and their successors (Childe 1957, 117). At Stein near Limburg (Netherlands) an important cremation cemetery was excavated in 1963 by Modderman (1964). In a cemetery at Omal near Liège burnt bones, possibly originally in wicker baskets, were placed in oval pits and sprinkled with haematite powder as a substitute for red ochre (De Laet 1958, 70). The communal character of most of these cremations should be noted.

In Britain cremation cemeteries have been found at ceremonial sites including Stonehenge, Cairnpapple (West Lothian), and Dorchester-on-Thames. At Stonehenge, about thirty-five cremations came from the Aubrey Holes and another thirty were found near by, some primary and others later (Atkinson 1956, 11–13). At Sites I and XI at Dorchester-on-Thames, there were cremations in pits arranged in a circle, and at Cairnpapple they were arranged in a semicircle. In all instances there were associated bone pins earlier than the Beaker period. Duggleby Howe round barrow (Yorkshire, East Riding) contained, above ten successively buried skeletons, more than fifty cremations, four with bone pins probably used to fasten a leather container (Mortimer 1905, 23–42). In Britain there are a few instances of cremations with beakers, mainly those of D.L. Clarke's 'Barbed Wire' and 'Northern/North Rhine' types, and with late beakers of other types probably resulting from contact with cremating immigrants from the continent (Clarke 1970, 453–4). Otherwise the spread of cremation in Britain seems to have been partly a reassertion of the cremation rite sometimes practised in the Late Neolithic. The earlier collared urns, in which the burnt bones were often placed, developed from the 'Secondary Neolithic' (Peterborough) types of vessel.

During the European Early Bronze Age the normal procedure was individual (as distinct from communal) cremation. After being picked from the pyre the burnt bones were deposited, sometimes in a bag, in an urn or beneath an inverted urn, and placed in a cist either below, on, or (if secondary) above the turf-line of a round barrow.

From the Middle Bronze Age onwards cremation cemeteries gained currency and spread over most of Europe where their emergence is clearly linked with the growth of villages and urban settlements. A cremation cemetery probably originally comprising at least two hundred urns, excavated at Troy in 1934, is dated to the end of Troy VI, *c.* 1400–1300 BC (Blegen 1963, 142–3). In southern England cremation cemeteries were often inserted into the south side of an earlier round barrow. From *c.* 1000 BC onwards urnfields occur in the Hallstatt cultures of central and western Europe. Elsewhere cremation and inhumation were both practised. The Villanovans (*c.* 900–*c.* 500 BC) of northern Italy cremated their dead and put the bones into 'hut-urns'; this custom was continued by the Etruscans around Chiusi and in certain other areas. Under Republican and Imperial Rome cremation was normal until the reign of Hadrian (AD 117–38) when it began to be superseded by extended inhumation.

In Anglo-Saxon England cremation was normal in Lincoln-shire and East Anglia and occurred occasionally elsewhere, some-times in round barrows as at Asthall (Oxon). In the Midlands both cremation and inhumation were prevalent (Meaney 1964, 15–16). During the Viking period both rites were practised but cremation was the rule at the great cemetery at Lindholm Høje in Jutland (Jones 1968, 334; Ramskou 1957). In AD 922 Ibn Fadlan, an Arab emissary to Russia from the Khalif of Baghdad, was told as he witnessed the cremation of a Viking chief on the Volga that 'we burn him . . . so that he enters paradise at once' (Jones 1968, 429).

Chapter Three

Dress and personal adornment

The ghost of Melissa appeared and said that . . . she was cold and naked,
the clothes, which had been buried with her, having been of no use at all,
since they had not been burnt. Herodotus. *History* v, 92.

Periander's reaction to this state of affairs was to get every woman
in Corinth to bring her best clothes which were then burned in the
Temple to enable the spirit of his late wife Melissa to be warm
and comfortable. The story emphasizes not only the idea that
offerings have to be burned to be of use to those who have been
cremated, but also that the dead should not be sent to the after-life
naked. Evidence for the shroud or dress in which the dead were
placed in the grave depends on the extent to which its contents
have been preserved. In Egypt the natural conditions have
favoured preservation of such items. In Denmark, the constant
water-logged environment of several oak-coffin burials of the
Early Bronze Age has protected the shrouds and clothing of the
dead from decay. In the frozen tombs (*c.* 400–350 BC) of Pazyryk
and elsewhere in Siberia the water entering through the robbers'
holes froze and resulted in the preservation of the clothing of the
dead and much else besides. For the rest of Europe, on the other
hand, nearly every perishable object, inevitably including almost
all the clothing, has disappeared and we are left with items such
as the pins or brooches used in fastening the shroud or dress, and
the buttons originally attached thereto, as our only means of
forming an opinion concerning the dress of the dead. Objects of
personal adornment, usually necklaces, armlets, anklets, or headgear consisting partly of objects of shell, bone or stone, or beads,
have often survived. The decoration of the body by painting or
tattooing can sometimes be inferred if red ochre or other colouring
material has been placed in the grave in quantities which imply
their use for that purpose. Barrow 2 at Pazyryk preserved the
magnificent tattooed decoration on the body of the dead.

From the earliest times objects of personal adornment have been
worn by both sexes; it cannot be assumed, therefore, that a skeleton with a necklace is necessarily female. If the bones are well
enough preserved they should enable the sex to be determined.
Only where they are inadequately preserved, or where their
former presence is indicated only by a stain in the soil (as with
many barrows in the Netherlands), may their sex be hazarded as a
last resort from the character of the objects of personal adornment
or grave-goods. As a general rule, grave-goods which indicate
'male' or 'female' activities are a safer indication of sex than objects
of personal adornment.

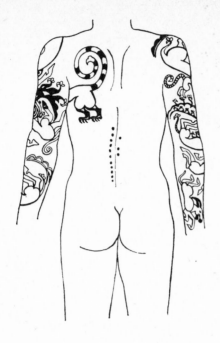

Upper Palaeolithic

Instances of Aurignacian burials with objects of personal adornment are numerous. From Grimaldi (the Cavillon cave opened
in 1872) comes a bonnet embroidered with over two hundred
Nassa shells covering the head of an adult male with a crown of
pierced stag teeth. At the left knee was a garter of forty-one *Nassa*
shells. From the Grotte des Enfants near by the skeletons of two
children were both dressed in a 'sort of petticoat' embroidered
with small *Nassa reticulata* shells, and the skeleton of a male adult
had a necklet of *Nassa* shells and pierced canine stag teeth. Other
objects of personal adornment were found on the skeleton of an
adult male from Barma Grande (1884) and on the skeleton of a
youth at Arene Candide (Italy).

Magdalenian burials include that of a male adult from Laugerie-
Basse ornamented by pairs of *Cypraea* shells, two on the forehead,
one near each humerus, four at the knees, and two at the feet.
From La Madeleine itself came a skeleton of a child with pierced
teeth and many small shells on a level with the head, neck, wrists,
and ankles. From the Magdalenian IV layer at Duruthy cave
(Landes) came a skeleton with a necklet of forty bear canines and
three of lion, all engraved with pictures of seal, pike, heads of
bears, and arrow-shaped signs.

14 Tattooed body from barrow 2
at Pazyryk. (After Rudenko)

Mesolithic

Burials of the Natufian culture in Palestine were decorated with
headgear, necklaces, pendants and anklets of shell, bone, and
stone (Garrod 1937). Some of the skeletons in the cemetery at
Hoëdic in Brittany had hair-nets, necklets, bracelets, and anklets.

A Tardenoisian burial of an adult male from Le Curgoul de Gramat (Lot, France) had on the left side of the skull a circlet of pierced shells. From the cave of El Aven del Rabasso, Tarragona, came skeletons with parts of necklaces, pierced shells, and schist beads.

Egyptian Neolithic, Predynastic and Early Dynastic

From the Badarian until the Early Dynastic period it was usual to place in the grave a slate palette, a grinder, and some malachite as cosmetic provision for the dead. During the Badarian and Amratian periods the bodies were wrapped in goat-skin (sometimes with the hair inside; Murray 1956, 87), woven cloth, or matting. During the Gerzean period the bodies were often wrapped in bark fibre or woven rhamie fibre (Murray 1956, 93). A Badarian adult male had a girdle of over five thousand steatite blue glazed beads. An Amratian female burial had beads at the neck, an ivory bracelet on the right wrist, two cowries by the left wrist, and a bone bangle on each wrist. Combs occur in graves from the Predynastic onwards, and mirrors from Dynasty VI onwards (Petrie 1937, 9–10).

The European Neolithic

For much and probably most of Europe the clothing was most likely animal skins, the only archaeological evidence being pins of bone or antler, such as those from Greenwell's long barrow CCXXII (Willberby Wold, Yorkshire, East Riding) and from Duggleby Howe round barrow in the same county. Some large holed objects often described as beads but found singly and really too large for normal beads, such as those from long barrows at Eyford and Notgrove on the Cotswolds, may really be dress-fasteners (Clifford 1950).

Deposits of burnt human bones from Late Neolithic pits at Stonehenge (the Aubrey Holes and others near them), Dorchester-on-Thames (in ring-ditches) and elsewhere are sometimes accompanied by bone skewer-pins. As these are usually partly burnt, it seems a little uncertain whether they were dress-fasteners, hairpins, or pins used for fastening the bags which contained the cremations (Atkinson *et al.*, 1951).

The Bronze Age

A remarkable female interment of Bell-Beaker culture at Marefy (Moravia) wore clothes trimmed with 101 bone beads, 6164 shell rings, and 421 dogs' teeth, some imitated in bone as otherwise more than twenty-two dogs would have been needed to satisfy this requirement (Neustupný 1961, 81).

The most important evidence of the dress of the dead in this period comes from Jutland, where seven almost complete sets of garments (four of men and three of women) have been recovered in almost perfect condition in bole-coffins (split hollowed oak trunks) beneath round barrows of the Early Bronze Age. Their preservation is due to the formation of an impervious layer beneath the coffin, causing it to be permanently water-logged, thereby protecting its contents from decay. In addition fragments of clothing have been recovered from oak coffins in numerous other Danish round barrows of the same period.

Men's clothing comprises a woven woollen cap covered with pile which would have been capable of taking some of the brunt of a blow, leather shoes, a woven woollen under-garment, and a sleeveless cloak of similar material. It has been noted that the cloak is of such a size that it could have been made from a stag's hide. Its external decoration of long pile suggests a reproduction in wool of what had previously been of skin – a woollen imitation of the skin garment of the Late Neolithic period.

Women's clothing normally comprised a hair-net of horse-hair or a woollen cap, leather shoes, an elbow-length sleeved jacket of wool, and a corded skirt of the same material, with a woven belt to which was fixed a large bronze circular disc with a central prong presumably for discouraging unwelcome advances from the opposite sex. Attached to the belt was normally a comb and sometimes a bronze dagger. The woman from the Skrydstrup barrow was wrapped from the waist downwards in two blankets or shrouds of wool and did not have a corded skirt.

The question arises whether these garments were the normal everyday clothing or for funerary purposes only. It seems almost certain that, with the possible exception of the blankets or shrouds from the Skrydstrup barrow, they were the clothes worn by the living.

In some instances at least, the clothed body was laid on a cow hide with the hair upwards, and covered by a second hide or an expanse of woven material.

Objects of personal adornment from these remarkable burials include gold earrings, a bronze collar, and bronze tubes fixed to the cords of the skirt (Broholm and Hald 1940 and 1948).

From the evidence of these Danish round barrows there seems very little doubt that it was the normal custom in many regions for the dead of the Early Bronze Age to be buried fully clothed. As a rule, however, archaeological evidence is confined to little more than the dress-fasteners of copper or bronze or other durable materials.

Evidence of Bronze Age clothing from traces of textiles in graves or cists beneath round barrows was assembled for the British Isles by Henshall (1950). Exceptional conditions resulting in the preservation of textile impressions include (i) contact with bronze implements, the corrosion of which has replaced the textile by metal oxide; (ii) replacement of the textile by carbonate of lime (as in the Manton round barrow, Preshute 1a, Wiltshire); (iii) preservation of the impression of textile on the clay floor of a grave or cist (as in barrow Milston 23, Wiltshire). On the head of the female skeleton in the Manton round barrow was found cloth of a type different from that on the body, implying a head-dress separate from the garment. Traces of cloth, probably wool, were associated with inhumations in oak coffins beneath barrows at Kellythorpe (Yorkshire, East Riding) and Rylston (Yorkshire, West Riding).

15 Costume of adult female
preserved in a water-logged oak
coffin beneath a round barrow at
Egtved, Jutland. Early Bronze
Age

The closest English parallels to the preservation of garments in the oak bole-coffins of Denmark are from round barrows at Gristhorpe (Yorkshire, East Riding) and Stoborough (barrow Arne 19), Dorset. The Gristhorpe round barrow, opened in 1834, had in its centre a large oak bole-coffin which was water-logged and therefore preserved its contents – a male skeleton (extended?), wrapped in the skin of an animal with soft and fine hair; this had been fastened at the chest of the body by a bone or horn pin. On the underside of the coffin was a small rectangular hole, a feature characteristic of the Danish Early Bronze Age coffins. In the centre of the round barrow at Stoborough (Dorset) was a large oak bole-coffin containing a human skeleton wrapped in a covering of several deerskins sewn together and a piece of gold lace is said to have been associated. It will be noted that in both these English interments the bodies were wrapped in hides, suggesting a continuance of Neolithic fashion into the Early Bronze Age. There is some uncertainty whether they represented shrouds or ordinary clothing; the writer, on evidence from Denmark, considers that in most instances the cloth or skin belonged to ordinary clothing.

Space does not permit a recital of all types of dress-fastener which occur in the inhumations of the Early Bronze Age in Europe. The V-perforated button is widely distributed and was sometimes used for buttoning garments in front, as occasionally shown by the position of the loops in the remains of clothing. Mortimer (1905, 84–5) noted jet buttons at the legs of a skeleton in barrow Acklam Wold 92 (Yorkshire, East Riding), implying the use of some kind of legging which buttoned up. What is important, of course, is to note the precise position on or near the body of every dress-fastener whether button, pin, brooch, clasp, or anything else, this being often the only remaining indication of the type of garment or shroud in which the dead was interred.

Objects of personal adornment cannot be discussed in detail, but it is not out of place to mention some of the gold objects excavated from tombs of the second millennium BC. These include crowns, diadems, pectorals and other objects from the tombs of the princesses of the Middle Kingdom near the pyramids at Dahshur and Lahun, and the slightly later pendants, pectorals and other jewellery from the royal tombs at Byblos, dated by the inscribed gifts to the reigns of Amenemhet III and IV of Egypt (*c.* 1830–1780 BC). In this category can also be placed the gold face-masks from shaft-graves in Grave Circles A and B at Mycenae, as well as a large variety of other gold objects, mostly dress-fittings, from the Mycenaean shaft-graves and chamber tombs, dated between *c.* 1550 and 1200 BC. At Arkhanes south of Knossos was found a Minoan burial of a princess (?) in a robe decorated with gold ornaments and wearing jewellery including more than 140 gold items (Sakellarakis 1967). Jewellery of gold with various inlays from the tomb of Tutankhamun (*c.* 1336 BC) included the celebrated funeral mask, several pectorals and pendants, and elaborate earrings.

Even from northwest Europe the recorded finds of gold from Early Bronze Age tombs, almost all of them round barrows, are by no means unimpressive. They include gold basket earrings

16 Gold face-mask from shaft-grave V, Grave Circle A, Mycenae. The so-called 'Mask of Agamemnon'

17 (*Opposite*) Gold brooch from
the Regolini-Galassi tomb,
Cerveteri, Italy

from a young man's grave at Radley (Berkshire) and possibly
from a cairn at Orton (Morayshire) which may also have contained a gold lunula (neck-ornament) of Irish origin. Other gold
lunulae may have come from barrows at Harlyn Bay (Cornwall)
and from a 'cromlech' near Magheramesk (Co. Antrim, Northern
Ireland), but the early records are too vague for certainty. Circular
gold discs, usually interpreted as 'sun-discs', often found in pairs
and with two holes near the centre suggesting that they were
dress ornaments of some kind, have come from round barrows
Mere 6a (Wiltshire) and Monkton Farleigh 2 (Wiltshire), both of
which also yielded bell-beakers. Other examples from Ireland
and northwest Europe have been discussed by Butler (1963,
167–75). It seems uncertain whether the later gold-covered bronze
'sun-disc' from a round barrow at Lansdown near Bath (Somerset) was a flat 'sun-disc' or the base of a bowl similar to that from
Gyldengård in Denmark (Grinsell 1972, 61). The 'Wessex' chieftain in Bush Barrow (Wilsford South 5, Wiltshire) had a lozenge-
shaped gold plate over the breast, but for the most part gold objects
from 'Wessex culture' round barrows comprise conical or biconical button-coverings, circular amber discs with gold mountings, and halberd-pendants in gold and amber, though a curious
assortment of objects came from bell-barrow Wilsford South 8
(Wiltshire). The most spectacular object found in any British
barrow is the gold cape from the barrow at Mold in Flintshire
(Powell 1953).

With the general spread of cremation after the Early Bronze
Age evidence of clothing becomes less and objects of personal
adornment, apart from items such as pins and brooches, become
comparatively rare in the cremated deposits.

The Iron Age

In several of the richer tombs of Etruscan Italy from about 700
BC onwards, we find a fantastic wealth of gold objects of adornment, especially in the granulation technique. Among the finest,
perhaps, are the animal-decorated gold clasp from the Bernardini
tomb at Palestrina near Rome, the magnificent gold brooch and
the gold bracelets (or earrings) from the Regolini-Galassi tomb at
Cerveteri, and the large and richly ornamented gold pectoral
from one of the chamber tombs on the Monterozzi by Tarquinia.
As the vast majority of the known Etruscan tombs were plundered
long ago, these finds must represent only a minute fraction of the
immense wealth originally interred with the dead, even in the
form of those objects of personal adornment which alone are the
subject of this chapter.

In and around Scythia frozen and other tombs from the fifth
to the third century BC have preserved an amazing array of relevant evidence. Barrows 2 and 5 at Pazyryk contained two adult
male corpses which were richly tattooed with animal designs
especially on the arms and legs. The dead in these frozen tombs
were normally interred only partly clothed – the men with their
coats over their shoulders, and the women with their bodices
across their breast. There is no evidence of men's trousers and it is

thought that these were not included in the burial dress. The dead were fitted with headgear, stockings, and shoes. The rarity of jewellery on the bodies is attributed to the activities of tomb robbers in remote antiquity. The bodies were normally laid on rugs placed on felt blankets (Rudenko, 1970).

What must have been among the richest tombs was found at Chertomlyk. This had clothes-hooks on the walls and ceilings, but the clothes had perished, leaving their numerous fittings of gold plaques on the ground beneath. The chieftain wore a gold earring on one ear and on all his fingers were gold rings. Two bodies in another chamber were each adorned with a torque, bracelets and rings of gold, and with a belt decorated with gold plaques; further gold plaques had been fixed to the clothing in which the bodies had been buried. In yet another chamber was the corpse of a woman wearing gold bracelets, finger rings and earrings, while numerous gold plaques, roundels and buttons had been attached to her clothing. Her purple headdress was decorated with fifty-seven gold plaques. The tomb had been robbed in antiquity and many of the best objects doubtless taken – yet all this and much other material remained for the modern archaeologist to recover (Rice 1957, 92–5).

The large barrow at Vix (Côte d'Or, France), opened in 1952, contained the burial of a woman, presumed to be a princess, of about 500 BC or slightly later, with a gold diadem weighing 0·48 kg, bracelets of schist and of amber beads, and several brooches of elaborate workmanship (Joffroy 1954). It was in fact an exceptionally rich wagon burial. Other wagon burials of women with gold jewellery have been found at Sirnau (Wurttemberg), Hochmichele near Heuneberg, Reinheim, and elsewhere. In central Europe chariot burials are mostly of men and without personal ornaments except in Bohemia where they occasionally have dress-fasteners in the form of brooches. An exception is at Pflugfelden where an adult male was interred in a splendid robe and wearing a gold diadem (Filip 1962, 31–50).

Of the La Tène chariot burials, mostly beneath small round barrows often surrounded by square trenches, those on the Yorkshire Wolds are poorly equipped compared with those of France. Only one – the so-called 'Queen's Barrow' at Arras – was equipped with a reasonable number of objects of personal adornment, including a gold ring (lost), rings of amber and bronze, a bead necklace, two bracelets, a brooch, and a pendant (Stead 1965, 102).

Details of the costume and personal adornment of the dead in Roman and later times are excluded for reasons of space.

Chapter Four

Human and animal sacrifice

The King is one who eats men and lives on the gods
A possessor of porters who dispatches messages; . . .
It is Khons who slew the lords
Who strangles them for the King
And extracts for him what is in their bodies,
For he is the messenger whom the King sends to
   restrain.
It is Shezmu who cuts them up for the King
And who cooks for him a portion of them
On his evening hearth-stones;
It is the King who eats their magic
And gulps down their spirits;
Their big ones are for his morning meal,
Their middle-sized ones are for his evening meal,
Their little ones are for his night meal,
Their old men and their old women are for his
   incense-burning. . . .

                    Pyramid Texts § 400–404.

Human sacrifice

In Egypt the royal burials from the reign of Djer to the end of
Dynasty I were normally accompanied by the subsidiary burials of
retainers and servants, perhaps in many instances killed to accompany their king or queen (Brunton 1946, 204). The funerary
monuments of Djet had 174 subsidiary burials at Abydos and
62 at Sakkara (at this period it seems to have been usual
for the pharaohs to have one tomb or cenotaph in Upper Egypt
and one in Lower Egypt). Similar subsidiary graves in rows surround some of the tombs of the nobility of this period (Emery
1961, 131). The burials accessory to the royal tombs were normally accompanied by jars of food and drink and objects appro-
priate to the vocation of each servant. The practice of having
servants and retainers buried around the main tomb continued in
Upper Egypt rather longer than in Lower Egypt. During the Old
Kingdom its place was taken by decorating the walls of the funerary chapels with scenes of servants about their tasks; in the Middle
Kingdom by models of these daily occupations; and from the
Second Intermediate period onwards by *ushabtis* or servant
statuettes (Emery 1961, 131–8, 152).

In the Sudan the royal tombs of the Middle Kingdom at Karma
(*c.* 2000–1800 BC) contain subsidiary burials of victims believed
to have been buried alive. It is astonishing that there was a recurrence of this practice at the burial of the Sudanese medieval kings,
a case in point being dated *c.* AD 1080 (Vycichl 1959).

18 Sacrificial burials in a royal tomb at Ur, *c.* 2200–1800 BC

In Mesopotamia human sacrifice was a marked feature of the royal tombs of the Third Dynasty at Ur (*c.* 2200–1800 BC). Each royal burial was normally accompanied by a few attendants in the tomb chamber and by a larger number (between six and eighty) of victims in subsidiary rooms or in a 'death-pit' near by. They had probably been either poisoned or slain (Gadd 1960). These victims, of both sexes, were not provided with food offerings but were carefully arranged in a manner which related to their various duties, posed ready for service. The human victims were sacrificed before the animals which lay above them (Woolley 1934, 33–42).

In Russia there is evidence of human sacrifice at the burial of the chief of the family from the Neolithic onwards. According to Gimbutas (1956, 79–80), it was an Indo-European custom for the wife to die with her husband. Archaeological evidence for this custom is provided by the high percentage of double interments of man and wife, often accompanied by those children who were too young to survive without either parent. One-third of the graves of the Balanovo culture were of this type. The most richly furnished of the Maikop burials (*c.* 2400 BC) included two persons sacrificed to the main interment. In the Early Bronze Age Globular Amphora and Catacomb cultures, the burial of the chief is likewise often accompanied by his wife and their youngest children in this way, and sometimes also by serfs. Some Iron Age burials in Transcaucasia were accompanied by sacrificed serfs, shown by anatomical study to have belonged to a racial type different from their masters (Sulimirski 1970, 122, 163, 223, 400). In Romania the La Tène II grave of a prince at Agighiol included

19 Sacrifice of T
pyre of Patroclus, from ..
Etruscan bronze cista. The pyre
of logs is right of centre, and on
top of it are the cuirass and two
shields of Patroclus. To the left is
Achilles plunging his sword into
the neck of one of the captives,
and other captives await their
fate

the sacrificial burial of a woman presumed to have been his wife
(Berciu 1967, 143–5).

Homer's description of the burial of Patroclus in Book XXIII
of the *Iliad* states that it was accompanied by twelve Trojan pri-
soners of noble birth slain for the occasion. The slaying of these
victims is portrayed on an Etruscan bronze cista in the British
Museum. At least two of the tombs at Salamis (Cyprus), probably
some centuries later than the custom described by Homer and
dated to the eighth and seventh centuries BC, revealed evidence of
human sacrifice. Tomb 2 contained in its *dromos* (entrance passage)
several sacrificed victims, at least one with hands tied. A servant
had also been sacrificed at a less opulent burial in tomb 83 in the
Cellarka at Salamis. Other possible instances of this custom have
been collected by Karageorghis (1967, 121).

The Scythian tombs of Russia and elsewhere (seventh to third
centuries BC) often contain a main chamber for the dead chief and
subsidiary chambers in which his sacrificed wife or wives, servants
and attendants were placed, carefully arranged for service to the
dead (Rice 1957, 96). They were probably poisoned or strangled.
This being such a large area, there is considerable variation in the
precise details of this custom.

Among the Viking burials of eastern Scandinavia are a few
which seem to perpetuate customs from Scythian times. The
extensive cemetery at Birka in eastern Sweden includes a grave
containing the burial of a richly attired woman accompanied by
the twisted body of a woman believed to have been a serf buried
alive to accompany her mistress (Brøndsted 1960, 273). This interpretation is supported by the well-known account by the Arab
Ibn Fadlan who witnessed a ship-funeral of a Viking chief on the
Volga in 922. The family of the dead chief asked his slave women
which of them wished to die with him, and one of them replied,
'I do.' From then onwards she was accorded special treatment and
the numerous male mourners had sexual intercourse with her
before she was killed with due ceremony (Jones 1968, 425–30).
Such instances of human sacrifice at burials appear, however, to
have been most exceptional during this period.

In the British Isles there has been much discussion on whether
there is any evidence of human sacrifice in the chamber tombs and
long barrows of the Neolithic period (Daniel 1950, 109–15;
Ashbee 1970, 83). Brothwell has recently shown that the badly
hacked adult male from the bank-barrow within Maiden Castle
(Dorset) is not Neolithic but probably Saxon (Brothwell 1971).

Sir Cyril Fox thought he had found evidence of child sacrifice in the Bronze Age round barrows at Sutton 268' (Glamorgan) and Pond Cairn in the same county (Fox 1959, 102, 104, 123).

Animal sacrifice

On present evidence the sacrifice of animals at human burials starts as early as the Middle Palaeolithic. In the Skhul cave at Mount Carmel, a Neandertal male burial had in its arms the jaws of a large wild boar (Anati 1963, 101). At the Early Neolithic site of Lepenski Vir in Yugoslavia (*c.* 6000 BC) many of the human burials were accompanied by the skulls and antlers of stag, and one by a dog (Srejović 1972, 120).

In Egypt the tomb of Queen Her-nit (Dynasty I) at Sakkara had at its entrance the burial of a dog, evidently her pet (Emery 1961, pl. 26). The Pan Grave people of the Second Intermediate Period often interred their dead accompanied by horns of animals including goat, and by the frontal bones of oxen (Brunton 1946, 223). The wall scenes of Theban private tombs of Dynasty XVIII often show the killing of a young bull as part of the funerary ceremony. From Dynasty XIX onwards these scenes stop, probably because of deteriorating economic conditions, and are replaced by scenes of the leg being cut from a male calf – a more economical offering (Abdul Qader 1966, 93, 170).

In Mesopotamia the excavations by Sir Leonard Woolley at Ur showed that the human victims sacrificed at the royal funerals were followed by the sacrifice of numerous oxen (Woolley 1934, 33–42).

At Jericho, Bronze Age tomb J3, of a warrior aristocrat, had the remains of three equids (probably asses) in the shaft above the tomb (Kenyon 1957, 225). Animal sacrifices occur in Hyksos tombs (*c.* 1800–1570 BC) at Tell Fara, Jericho and Lachish. Horses and donkeys were sometimes buried with the dead at Tell el-Ajjul (Anati 1963, 394–5, 406).

In Mycenaean Greece the tholos tomb at Marathon had, at the outer end of its *dromos*, an interment of two horses without any indication of a chariot (Vermeule 1964, 298 and pl. XLVIIB). Other Mycenaean horse-burials have been noted from graves at Nauplia and Argos (Karageorghis 1967, 117), and many more may be found when excavations are directed specifically to the *dromoi* of tombs. At chamber tomb 2, Dendra, the slaughtering block(?) and sacrificial table used for animal sacrifice were found (Persson 1931, 77–9).

In Minoan Crete there is the scene of the sacrifice of a bull on the sarcophagus of Hagia Triada, now paralleled by the remarkable find of the skull of a sacrificed bull in the doorway between the main and inner chamber of tholos tomb A at Arkhanes south of Knossos. To the right of this door were the remains of a horse that had been cut to pieces (Sakellarakis 1967; 1970).

In and around Russia, the sacrifice of horses with the dead in Caucasia and south Russia dates from the third millennium BC (Gimbutas 1956, 68, 75, 92, 131, 144), and continues here and there through the Bronze Age and Iron Age (Sulimirski 1970,

20 (*Opposite, upper*) Dog burial at entrance gate of the tomb of Queen Her-nit, Sakkara. Dynasty I

21 (*Opposite, lower*) Horse sacrifice in the dromos of a Mycenaean tholos tomb at Marathon. There was no evidence of any vehicle

22 Slaughtering block (?) from a chamber tomb at Dendra, Greece

368). The La Tène II prince's barrow at Agighiol in Romania
contained a sacrificed horse (Berciu 1967, 143–5). In this period
there are also many instances of the sacrifice of sheep and cattle.

At Trialeti near the Turkish border, an important group of
Early Bronze Age barrows includes one (*c.* 1700–1500 BC) covering an interment with remains of a four-wheeled wagon drawn by
oxen whose bones were found. At Usatovo, on the north coast of
the Black Sea, a Bronze Age cemetery included tombs some of
which had offering holes containing the skulls of bulls, while others
were surmounted by stelae carved with bulls' heads. Another tomb
in this group was corbelled somewhat in the Minoan manner, and
influence from Minoan Crete with its bull cult seems highly
probable (Sulimirski 1970, 183, 238, 271–2). The Copper Age
cemetery at Basatanya in Romania had skeletons of dogs near the
feet of several interments, and other instances of dogs buried with
the dead about this time have been noted from Moravia and the
Great Hungarian Plain (Bognár-Kutzián 1963, 378–9). These
interments of dogs must surely have been made to eliminate the
risk of their pining away after the death of their owners.

At the Homeric funeral of Patroclus (*Iliad*, Book XXIII), the
body of the deceased was covered with fat of animals whose
carcasses were placed around the bier, together with those of four
newly slain horses and two dogs. At Salamis in Cyprus excavations
since the Second World War have brought to light a remarkable
cemetery of the eighth and seventh centuries BC. Nearly all the
tombs are approached by a passage (*dromos*) in which was a vehicle
(hearse or chariot) drawn by two horses (if a royal burial) or by
two donkeys (if a non-royal burial). Almost invariably, after the
first animal had received a fatal blow, the second took fright and in
its effort to escape somehow twisted its neck around the yoke and
then fell in the opposite direction to its neighbour (Karageorghis
1969, 31–2, 53–4, 72–3).

In the great Scythian barrow at Kostromskaya, the twenty-two
sacrificed horses were carefully arranged in rows, with their heads
towards the circumference of the mound (Rice 1957, 102–3).

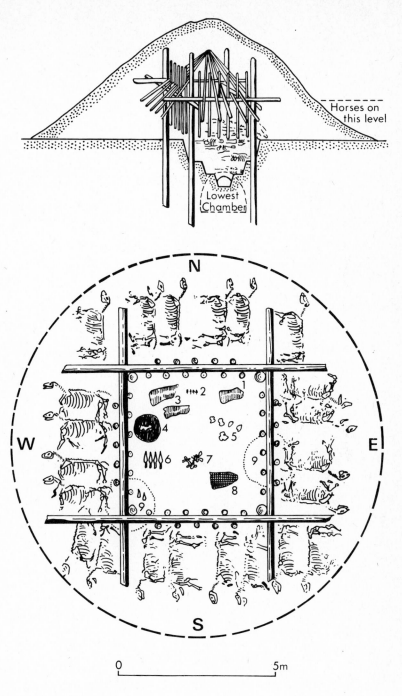

24 Arrangement of sacrificed horses in barrow at Kostromskaya, southern Russia. (After Rice)

1 Grindstone
2 Arrowheads
3 Leather quivers
4 Iron shield with deer
5 Potsherds
6 Iron spearheads
7 Bits
8 Scale armour
9 Plunderers' pits

In Roman law, a grave was not legally a grave until a pig had been sacrificed at the interment (Toynbee 1971, 50, quoting Cicero, *De Legibus*, ii, 22, 57).

At the Viking ship funeral on the Volga, witnessed by Ibn Fadlan in 922, a dog, two horses, two cows, a rooster and a hen were sacrificed (Jones 1968, 427). The Viking cemetery of fifteen graves on Westray Island, Orkney, contained burials accompanied by skeletons of horses, and one by the bones of a dog (Shetelig 1954, 68–9).

Where British prehistoric barrows are concerned, we may note the bones of a dog from Eyford (Gloucestershire) from a chambered long barrow (Daniel 1950, 106; the Tinkinswood cat was eliminated by Greenaway 1958). From Bronze Age round barrows come instances of a dog buried with its master in barrows Weymouth 22 in Dorset (Grinsell 1959, 142) and Collingbourne Kingston 19 (The Hunter's Barrow) in Wiltshire (Grinsell 1953, 171), where it accompanied a cremation with five flint arrowheads and a circular wreath of antlers. There are also instances of dogs buried in round barrows in Staffordshire and Yorkshire (Thurnam 1871, 539).

Chapter Five

Grave-goods

The equipment of the dead was subject to a number of considerations: his status in life, his own wishes, the respect or covetousness of his relatives, possible religious considerations, the nature of his death, etc.; in other words, factors which no archaeologist can ever hope to distinguish. J. Mellaart. *Çatal Hüyük* 1967, 207.

As was stated at the beginning of Chapter Three, perishable objects placed in tombs have been preserved only in a few exceptional conditions: the dry and warm desert climate of Egypt; the frozen state of parts of Siberia; the unique chemical conditions applying at the Bronze Age tombs of Jericho; and the permanently water-logged environment of the oak bole-coffins of the Danish Early Bronze Age. Occasionally we may be fortunate enough to have illustrations of perishable grave-goods carved on tomb walls.

The subject of grave-goods is so vast that the material from ancient Egypt alone would require several volumes for adequate treatment. Only a few fundamental aspects will therefore be considered here.

Offerings of food and drink

In Egypt offerings of food and drink date from Predynastic times. An early example of exceptional importance comes from an Early Dynastic tomb (no. 3477) at Sakkara excavated by Emery (1962). Beside the burial pit was a complete funerary meal comprising bread, porridge, fish, pigeon stew, quail, kidneys, beef, stewed fruit (probably figs), honey cakes, cheese, and grape

25 Funerary meal of the Egyptian Early Dynastic period from a tomb at Sakkara

wine, each on a separate dish or in some other container and already cooked. The tomb had escaped the attention of the tomb robber because it contained nothing of intrinsic value. The storerooms of the Step Pyramid of King Zoser (Dynasty III) contained at least eight thousand stone vases and many of them must have contained food or drink when deposited. The practice of depositing such offerings with the dead continued until at least the end of the Middle Kingdom and it was reinforced by spells in the *Coffin Texts* such as no. 365 which provides water for the dead. In later times food and drink were gradually replaced by substitute offerings described in the next chapter.

A few other instances from the Near East must be given. At Çatal Hüyük (*c.* 7000–6000 BC) the dead were accompanied by wooden bowls and baskets of food which included berries, peas, lentils, grain, eggs and meat (Mellaart 1967, 208). At Jericho the Middle Bronze Age tomb chambers contained multiple inhumations surrounded by supplies of food including fruit and flesh, and pots, arranged to imply communal feeding (Kenyon 1960, 263–5). At Ur Woolley noted that 'in every undisturbed grave the dead man holds between his hands, in front of his face, a cup or drinking vessel of metal, stone, or clay; in practically every grave there is some kind of jar or bottle, presumably for the replenishing of the cup; and in most, if not in all, there is a saucer for solid food' (Woolley 1934, 144). The sacrificial burials of between six and seventy to eighty servants or slaves with each royal burial at Ur were not accompanied by food offerings.

In the mid-third millennium BC Urukagina, King of Lagash, having decided that too much food and drink and other equipment was being placed with the dead, issued a decree limiting grave offerings to an extent summarized below:

> Beer: 3 jars (previously 7)
> Bread: 80 flat loaves (previously 420)
> Grain: 3 measures (previously 12 measures)
> Garment: none (previously, one)
> Bed: one, as before
> Head support: one, as before
> Chair: none (previously one)

He also directed that the bed be recovered from the tomb after the funeral (Heidel 1946, 151).

The Bronze Age tombs in the cemeteries of Cyprus, such as Vounous/Bellapais are remarkable for the large quantity of pots placed in each tomb. Most if not all of them are likely to have contained food or drink when deposited, excepting some of the small ones which may have contained perfumes or unguents.

In Greece and the Aegean Weinberg (1965) has made an important study of the question whether the pottery vessels, in which the food and drink were placed for the dead, were the ordinary domestic wares re-used for that purpose or were 'funerary pottery' made for the occasion. He concluded that much of it was made for funerary uses only, and that the latter can often be distinguished by one or more of the following characteristics:

(i) pots too large or too small for everyday use; indeed some of

the larger ones would have fallen to pieces if handled more
than once with their contents
(ii) pots of normal size but too coarse or poorly fired for daily use
(iii) pots with decoration too evanescent for continuous use but
adequate for the single occasion of the tomb offering
(iv) pots of non-utilitarian shapes perhaps for funerary ritual

These criteria can be applied, within limits, to the study of pottery
from tombs in other regions. For example, it has been noted that
the tombs of the Lausitz and La Tène cultures in Czechoslovakia
often contain 'funerary' pots less carefully fired than for normal
purposes, or of inferior quality (Neustupný 1961, 123, 245).

From the context of Minoan Crete, Branigan (1970, 92) is
commendably open-minded on whether dishes or pots already
contained food or drink when placed in tombs. For the rest of
Europe, it must suffice to state that it was the custom to deposit
food offerings at any rate with the inhumed dead in the Neolithic
sometimes, and as a rule in the Early Bronze Age until inhumation had been superseded by cremation. The evidence for this
comprises either the pots which contained the sustenance or the
animal bones from the meat offerings; but the latter must be carefully distinguished from the remains of funeral feasts consumed
by the mourners.

In Britain Neolithic bowls now and then deposited with the dead
in long barrows or chamber tombs imply food offerings. With
regard to beakers of the Late Neolithic/Early Bronze Age overlap,
their former name 'drinking cup' carries the nineteenth-century
view of their purpose. They were placed by the head or feet of
the inhumed dead, usually beneath round barrows. It is fairly
safe to assume that when deposited they contained food or drink,
and beer has been suggested (Childe 1947, 91). The latest and most
exhaustive study of *The Beaker Pottery of Great Britain and Ireland*
(Clarke 1970) seems to be silent on what they contained, as far as
one can tell from such a large book having no index. Food
vessels of the Early Bronze Age, placed with the dead beneath
round barrows mostly in northern Britain, have in several
instances been shown to contain the remains of food (Abercromby 1912, I, 110, 147, 155). Animal bones, often not in pots,
sometimes indicate flesh offerings. After cremation was generally
adopted there is less evidence of food offerings. Iron Age burials
in Yorkshire and elsewhere normally include gifts of pig. It is
plausible to consider all these food offerings as intended to provide
for the needs of the dead during his last journey which it might
have been thought he would have completed by the time the
flesh had gone from the body; but this is reading twentieth-
century concepts into the ideas held by later prehistoric man.

Means for post-funerary transmission of food to the dead

Some of the Copper Age megalithic tombs around Otranto (heel
of Italy) have holed cover slabs, suggestive of a channel for
making offerings of sustenance (Trump 1966, 88; Guido 1972,
155–6). Similar 'dolmens' with holed cover slabs occur in Malta

(J. D. Evans 1971, 192–8), and it is believed that they were introduced by immigrants from the heel of Italy. Similar holes in the stones of Minoan tombs Branigan (1970, 93) believes were for pouring libations into the tomb *during* the funeral. Some of the dolmens of Abkhazian in the northwestern Caucasus have at their entrance a hole thought to have been for post-funerary offerings of food; when not in use these holes were covered by a stone disc (Sulimirski 1970, 125–6 and pl. XII).

Some centuries later, during and after the Greek Geometric period, appear vases made it would seem exclusively for funerary use, with their base either pierced or non-existent, so that drink or libations poured into them would flow straight into the grave, perhaps even into the mouth of the dead or over his bones (Nilsson 1950, 618; Kurtz and Boardman 1971, 57–8, 152). The base of some of these vases, however, was pierced to enable them to be affixed to the top of the tomb. At Syllyum on Turkey's southern shore are Hellenistic(?) tombs some of which are provided with a hole for pouring libations to the dead (Bean 1968, 64).

From various parts of the Roman Empire have come pipe-burials usually beneath altar-tombs. From an altar on top of the tomb a pipe or tube of lead or pottery extends and leads vertically or obliquely down into the tomb, the purpose being the same as in the case of the Greek vases. Such interments with lead pipes have been found at various localities including Rome, Pompeii and Carthage; examples with earthenware pipes have been noted from Syracuse and Poitiers. In Britain they have been published from Colchester (an inhumation in a lead coffin with lead pipe extending) and Caerleon (a cremation in a lead casket with lead pipe extending). These pipes or tubes could also, perhaps, have been used for inserting a cremation of later date (Wheeler 1929; Toynbee 1971, 51–2).

Other grave-goods

Whether or no we interpret the presence of rich grave-goods as an index to the prosperity of the period, or at least of the person buried in the tomb, poverty of grave-goods does not necessarily indicate an impoverished economy. 'On the contrary . . . among most societies, the graves grow progressively poorer as material wealth, the number and variety of available articles of use or enjoyment, increased' (Childe 1945). In particular, Childe contrasted the often well-equipped graves of the Copper and Early Bronze Age inhumations over much of Europe with the frequently unaccompanied cremations (apart from those of chieftains and tycoons) from the Middle Bronze Age onwards, after a technological revolution had greatly increased the variety of objects which could have been placed with the dead. He also noted that the poorest-furnished graves at Syracuse were of the period of the city's greatest prosperity – the fifth to fourth centuries BC. 'In brief, of the new sorts of possessions and wealth, created by technological progress, only a few classes, and mostly those approved by tradition from the Pleistocene, were generally regarded as suitable grave furniture' (Childe 1945). In some periods

26 Bronze dagger, inlaid with gold, silver and niello, showing a lion hunt; from shaft-grave IV, Grave Circle A, Mycenae

and regions the quantity and type of objects placed with the dead may have been regulated by legislation or conditioned largely by custom.

The tombs of the great (or those pretending to be great) are often distinguished in antiquity by the presence among the grave-goods of status symbols such as the gold crook and flail of the Egyptian pharaohs; the bronze swords and daggers inlaid with gold and other materials from the Mycenaean world; the sceptres and maces of Bronze Age Europe; the trappings with the Wessex chieftain in Bush Barrow, Wiltshire (pp. 211–12); finely wrought and jewelled swords of the Late Bronze and Early Iron Age; and ceremonial objects from the rich Saxon and Viking burials, such as the fine sword, whetstone, shield, helmet and other objects from the Sutton Hoo (Suffolk) ship-burial. Chariot burials, predominantly of the Iron Age, are also often regarded as status interments. Within certain limits the presence of objects of these classes may enable a distinction to be made between the tombs of the chieftains and those of the tycoon containing merely objects of pleasure such as gaming boards and musical instruments.

Gaming boards, pieces, and boxes occur in Egyptian tombs from Dynasty I (the tomb of Hemaka) to the Ptolemaic period, and for much of the Dynastic period they are also represented on tomb walls. Elsewhere it does not seem to have been the custom to deposit such objects with the dead. There are, however, several instances of bone draughtsmen having come from Anglo-Saxon graves in Britain (Meaney 1964, 15, 74). Musical instruments, including lyres and reed pipes, were found in the royal cemetery at Ur; and those from Egypt include reed pipes and a sistrum from tombs of the Middle Kingdom (Sachs 1940). The remains of a harp came from barrow 2 at Pazyryk, and most of the Pazyryk barrows yielded drums (Rudenko 1970, 277–8). Another notable instrument is the harp from the Sutton Hoo ship-burial.

An effort to identify the group of thirteen Pylos furniture tablets as an inventory of the contents of a Mycenaean royal tomb has not met with general acceptance (Vermeule 1964, 175, 300).

Determination of the sex from the grave-goods (where the body has been removed, or has been dissolved by acid soil) is often difficult. The presence of archery equipment is generally indicative of a man, and this includes not only arrowheads of flint or bronze, but also their shafts which are occasionally preserved even in the British climate of the Early Bronze Age

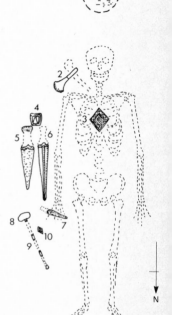

27 Arrangement of grave-goods in Bush Barrow, Wiltshire. (After Ashbee)

1 Remains of a wooden shield (?)
2 Flanged axe
3 Gold lozenge
4 Gold scabbard hook
5 Dagger
6 Dagger
7 Knife-dagger
8 Mace-head
9 Mounts of shaft
10 Gold object

(Grinsell 1953a, 36); and in barrow 3 at Pazyryk, twenty-four of them were still present although their metal arrowheads had been taken by tomb robbers (Rudenko 1970, 218). Even more rarely a complete bow has survived, as for example from a grave of the Russian Bronze Age Catacomb culture (Sulimirski 1970, 223). The great barrow at Kernonen-en-Plouvorn, Finistère, contained with the primary (?) interment nearly fifty barbed-and-tanged flint arrowheads and an amber wristguard (Briard, 1970). Arrow-shaft smoothers, usually of sandstone, have come from numerous Early Bronze Age graves extending from Russia to Britain. Bronze daggers and swords placed with the dead likewise normally indicate the male sex. Male interments may also be distinguished by the type and position on the body of dress-fasteners.

Identification of the sex of interments accompanied by objects of personal adornment is complicated by the fact that these were sometimes worn by both sexes. During the Egyptian Middle Kingdom, for example, necklaces, cosmetics and mirrors were used by both sexes (Hayes 1953, 242). In the great Copper Age cemetery at Basatanya (Yugoslavia) objects of personal adornment occurred with both sexes (Bognár-Kutzián 1963, I, 373). At Radley (Berkshire) a skeleton of a young man was accompanied by a beaker and a pair of gold basket earrings (Williams 1948, 5–6). Nonetheless, the fact remains that the tendency is for more objects of personal adornment to accompany female than male interments. At Çatal Hüyük, Mellaart noted that some of the female burials had bone spools and spatulas used for feeding children (Mellaart 1967, 207–9); others were accompanied by awls for sewing and bodkins for basketry. In Britain, many of the Early Bronze Age female interments have small knives or knife-daggers readily distinguishable from the more masculine daggers of the males.

Apart from objects identifying the sexes, such as those just discussed, it is only exceptionally that the archaeological record indicates the vocation of the dead by the grave-goods. Egyptian Dynastic tombs of quality usually have inscribed on their walls a list of offices held by the person buried in the tomb and there is no need to resort to any unplundered grave-goods for confirmation. Elsewhere the situation is very different. In Crete, Branigan has attempted to identify from the grave-goods the tombs of Minoan leather-workers, carpenters, stoneworkers, and obsidian-workers (Branigan 1970, 91–2). The Early Bronze Age barrows of leather-workers in Britain have been studied by Smith and Simpson (1964). In Russia a few graves of foundry-masters have been identified from the presence of moulds, crucibles, and other appliances for metalworking (Sulimirski 1970, 254, 280), but this is most unusual. By way of contrast, the decorations on Gallo-Roman tombs illustrate many vocations, including those of arboriculturist, blacksmith, butcher, butcher's wife, carpenter, clothier, cooper, currier, gardener, hairdresser, innkeeper, leather-worker, locksmith, musician, scribe, shoemaker, and weaver (Hatt 1951, 293–5).

The practice of depositing objects designed to protect the dead was developed in ancient Egypt from Dynasty V onwards.

With the advent of the New Kingdom they became very common, and even more so from Dynasty XXI onwards when they tended to replace the deposit of normal grave-goods, following the period of the great tomb robberies. Among the most interesting funerary amulets is the Heart Scarab, inscribed with chapter XXXB of the Book of the Dead, to protect the dead from his own conscience at the final judgment. There can be little doubt that among the grave-goods from other areas are numerous objects intended specifically for the protection of the dead. This may well have been the purpose of double-axes in Minoan tombs, one of which, the Tomb of the Double Axes at Knossos, was shaped in this form. In general, however, protective amuletic objects are to be sought among those grave-goods not obviously utilitarian. Certain objects of adornment may have been protective, including those of amber, jet, and faience (Grinsell 1953*b*, 272–7).

28 Egyptian Heart Scarab of Web-priest Neb-seny, inscribed with text from the Book of the Dead. Dynasty XVIII

In children's graves the presence of toys is of course frequent. They sometimes include models of boats, wagons and chariots, the latter occurring especially in boys' graves. When such objects are placed with adults they are usually interpreted as symbolic vehicles for a journey to the after-life (Chapter Nine).

Lamps occur quite frequently. Most of the Early and Middle Bronze Age graves at Jericho contained a lamp placed in a niche in the wall; the roof of this niche has often been blackened by soot from the lamp (Kenyon 1965, 551). The niche frequently inside the door of 'Giants' Tombs' in Sardinia may have served the same purpose, and this was certainly the case with the niches in the walls of Punic tombs on the same island (Guido 1963, 92, 205–6). In Greece lamps occur in tombs chiefly at Corinth from the fourth century BC (Kurtz and Boardman 1971, 211). In Roman times provision was sometimes made for the lighting of lamps in graves on occasions when the dead were commemorated (Toynbee 1971, 63–4). In England three richly furnished Roman cremation tombs near Chichester were provided with brackets on which lamps were placed (Winbolt 1935, 49, 54, 67).

In conclusion, a word must be said on the reasons for depositing objects with the dead. Their presence does not always prove a belief in an after-life. In some societies there was probably an idea that the possessions of the dead should be buried with him because of a repugnance against their use by the living. This question, however, does not arise with objects made for funerary purposes only, and these include the substitute offerings next to be described.

Chapter Six

Substitute offerings

Such as can not afford wine may have recourse to it's substitute, beer.
C. Lucas. *An Essay on Waters* 1756, III, 165.

As early as the Egyptian Predynastic period substitute offerings were made for placing in tombs. Among the earliest are the clay models of garlic deposited in Predynastic tombs, presumably in the hope of providing the dead with the pleasant taste of garlic without having to endure its obnoxious smell. Substitute tomb offerings were usually produced partly in the interests of economy and partly because it was no doubt hoped that these, being symbolic of the real thing, could be made useful to the dead, perhaps with the assistance of the recitation of a religious formula (as in ancient Egypt), while being of little or no use to the potential tomb robber.

In the Badarian period the adult male dead were sometimes provided with statuettes of women to serve as their companions or to satisfy their sexual needs. Some of the Early Dynastic royal tombs (or cenotaphs) at Abydos, notably that of Khasekhemuy, contained wafer-thin copper models of axe-heads, chisels, and barbed fish-spears. Models of implements and weapons continued to be placed in tombs until the Middle Kingdom. During the Old Kingdom vessels for food offerings include many stone vases, solid except possibly for a saucer-depression on the top, to receive token offerings. Real offering vases were sometimes filled with mud or sand to symbolize food or drink. The mortuary temple of the pyramid of Neferirkare at Abusir contained vases of gilded wood inlaid with coloured faience, in imitation of gold vessels inlaid with semi-precious stones (Fakhry 1969, 177). There are many other such instances of substitution from the Old Kingdom. The scenes of everyday life which adorn the walls of the more opulent private tombs, especially of Dynasties V and VI, should perhaps be interpreted as symbolic of a continuation into the hereafter of the activities of this life, including food production, the making of utilitarian objects, and recreation. The tomb of Perneb (Dynasty V) at Sakkara contained numerous model vases, and a complete model table service was found in another Memphite tomb of the same general period.

The disturbed conditions of the First Intermediate Period led to the development of other substitute offerings in the interests of economy. In particular there originated the custom, in several cemeteries of Middle Egypt, of depositing in the tombs wooden models of scenes of daily life, including bread- and beer-making, butchery, weaving, boating, shops, and so on. These continue into the early Middle Kingdom. Above the tombs were often placed earthenware 'soul-houses' (Dynasties IX to XI) which

developed from offering trays. In the gardens or courtyards of these 'soul-houses' model offerings of birds, joints of meat, and other food are frequently found. The tomb of Meket-Re (Dynasty XI) at Thebes contained the finest known series of these tomb models, and also more than 1200 model weapons and tools (Hayes 1953, 166–7, 262–7).

During the Middle Kingdom wooden dummy sandals, placed at the feet of the mummies, are more common than real sandals. Wooden models of bronze mirrors too occur in tombs of this period. They also contain jewellery of two kinds – the genuine article, often showing signs of wear, and the imitation jewellery of gilded plaster, gilded wood, faience, or other cheap substitutes for gold and semi-precious stones, made for funerary use only. Other substitute offerings in tombs of this period include models in clay and painted wood of metal vases, and model carpenters' tools (Hayes 1953, 261, 288, 306–7).

Towards the end of the Middle Kingdom the placing of wooden models and servant statuettes in the tomb was largely discontinued. It was followed by the introduction of *ushabtis,* figurines of servants to do the chores for the dead in the hereafter. At first of wood, they increased in number and popularity during the Second Intermediate Period and the New Kingdom when they were made of pottery, faience and other materials. Hundreds of them were placed in each well-equipped tomb.

29 Egyptian model granary from the tomb of Meket-Re, Thebes, which yielded the finest known series of tomb models from any Egyptian tomb. Dynasty XI, *c.* 2000 BC

30 Egyptian model tools (axes, chisels and knife) from a tomb at Sidmant. Dynasty IX–X, c. 2100 BC

Pottery statuettes of 'wives', laid on a couch of the same material, sometimes occur in tombs of late Dynasty XVII and early Dynasty XVIII (Petrie 1937, 8–9). Some of the royal tombs of Dynasty XVIII, notably that of Tuthmosis IV, contained model offerings of weapons and vessels. Solid dummy jars of wood, painted to resemble stone, sometimes occur in tombs of this dynasty (Hayes 1959, 149, 228). There was a wooden model granary in the tomb of Tutankhamun (Desroches-Noblecourt 1963, pl. 47). The practice of depositing grave-goods of all kinds with the dead was largely discontinued after its futility had been exposed by the great tomb robberies of Dynasty XX. Models of offerings do, however, continue occasionally even into the Late Dynastic period.

The Late Hellenistic cemetery at Myrina in Turkey included solid clay dummy bottles for symbolic offerings. (Bean 1966, 108). In Minoan Crete ordinary drinking cups and goblets were superseded for funerary use by small conical cups for token toasting only (Branigan 1970, 100). In the undisturbed tholos tomb at Pylos, excavated by Blegen, the final burial (of an adult male) had a female figurine on its chest, presumably a substitute wife or concubine (Taylour 1964, 81).

In Cyprus, the Vounous/Bellapais Early Bronze Age cemetery contained pottery models of daggers and their sheaths and pottery copies of brushes or combs (Stewart 1950, pls. XCVI–XCVIII). Tombs in the same cemetery contained earthenware models of a ploughing scene showing two ploughs each drawn by two oxen, and a scene interpreted as of a sacred enclosure (Karageorghis 1969, pls. 48, 49). These models are broadly contemporary with those of the early Middle Kingdom in Egypt (Grace 1940, 51). In the Iron Age cemetery at Salamis, Cyprus, tombs 2 and 47 contained earthenware jugs tin-plated to imitate those of silver. Many of the clay bottles from the pyre of the cenotaph of King Nicocreon (tomb 77 at Salamis) had been gilded to imitate gold bottles (Karageorghis 1969). Earthenware copies of jewellery and other objects occurred in the pyres of tombs in the Cellarka.

A Mycenaean chamber tomb on the northern slope of the Areopagus, Athens, contained a skeleton of a warrior accompanied by a set of twelve pottery vases tin-coated to simulate silver tableware. Similar 'false' silverware has come from chamber tombs at Dendra, Mycenae, Isopata and Ialysos, all late fifteenth or early fourteenth century BC (Immerwahr 1966).

In Sicily, there was a tendency in the Late Bronze Age for miniature replicas of bronze weapons instead of real ones to be

31 Villanovan pottery reproduction of a helmet, made for funerary use

used for funerary purposes (Childe 1945, 16). In Italy the cinerary urns of the Villanovan culture were sometimes covered by the warrior's bronze helmet but more often by an imitation helmet of pottery. From *pozzo* graves (small cremation pits) of the same culture come pottery model boats probably representing the owner's ship, as the original would have been too large and valuable to place in the tomb (Hencken 1968, 30–1, 48, and pls. 76, 77), and pottery models of chariots and their horses.

At Carthage, some of the tombs of the sixth century B C contained stone models of chairs, tables and stools (Harden 1962, 142–3 and fig. 39). In the Hypogeum at Hal Saflieni, Malta, some of the human skeletons were accompanied by greenstone axependants holed for suspension; but it is uncertain whether these can be regarded as substitute axes in the context of this chapter (Evans 1959, 160).

From various areas in northern and western Europe, and from several periods, Piggott (1962c) has assembled instances of the

32 Limestone models of furniture from Phoenician tombs at Douimes near Carthage

33 Villanovan pottery funerary model of a boat

offering of the heads and feet only of horses and oxen with human interments. They occur for example in the Timber Grave and Catacomb Grave cultures of south Russia and even probably in British long barrows (Thurnam 1870, 182). These could well be token offerings in the interest of economy.

In the Iberian peninsula substitute offerings often occur in pre-historic tombs. They include lunulae of limestone from pre-beaker contexts, presumably reproductions of those of scarcer materials but apparently much earlier than the Irish gold lunulae. Stone or ivory models of combs (with teeth unseparated), stone models of hoes in their handles (with simulated binding), and

34 Villanovan pottery funerary model of a chariot

stone models of sandals all occur in megalithic or rock-cut tombs around Lisbon (Savory 1968, 121–2, 125, 128–9, 131, 145, 148). Somewhat later, between the tenth and fifth centuries BC, are the decorated funerary stelae of western Spain. These usually portray the deceased warrior in highly stylized form, with sword, shield, spear and accessories, and sometimes with a two- or four-wheeled chariot drawn by two animals. Among the best is that from Solana de Cabañas (Cáceres), Spain (Savory 1968, pl. 62). The whole group is described by Almagro (1966). It seems uncertain whether these stelae provide illustrations as substitutes for the actual grave-goods.

In Denmark a round barrow in Jutland contained, in an oak coffin, a sword scabbard within which had been placed a simple dagger instead of a sword. Some of the urns containing Late Bronze Age cremations include a miniature sword symbolic of the real thing, which would in any case be too large to go into the urn (Klindt-Jensen 1957, 63, 75).

In France an Early Bronze Age grave at Lescongar-en-Plou-hinec (Finistère) contained, just outside the disturbed funerary chamber, bone copies of two large bronze daggers with six rivets each (also copied in bone) and of two small bronze knife-daggers (Briard 1968). It is a question whether the decoration in the interior of the megalithic tombs of France (especially Brittany) was sometimes a substitute for the deposit of grave-goods. This seems especially probable with carvings of axe-heads of green-stone or other material, whether hafted or not, and of spears and daggers, which would have been sought after by the average tomb robber. The carving of such objects on the tomb walls could be considered as supplying the needs of the dead in a manner which eliminated the risk of robbery. A case in point is the group of eighteen 'jadeite' axes on a wall-slab from Gavrinis. Some of the

carvings of subjects not yet satisfactorily interpreted could then be of perishable objects not known to have survived.

In the British Isles, carvings of axe-heads in stone cists at Nether Largie (beneath a round barrow) and Ri Cruin, both in Argyllshire, and of axe-heads and hilted daggers on a slab from the Badbury Barrow (Dorset) could have been substitute offerings (Grinsell 1959, 73). A cairn known as Crug-yr-Afan (Glamorgan), resembling a Wessex bell-barrow in plan, contained with an interment a non-metallic (probably fossil mammoth-tusk) copy of a Wessex-type grooved ogival bronze dagger, evidently a close parallel to those just noted from Finistère (Burgess 1962).

From the Roman period comes a group of bronze miniature models of agricultural tools and other objects from a barrow in Sussex, believed to be a votive deposit dedicated to Sabazius, a Thraco-Phrygian agricultural god, and probably associated with a burial. Similar models, found with burials of adults, are centred on and around Cologne (Manning 1966).

In Saxon contexts it is by no means unusual for miniature combs, shears, tweezers, and knives to occur among the grave goods (Meaney 1964, 16).

It is of interest that in Japan, wreaths of paper are still used at funerals (Habenstein and Lamers 1960, 45); and in China, special types of paper money were printed for burning with the dead until the custom was prohibited by the Chinese Communist government a few years ago.

35 Sepulchral slab of warrior with shield, sword, mirror (?), bow-brooch and cart. Solana de Cabañas, Cáceres, Spain. Sixth century BC

Chapter Seven

The breaking or 'killing' of
funerary objects

In the eyes of the people who practise it the breaking of the object is the equivalent of the death of the human being to whose service it is dedicated. It is thus killed in order that its ghost may follow the ghost of the dead into the spirit world, there to serve the purposes which it served in this world when made. E. Sidney Hartland, in Hastings' *Encyclopaedia of Religion and Ethics* IV, 1911, 430.

(For full documentation, where not here given, see Grinsell 1962 and 1973*a*.)

In this chapter it will be shown that the reasons for this custom are much more complex than Hartland suggested. We are here concerned not only with the breaking but also, in some contexts, with the 'killing' of grave goods by bending or rolling them over, as sometimes with iron swords of various periods. In almost all cases the purpose is to end the life of the object placed with the dead. The following reasons have been given for this custom which is widespread both ethnographically and archaeologically:

   (i) To release the spirit in the object to accompany the dead to the after-life.

  (ii) To reduce the risk of tomb robbery by rendering the grave-goods of little or no value to the living (as among the Eskimo).

 (iii) To prevent quarrels among the surviving relatives regarding disposal of the dead person's property (as among some of the Nicobar Islanders).

 (iv) To prevent the efficacy of the funerary ritual from being spoiled by the subsequent use of funerary objects for profane purposes; there are many ethnographical instances of the breaking of funerary equipment for this reason.

  (v) To reduce or eliminate risk of pollution, especially where all the property of the dead is destroyed following death from a contagious disease.

 (vi) Exceptionally, to frighten away Charon and thus prevent him from claiming another death, as in parts of the Aegean in recent times. This is probably a later reason invented to explain an early custom, the original meaning of which had been forgotten.

 (vii) Swords and other symbols of authority may have been 'killed' because of their close association with the dead, and from the idea that it would be improper for them to be used again by someone less worthy. This explanation applies particularly to swords and certain other objects from the pre-Roman Iron Age to the Viking period.

(viii) Sometimes, the cups or other vessels in which a toast to the dead was drunk were shattered and the fragments fell at or near the tomb, as in the Mycenaean Age and occasionally in other periods. Thus Propertius wrote, 'Was this also a burden . . . to appease mine ashes with wine from the shattered jar?'

 (ix) Exceptionally, notably in the Egyptian Old and Middle Kingdoms, certain types of object were broken to symbolize the destruction of the enemies of the deceased. This idea apparently lay behind the ceremony of the Breaking of the Two Red Jars (representing the pharaoh's enemies) described in the Pyramid Texts (Utterance 244), and it may also explain the 'cursing statuettes' of the Middle Kingdom, found near the pyramid of Teti at Sakkara, and elsewhere.

  (x) Objects too large to go into the grave or other funerary enclosure were sometimes partly dismantled to enable them to fit into it. This occurred with the boat of Kheops near the Great Pyramid at Giza; with the chariots in the tomb of Tutankhamun; with the carriage from the chief burial in the Regolini-Galassi tomb at Cerveteri; and with chariotry equipment in various Iron Age burials. The bending or rolling up of the blades of Greek swords, to enable them to fit into the cremation pit, is another instance.

 (xi) Broken objects may sometimes have been placed with the dead by relatives who were too mean to deposit unbroken offerings. This explanation seems, however, a little far fetched, as such people are more likely to have refrained from making any offering at all.

(xii) Hacked and battered arms and armour buried with the dead may merely indicate that he had died a warrior's death as shown by the condition of these offerings. This is sometimes illustrated in medieval funerary art (Boase 1972, 116).

Characteristics of some ritually 'killed' objects

It is often difficult to ascertain whether broken objects in and around tombs were broken ritually at the time of the interment or at subsequent ritual acts such as periodical drinking to the health of the dead, or much later by tomb robbers, by the collapse of the superstructure of the tomb, or from any other cause. It was probably natural at all periods for a tomb robber, annoyed at his disappointment at finding no gold, to smash in a frenzy whatever else he did find. Only a critical weighing of the evidence from a tomb excavation can result in reliable conclusions as to the cause of breakages, excepting in certain special instances enumerated below:

  (i) Stone or pottery vessels with holes neatly made in or near their centre, when found in or near graves, can normally be considered to have been ritually 'killed'. Examples are known from ancient Egypt, from present-day Sudanese tribes, contemporary natives in the Blantyre region in Malawi, among various American Indian tribes, and from parts of the Roman Empire including Britain, notably at the Infirmary Field cemetery at Chester.

(ii) The breaking or bending of swords, sceptres, or other emblems of authority, as a funerary rite, the object broken sometimes being afterwards placed in or near the grave. Some of the bent or broken swords from Late Bronze Age, Iron Age, Saxon and Viking funerary contexts come into this category. Roman interments found near Brough (Yorkshire, East Riding) in 1936 had sceptres which had been bent across the knee before being placed in the grave. The Pope's signet ring (Fisherman's Ring), which dates at least from 1265, has at any rate since 1521 been ceremonially broken on the death of each holder of the office; this ritual was duly performed on the death of Pope John XXIII in 1963. On the death of the British sovereign the Lord Chamberlain's staff of office is ceremonially 'killed'; and the Swedish monarch's coat of arms is ritually broken on his death.

(iii) The 'killing' of metal vessels and other metal objects by thrusts from swords, spears, daggers, or other weapons, leaves the object with strong evidence of the ritual act. Cases in point are the helmet from the Sutton Hoo barrow (Suffolk) which was pierced from the inside, and the three bronze bowls from a Saxon interment on Loveden Hill (Lincolnshire), all of which had their base pierced before burial.

(iv) Identification of sherds from ritually broken pottery vessels can be made in certain instances, for example when a

36 Ceremonially 'killed' bronze bowl from a Saxon grave at Loveden Hill, Lincolnshire. The bowl was 'killed' by making in its base three holes (not visible in this photograph)

libation of resinated wine, or other liquid leaving permanent traces, extends over the fractured surfaces of the sherds,
as with the amphorae from the Roman barrow at Holborough (Kent), or when the sherds had afterwards been
placed on the pyre and their fractured surfaces become
burned, as at a barrow at Long Crichel (Dorset).

The evidence from tombs

Perhaps the earliest known instance of this custom is from Poland.
What has been described as the richest Tardenoisian burial in
Europe (Middle Ancylus period, *c.* 7000 BC) was found at Janis-
lawice in the province of Lodz. This extended inhumation of a
male adult in an oblong grave was accompanied by many finely
worked microliths, points of bone and antler, and other bone
implements, some for fishing. Most of the implements had been
deliberately broken.

In Egypt the breaking of grave-goods before being placed with
the dead dates from the Predynastic period, when flint implements including forked lances and stone mace-heads were broken
for this purpose. During the Early Dynastic period the custom continued and stone vessels were later included. The Petrie collection at
University College, London, includes stone vessels of Dynasties
III–IV with holes made in their base before being placed with the
dead. Many of the vases from the tomb of Sekhemkhet at Sakkara
(Dynasty III) are thought to have been ritually broken. The
practice continued through the Old Kingdom. A good example
from the end of Dynasty VI comes from the antechamber of the
pyramid of Pepy II at Sakkara where Jéquier found fragments of
vases of diorite and alabaster inscribed with that king's and other
royal names; he was convinced that these vases had been deliberately broken as part of the funerary ritual. During the Middle
Kingdom the custom was often expressed by the breaking of bows
before placing them with the dead. Examples of such ceremonially
broken bows, from tombs of Dynasties XI and XII at Thebes
and Lisht are in the Metropolitan Museum in New York, and
other examples are housed elsewhere. The tomb of the little-
known pharaoh Hor (Dynasty XIII) at Dahshur contained, among
other things, sticks and wands which had been broken before
being placed in the tomb. During the Second Intermediate Period
the practice continued of ritually 'killing' pots by holing their
base before placing them with the dead. During the New Kingdom evidence for this custom seems to decline but it is believed
that some faience vessels of this period were ritually 'killed' for
funerary purposes. The tomb of Tutankhamun seems to have
yielded little or no evidence of ritual breakages apart from the
dismantled chariots; but the situation is complicated by the
intrusion of tomb pilferers on two occasions shortly after the burial
and the definitive account of the contents of this tomb is still
awaited. From the late Ramesside period onwards the shock of
the large-scale tomb robberies which took place in the Valley
of the Kings acted as a deterrent to the placing of offerings with
the dead.

In Palestine the custom of breaking grave-goods was exceptional. Dame Kathleen Kenyon found no evidence of it in the Bronze Age cemeteries at Jericho.

In the Aegean there is plenty of evidence of the ritual 'killing' of funerary objects from the Neolithic onwards. In Cyprus the Neolithic site at Khirokitia included burials with stone vases considered to have been ceremonially broken. Some of the Bronze Age tombs at Vounous/Bellapais, and other tombs in Cyprus, have yielded metal weapons and other objects broken, it would seem, ritually. Mycenaean Greece also provides evidence of this custom. At Vaphio two spears placed in the rotunda of the pit-grave must have been broken if deposited with their shafts as the pit was too small to take the shafts whole. An undisturbed tholos tomb at Pylos, excavated by Blegen, contained a rapier which had been bent probably as a ritual act. It has been held by several authorities of high standing, including Blegen, Mylonas, Persson, and Wace, that in the Late Helladic period at Mycenae and other sites in the plain of Argos, one of the last acts in the funerary ritual at chamber tombs, and probably also at tholos tombs, was to drink a toast or pour a libation in honour of the dead from a stemmed cup (*kylix*), or from several of them, and then shatter the cup against the entrance to the tomb. Fragments of many of these cups have often been found at tomb entrances in numbers sufficient to suggest this practice. Some centuries later the funerary vases known as Attic white *lekythoi* were believed by Beazley to have been sometimes deliberately shattered at the grave. The custom of breaking pots continues as a funerary rite in parts of modern Greece.

In Italy Copper Age tombs at Osimo near Vescovaro (Ancona) have yielded daggers believed to have been ritually broken before deposit. Late Bronze Age Villanovan biconical urns usually have one of their two handles knocked off when used for funerary purposes. From early Latin authors we get occasional glimpses of the ritual of drinking a toast to the dead. So Petronius, describing the belated arrival at Trimalchio's banquet of Habinnas who had been detained at a funeral, quotes him as saying that the occasion was 'pleasant, though we had to empty half our drinks upon his bones'. In Italy as in Greece, the ritual breaking of pots at funerals continues in some regions to the present day, notably at Pavia.

In Russia there is evidence that in some Neolithic cemeteries of the Dnieper-Donetz culture the pots were shattered probably at the funeral feast and the sherds scattered over the surrounding area. In Poland, the breaking, bending, or burning of grave-goods was practised during the pre-Roman Iron Age and continued into the Roman period.

In Spain Copper Age graves sometimes contain flat copper axes broken across, and the piece containing the cutting edge is sometimes missing. Graves of the Lusitanian and other Iron Age tribes of southern Spain often have their weapons mutilated 'to prevent re-use or desecration' (Arribas 1964, 139).

In France, of more than a hundred greenstone axes from the megalithic tomb of Mané-er-Hroek (Morbihan), several had been deliberately broken into two or three pieces. Instances of the breaking, twisting or bending of Iron Age swords with inhumations have been noted from the cemeteries of Notre-Dame-du-Vaudreuil and Hallais near Brouelles, and from graves in the Marne region. The Viking grave at L'Ile de Groix (Morbihan) contained swords which had been intentionally bent and damaged, and shield bosses, one of which had received a violent blow.

In the Low Countries pottery and tools were sometimes broken before being placed in tombs of the Michelsberg culture, notably at Spiennes in Belgium. Some of the 'hunebeds' of the Netherlands have also yielded broken flint implements, believed to have been ritually 'killed'. From a cremation at Chevaudos near Namur (Belgium) came an intentionally broken Iron Age sword. In the Hallstatt tombs of the Low Countries, 'only rarely was the sword intact when deposited in the grave. Very frequently the bronze sword was broken, and the iron one ritually bent' (De Laet 1958, 139). The well-known Romano-Belgic barrows in Belgium have also yielded numerous objects considered to have been ritually broken – for example the barrows at Fresin, Penteville, and Tirlemont.

In Scandinavia, from the Iron Age onwards there is abundant evidence of the bending or rolling of iron weapons before placing them with the cremated dead, especially in Norway and Sweden. The larger cremation urns of this period usually have their lugs knocked off, perhaps to signify that they should never again be lifted from their place: an explanation which might well apply also to the Italian Villanovan cremation urns already described. Removal of one or both lugs or handles of a large urn would in any case create a problem for a tomb robber. There are numerous instances of the breaking, bending or twisting of swords and other weapons placed in graves of the Viking period in Scandinavia.

The evidence from the British Isles can be stated briefly. From the Neolithic period there are numerous instances of broken flint leaf arrowheads found more or less in association with interments in long barrows – notably Wayland's Smithy (Berkshire); Windmill Tump, Rodmarton (Gloucestershire); long barrows Alton 14 and Milton Lilbourne 7 (Wiltshire); and in round barrow Calais Wold 275 (east Yorkshire) which had Neolithic features.

Evidence of ceremonial breaking of grave-goods in Bronze Age round barrows is remarkably slight when compared with the large number of excavation records available; but most of these date from the nineteenth century or earlier when the finer points of funerary ritual were seldom looked for. It has been noted that the rarity of dagger-pommels with Early Bronze Age interments could be explained on the assumption that the pommel was broken from the dagger before the latter was placed in the grave. Sherds from barrow Long Crichel 14 (Dorset) had been burned after the pot from which they came had been broken. Round barrows Wimborne St Giles 9 and Winterborne Herringston 1 in the same county had fragments of stone or flint axes above the primary interment. Round barrow Charlton Horethorne 1 (Somerset), opened in 1877 by Pitt-Rivers, contained twenty

37 Bronze axe-heads (all but one broken across) from a votive deposit in a round barrow on Combe Hill, Jevington, Sussex

flint flakes which the excavator considered 'had been chipped during, or only shortly before, the erection of the mound, for the purpose of funeral ceremony'. A deposit of three flanged copper or bronze axes of which two had been broken across, and half an axe, in a round barrow at Jevington (Sussex) is likely to have been contemporary with the primary burial in the barrow. This find is a good parallel to the broken flat copper axes already noted from Copper Age graves in Spain. Round barrow Knook 1a (Wiltshire) contained an interment with a bronze dagger which had been broken in two. Pots or urns broken before burial have been retrieved from various round barrows excavated by modern methods, including Ogbourne St Andrew 6 and Snail Down XVII (Wiltshire), and Sutton (Glamorganshire) where Sir Cyril Fox found sherds of a beaker placed on and around the skull of a crouched interment. Mortimer's round barrow Aldro 88 (east Yorkshire) contained, in the remains of its original shaft, a lozenge-shaped flint arrowhead the tip of which had been broken off before the arrowhead was placed in the shaft. The round barrow at Sutton (Glamorganshire) yielded among the grave-goods seven flint arrowheads, some of which appear to have had their shafts ritually broken.

Iron Age interments in Britain are rare with the exception of Marnian burials in and around Yorkshire. The Iron Age chariot burial recently excavated at Garton Slack (east Yorkshire) had the shaft of the chariot broken in two to fit into the grave. An Iron Age burial in barrow Bincombe 11 (Dorset) was placed beneath an antler broken in half. At Lexden near Colchester (Essex), the barrow, possibly of Cunobeline or one of his family, contained an assortment of funerary offerings most of which had been deliberately broken before deposit.

Some Roman barrows in southeastern England, notably at Holborough (Kent) and possibly also Plumberow Mount (Essex), yielded evidence that amphorae or other vessels had been smashed as part of the funerary ceremony. The five amphorae from the Holborough barrow had been filled with wine or oil which had spread over the fractured surfaces of the sherds.

The Saxon period is represented in the present context by the Sutton Hoo harp which had been dismantled before being placed in the hanging bowl; and the escutcheons from the upper bowl had been removed and placed in the lower bowl. The three ceremonially 'killed' bronze bowls from the barrow on Loveden Hill (Lincolnshire) have already been mentioned. A Saxon interment in barrow Alvediston 1c (Wiltshire) was accompanied by an iron spearhead, ferrule, shield boss, and bracelet, nearly all broken in two before being deposited.

Viking graves with ritually 'killed' grave-goods include that from Hesket-in-the-Forest (Cumbria), which contained a sword bent nearly flat, a bent spearhead, and a shield-boss which had received a hard hit; and a burial at Kilmainham near Dublin was accompanied by three bent swords and three shield bosses, the tops of which had been damaged. The breaking of plates, saucers, and possibly earthenware tobacco-pipes has been reported at recent funerals in various parts of Ireland.

Chapter Eight

The funerary ritual and related considerations

Throughout the rites and observances attendant on death, two motives – two principles – are found struggling for the mastery. On the one hand, there is the fear of death and of the dead. . . . On the other hand, there is the affection, real or simulated, for the deceased. E. Sidney Hartland, in Hastings' *Encyclopaedia of Religion and Ethics* IV, 1911, 426a.

There is no necessary relationship between (i) the scale of the funerary ritual; (ii) the size of the tomb; and (iii) the importance or otherwise of the person buried therein. This was recently illustrated by the State Funeral of Sir Winston Churchill in 1965, followed by his interment in the village churchyard at Bladon in Oxfordshire. Ucko (1969) noted that in ethnographical contexts a large and imposing tomb may indicate construction by a burial society to which members subscribe. It could also serve as an advertisement for the undertakers or architects rather than a memorial to the dead.

In Egypt during the New Kingdom, and most probably at other periods, the costliness or otherwise of the tombs generally reflects the prosperity or poverty of the period (Abdul-Qader 1966, 13). This must surely have been the case in most other archaeological contexts unless expenditure on the tomb was limited by custom, or by legislation as in Athens during the time of Demetrius of Phalerum (*c.* 325–307 BC). Some peoples, such as the ancient Egyptians, were obsessed with the idea of having an imposing tomb; others, such as most of the Iron Age tribes of Britain, cared very little about burial except for that of their chiefs.

In some societies it was (and is) usual for funerary acts to be the opposite of those connected with the living. Among the Ainu of Japan and some Oceanic tribes it is customary to dress the dead in clothes turned inside out (Watanabe 1955). Archaeological parallels are provided from Egypt and by Scythian barrow 2 at Pazyryk in which a person was interred in a coat of squirrel worn furry-side inwards (Rudenko 1970, 91). Eight inverted silver bowls with a Sarmatian royal burial at Novocherkassk may be another instance of this (Kaposhina 1963).

The main purpose of this chapter is to draw attention to various contemporary pictures of funerary processions and to related matters not already covered.

Egypt

The funerary evidence from Pharaonic Egypt is so vast that only a few aspects will be considered here. From the Old Kingdom

onwards the deceased is portrayed in the tomb sitting at a table laden with food, with the menu of the funeral meal (the *pancarte*) on the wall near by. The scene continues though with less frequency until the end of the Pharaonic period, and the sepulchral banquet scenes in Greek, Etruscan and Roman tombs may or may not be derived from it.

A detailed study of the Theban tombs of the New Kingdom (Abdul-Qader 1966) shows that the scenes of the funeral procession occur throughout the period, but other scenes of the after-

38 Egyptian limestone offering-table and pancarte (menu of funerary meal) from the tomb of Princess Meryt-yetes II. Dynasty IV

39 Tomb of Ramose, Thebes: general view of funeral procession – perhaps the most complete from any known Egyptian tomb. Late Dynasty XVIII

40 Tomb of Ramose, Thebes: detail of the group of wailing women

life date from late Dynasty XVIII. Scenes of the funeral procession differ from tomb to tomb, but that in the tomb of Ramose (no. 55) at Thebes is among the finest and is easy of access. It was probably begun in the reign of Amenophis III and continued into that of Akhenaten when the upper register showing part of the funeral ritual was plastered over. However, the register still visible includes bearers of funerary furniture and flowers; perhaps the most beautiful of all are the groups of wailing women who face backwards towards the rest of the procession which is headed by a man carrying the dead man's sandals; the rest bring more funerary furniture including the bed, head-rest, and coffin. The wailing women depicted in these tombs are probably professional wailers as in modern Egypt (Werbrouck 1938). Scenes in other tombs show the weighing of the heart of the dead; the mummification ceremony; the sacrifice of a calf, or a calf having its leg cut off. The deceased is led from the entrance to the West to the after-life by various deities. The tomb chapel was a place where the priests,

relatives, and friends of the dead could meet periodically, perform
ritual, make offerings, and generally keep in touch with the dead.

41 Long side of painted
limestone sarcophagus from
Hagia Triada, Crete, *c.* 1400 BC

The Minoan-Mycenaean World

The sarcophagus from Hagia Triada (Crete), dated to *c.* 1400 BC,
has on its four sides painted scenes believed to illustrate the funeral
rites, but they are difficult to interpret and probably include
Egyptian elements. One long side shows a procession of three
figures in long dresses, headed by a dark-skinned flute-player who
is to be seen behind a tied and sacrificed bull on an offering stand,
beneath which are smaller animals presumably for sacrifice. On the
right is a priest (?) before an altar, behind which are a double-axe
on a tall plinth surmounted by a bird, and a sanctuary supporting
a small tree with two 'horns of consecration' on either side of it.

The other long side shows, from left to right, two pairs of double-axes mounted on a tall plinth, with a bird above each plinth; two female offering-bearers and a lyre-player all moving left; one of the offering-bearers pours blood of the sacrificed bull (?) into a large bowl. Next come three men moving right, the front one carrying a boat and the two rear ones each a small bull or model of a bull. Facing the front offering-bearer is a figure (of the deceased?) behind a stylized tree and three steps, and in front of a tomb (?) decorated with running spirals. There is little doubt that this scene continues from the previous one. The short sides each show two female figures in a chariot, in one case drawn by a pair of goats, in the other by a pair of winged griffins, above which is a bird. The birds in these scenes doubtless represent the soul of the departed. The sarcophagus may have been painted by an artist who had visited Egypt or was familiar with New Kingdom Egyptian funerary art, for a client who may have been Mycenaean rather than Minoan and who might also have visited Egypt.

The evidence from this sarcophagus can be supplemented by that from various tombs of the same general period. The sacrificed bull is paralleled by that found between the main chamber and the side chamber of a tholos tomb at Arkhanes, south of Knossos (Sakellarakis and Papademetriou 1970). Balances found in richer

Mycenaean tombs are of uncertain purpose and comparison with the scales used for the weighing of the heart in ancient Egypt is at best a rash conjecture. The placing of a gold death-mask over the face of the dead, as in Grave Circles A and B, is a feature of 'royal' interments here. Chariot scenes on the stelae from Grave Circle A at Mycenae have been interpreted as evidence of chariot races as part of the funerary games, and such chariot scenes also occur on Mycenaean vases (Vermeule 1964, 91, 297–8; Press, 1969). The dromos of a tholos tomb near Pylos, excavated in 1956, contained dozens of stone arrowheads, apparently fired as volleys towards the tomb in final salute to the dead, or possibly to frighten away evil spirits (Marinatos 1957). The more usual custom of drinking the health of the dead and smashing the drinking vessel against the tomb has been described in Chapter Six. It may here be added that in Minoan Crete, after the toast to the dead had been made, the drinking vessels were not smashed but were placed around the body of the dead, either upright as at Hagia Triada, or inverted as at Vorou and Kamilari (Branigan 1970, 100). Processions of female mourners with their arms above their heads are sometimes shown on Mycenaean vases and pottery coffins (Iakovidis 1966). Lamps for lighting the tomb for the funerary or subsequent ritual have been found in tholos tombs at Dendra, Mycenae, and Vaphio. There is evidence of fumigation and the burning of incense in the tombs before each burial.

The Homeric description of the funeral of Patroclus (*Iliad*, Book XXIII)

The funeral of Patroclus was directed by Achilles. Many trees, especially oaks, were felled and cut into logs to form a pyre *c.* 30 metres square. Cupfuls of blood from oxen, sheep, goats, and hogs slaughtered for the funeral feast were poured around the corpse which was placed on top of the pyre. Sheep and cattle were flayed and placed at the foot of the pyre; fat from them was spread over the corpse, and the carcasses of the animals were then placed around the body. Some two-handled jars of honey and oil were laid against the bier. The bodies of four horses and two of Patroclus' nine dogs were added, and finally twelve sons of Trojans of noble birth were put to the sword and placed on the pyre which was then fired with the aid of libations to assist the flames. It had been agreed that the bones of Patroclus and Achilles should eventually be placed in the same golden urn provided by Achilles' mother.

When the pyre had nearly burnt out, the smouldering embers were extinguished with wine. The bones of Patroclus were picked out, placed in a golden urn which was sealed with a double layer of fat and covered with a linen shroud. A barrow was planned by surrounding the pyre with a stone retaining wall and building within the enclosed area a mound. This mound was of medium size, it being understood that it would be enlarged after Achilles had been interred in it.

When the barrow was provisionally completed by the troops, they assembled in a wide ring where the funeral games would be

42 (*Opposite, upper*) Second long side of the sarcophagus from Hagia Triada. This scene probably continues from Ill. 41

43 (*Opposite, lower*) Short side of the sarcophagus from Hagia Triada showing two female figures in a chariot being drawn by goats

44 (*Above*) Second short side of the sarcophagus from Hagia Triada showing two female figures in a chariot being drawn by winged griffins

73

held. These comprised a chariot race, boxing, wrestling, running, armed combat, disc-throwing, archery, and javelin-throwing. It is noted that the prizes, ranging from skilled women to tripods and pans, were 'brought out from the ships' and were apparently not the possessions of the deceased.

Many have seen Mycenaean elements in the Homeric funeral, but the normal Mycenaean rite was inhumation of the unburnt body, whereas Patroclus was cremated.

Classical Greece

It is outside the scope of this work to do more than touch upon Greek funerals of the Classical period. Much is known about them from contemporary literature and from illustrations on Attic black-figure vases and stone sarcophagi. The deceased is shown lying in state on a high-legged bier accompanied by male mourners on foot or on horseback, with their right arm raised in respect to the dead, and by wailing women tearing their hair and sometimes wearing torn clothing (Weller 1970). Other vases show the coffin being lowered into the tomb, and the barrow above. The funerary feast was often held at the house of the departed; remains of food near the burial should therefore indicate offerings to the dead rather than remains of the funeral feast. A vase by the Sappho painter shows the dead being placed in the coffin by lamp-light, thereby hinting at one use of the lamps from Mycenaean tombs;

45 Lying in state (*prothesis*) with mourners on each side on an Athenian Geometric-style vase. Before 700 BC

46 Funeral procession (*ekphora*) on an Athenian Geometric-style vase. Before 700 BC

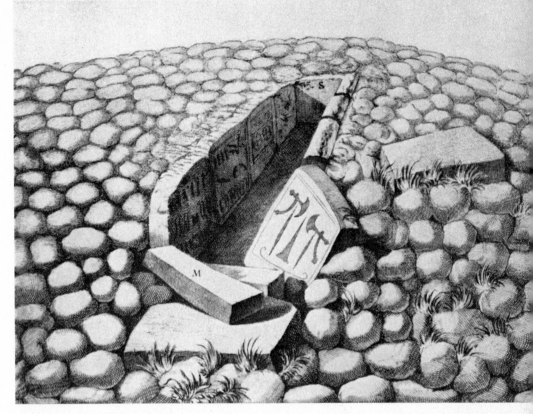

but only the idea of subsequent use would explain why they were left in the tomb and recovered by modern archaeologists. There are various references in the literature to the mourners cutting their hair in grief (Lattimore 1942, 202–3). Portrayal of the sepulchral banquet is a favourite motif on grave-reliefs (Kurtz and Boardman 1971, 142–61 and 234).

47 The Kivik Cairn, Scania, Sweden. General view at the time of its discovery in 1748. Some of the decorated slabs were damaged before their importance was realized

The Bronze Age in Scandinavia

It is a long way from the Aegean to the Baltic, but the distance was bridged in the Bronze Age by the Amber Route, and amber objects including space-plates of necklaces have come from Grave Circles A and B at Mycenae and from a chamber tomb at Kakovatos in western Greece.

At Bredarör near Kivik in Scania (southern Sweden) a cairn 75 m in diameter, and which should probably be dated between 1400–1000 BC, was broken into in 1748. It revealed an interior cist 3·8 m long and 1 m wide, whose two long sides are each formed by four slabs and the short sides by one slab. Seven of the slabs forming the long sides are incised with scenes probably connected with the funerary ritual. They include:

1 An 'obelisk' with a long object and a hafted Early to Middle Bronze Age axe on each side and a sledge or boat beneath. This slab is now destroyed and is known only from drawings.

48, 49 The Kivik Cairn, Scania.
Slabs 1–4 (upper); slabs 5–8
(lower). The slabs are numbered
from right to left

2 A boat with crew of six. The upper part of this slab has dis-
integrated and its decoration is uncertain.

3 Above, two horses facing right; below, two horses facing
each other; a zigzag motif between the two groups.

4 Two wheeled crosses (solar symbols ?) with zigzag motif
above and below.

5 This slab is undecorated except for three short lines.

6 Above, two scrolled crescents (lunar symbols ?); below, two
wheeled crosses (solar symbols ?).

7 A procession comprising a warrior with sword in a two-
wheeled chariot drawn by two horses; four men, two with
swords; two animals facing one another; a symbol doubtfully interpreted as a fish, and a spidery quadruped beneath;
and a procession of eight tall thin figures (mourners in
disguise ?) led by a man with arms upraised.

8 The procession in slab 7 has now apparently come to a
standstill. Beneath a thick symbol difficult to interpret is a

group including two musicians playing *lurer*, one figure holding a rectangular object, perhaps a rattle, and one with arm outstretched towards a U-shaped frame enclosing two people holding or striking a pair of circular discs attached to a frame; the act being performed in this U-shaped frame has been interpreted as fire-making, but its proximity to musicians suggests two musicians striking cymbals. Below this group the 'mourners' again appear, now rearranged four on each side of a coffin, altar, or cauldron. Beneath these are two Omega-shaped enclosures each with three figures without arms and one with arms before the open end. These possibly represent victims being led into the enclosure by an escort.

50 The Kivik Cairn, Scania: reconstruction of slab 8

Interpretation of these scenes is largely guesswork, but it seems logical to believe that we are here in the presence of a series of funerary pictures including a boat for the journey to the after-life; animals probably sacrificed; solar and lunar symbols; a warrior on a chariot, perhaps indicating the status of the dead; and a group of (female ?) mourners in disguise. An important detail is that several of the elements are in pairs. In 1942 the writer (Grinsell 1942) compared these scenes with those on the Hagia Triada sarcophagus, and others have followed (e.g. Gelling, in Gelling and Davidson 1969). The Hagia Triada sarcophagus is unlikely to be much later than 1400 BC, and the Kivik cairn could perhaps be of any date between 1400 and 1000 BC. Influence from the Aegean is likely therefore only if the Kivik cairn can be dated between 1400 and 1300 BC. A large symbol closely resembling the Minoan 'horns of consecration' occurs on a rock surface in Uppland (Gelling and Davidson 1969, pl. 4), and curiously enough there is a similar but very small symbol of the same kind on the foot-carved cist-slab from the Bronze Age round barrow at Pool Farm, West Harptree (Somerset), England. Certain elements of the Kivik slabs occur elsewhere in the Scandinavian Late Neolithic and Bronze Age, e.g. boats and solar symbols on cover-slabs or wall-slabs from chambers or cists in barrows (Grinsell 1941).

A suggestion has been made that the ploughing of the ground on which some Danish Bronze Age barrows were built may have formed part of the funerary ritual (Klindt-Jensen 1957, 62; Pätzold 1960).

The Viking ship burial in the Rus area on the Volga

In 922, Ibn Fadlan witnessed the funeral of a leading Viking near the modern town of Bulgar. The funerary ritual began by the chief being placed for ten days in a grave with a roof over it, and in the meantime garments were prepared for clothing his body for burial. His possessions were divided into three parts – the first for his wives and daughters; the second to pay for his funerary garments; and the third for making an intoxicant which the mourners drank between the death and the funeral. A slave-girl, who gave herself to be killed on the day of the funeral to accompany her master, drank, sang, and indulged in other pleasures until the day. The dead chief's ship was brought to the riverside and placed on a

wooden framework made for the purpose, and a pavilion was
built in its centre. After the deceased had the clothing in which
he died replaced by the garments made for his burial, his body,
newly clothed with trousers, stockings (?), boots, tunic, caftan of
brocade with gold buttons, and hat of brocade and fur, was placed
on a cushioned mattress in this pavilion. His weapons were placed
by his side. Various foods and flowers were arranged around his
body. A dog, two horses, two cows, a rooster and a hen were then
flayed and placed in the ship. The master of each tent is now said
to have had sexual intercourse with the female slave, who was
afterwards killed and put on the pyre. The pyre was ignited by the
dead man's nearest relative and took about an hour to burn out.
A mound was then raised (over the pyre ?) and on top of it was
erected a post of birch-wood inscribed with the name of the dead
man and the name of the Viking king (under whom he had lived ?)
(Jones 1968, 425–30).

The Bronze Age in Britain

The British Isles have so far yielded no prehistoric tomb whose
decoration has helped materially to reconstruct the funerary ritual.
However, the purpose of earthworks of the *cursus* type, which
often occur near the larger barrow cemeteries, has still to be considered. The best known examples are the Greater and Lesser
Cursus near Stonehenge, the Dorset Cursus on Cranborne Chase,
and ploughed-out examples at Dorchester-on-Thames, Thornborough (Yorkshire, North Riding) and elsewhere. Many other
ploughed-out examples doubtless await discovery by air photography. They vary in length from over 100 m to 10 km (the length
of the Dorset Cursus, which may, however, be two examples
placed end to end). They were first so-called by Stukeley, who
named the Stonehenge Cursus, from his belief that they were
for chariot and other racing (Stukeley 1740, 41–3). Some at least
were constructed in the Late Neolithic or Early Bronze Age, and
the cursus at Thornborough was overlapped by one of the henge
monuments. Surely the only possible purpose of such earthworks
would have been for racing of some kind, not necessarily specifically funerary, as it is possible that funerary games would have been
held in the same places devoted to secular sports. Is it, perhaps,
possible that the circular henges with no visible interior structures
(i.e. Priddy in Somerset, and Thornborough) may have been
arenas for boxing, wrestling, and other games for which a circular
arena was preferable? The occurrence of up to four of such rings
together (as at Priddy) could then be explained if each was devoted
to a particular form of sport.

Nothing is known of the purpose of the 'Wilsford Shaft', to all
appearances a pond-barrow in a group of barrows south of Stonehenge. The central 'dip' of this barrow proved to be 1·8 m in
diameter and 30 m deep. If not a well, it might have been a means of
communicating with the dead. Radiocarbon analysis of wood
samples suggests that it dates from between 1470 and 1290 BC
(roughly a century earlier if bristlecone-pine calibrated) (Ashbee
1963; 1966).

A minor detail is evidence for the shaving of the eyebrows at a Bronze Age funeral in Wiltshire (barrow Winterslow 3) – a Bronze Age urn from this barrow contained hair shown by analysis to have been from the eyebrows of several individuals (Grinsell 1951).

Fertility and the tomb

From various prehistoric tombs in Europe, mostly of the Bronze Age, come carvings of statues or other objects suggesting fertility or perhaps the idea of rebirth. The Karmi/Paleolona cemetery in Cyprus includes a tomb with a rock-cut female statue. A Giant's Tomb at Perdu Cossu, Sardinia, had in the passage two slabs, one carved with a female breast and the other with a phallic relief (Guido 1963, 94); some of the other tombs of this type have in their forecourt a baetylic stone carved with bosses or breasts. In the Iberian peninsula similar baetylic stones occur near tombs at Los Millares and elsewhere (Gorbea 1968). Some of the French megalithic tombs include mural designs of females, especially in the Marne area and Brittany (Piggott 1965, 61–2 and pl. VI).

Evidence of seasons for burial

The Early Neolithic burials beneath the house floors at Çatal Hüyük are believed to have been inserted each spring, after which the floors were re-plastered (Mellaart 1967, 204–9). At the Giants' Hills long barrow (Lincolnshire) the quantity of hazel-nuts scattered throughout the mound suggested that the builders had fed on them while constructing the barrow, which must have been in late summer or autumn (Grinsell 1953a, 49). A burial of the Bell-Beaker culture at Bohdalice (Moravia), accompanied by an offering of a lamb, must have been made in early spring (Neustupny 1961, 241 and pl. 38). It has been suggested that nomadic and semi-nomadic peoples tend to bury their dead in spring and autumn, when the tribe has to migrate in search of fresh grass (Rice 1957, 87). Sometimes, as among the Scythians, this involved a form of embalming to preserve the body for eventual burial.

Chapter Nine

The journey to the after-life

> But now farewell. I am going a long way
> With these thou seest – if indeed I go
> (For all my mind is clouded with a doubt) –
> To the island valley of Avilion;
> Where falls not hail, or rain, or any snow,
> Nor ever wind blows loudly; but it lies
> Deep meadow'd, happy, fair with orchard-lawns
> And bowery hollows crown'd with summer sea,
> Where I will heal me of my grievous wound.
> Alfred Lord Tennyson. *Idylls of the King*. The Passing of Arthur.

Mesopotamia

In the grave of King Abargi (possibly *c.* 3000 BC) at Ur, Woolley found two model boats, one of copper which had largely dis-integrated, and one of silver which was in excellent condition. The silver boat is 60 cm long, has a high prow and stern, and is equipped with five seats. Its purpose can only be conjectured. Full-size bitumen boats are frequent in tombs of the Sargonid age (Woolley 1934, 145).

Egypt

Space permits only a brief treatment of the large quantity of Egyptian evidence on this subject. Some of the Early Dynastic royal tombs at north Sakkara included a wooden boat placed in a brick-lined hollow adjoining the tomb. Beliefs concerning the character of the journey to the after-life are clearly stated in various parts of the *Pyramid Texts* of Dynasties V and VI. Special promi-nence is given to the journey by a primitive pair of reed-floats or by a boat across the sky to the horizon to the sun-god Re (Grinsell 1947, 92–3; Mercer 1952, 5). Efforts have been made to compare these references with the five boat-hollows near the pyramids of both Kheops and Khephren at Giza, and with boat-hollows placed beside other pyramids of the Old and Middle Kingdoms (Hassan 1946). The boat found in the eastern of the two boat-hollows south of the pyramid of Kheops was not a solar boat but a yacht-type boat with prow and stern in the form of a papyrus flower; it has a cabin near the stern, one (possibly two) steering oars, and ten rowing oars. It was 43·4 m long, 5·53 m wide, and about 7·9 m high including the cabin; it had been dismantled and put into a hollow 32·5 m long and 5 m wide (Nour *et al.*, 1960). One can only assume that magic would have reassembled it for the use of the king. The purpose of the boats buried near each pyramid has been much discussed, but it seems clear that at least one of them was to enable the pharaoh to make a voyage to the after-life. The Pyramid Texts also make frequent mention of the ferryman,

51 Funerary boat of cedar from a boat-hollow near the east end of the south side of the pyramid of Kheops, Giza

usually called 'he who sees behind him', or 'the man whose face is behind him', who has to ferry the pharaoh across the Marsh of Reeds, the Winding Watercourse or other waters to reach the hereafter.

A ladder or stairway (a different word for each was used in the Pyramid Texts) was another means of reaching the after-life. The stepped pyramids, and the stepped internal structure of many of the later pyramids of the Old Kingdom, seem to have been to symbolize the pharaoh's stairway to the sky. In some tombs model ladders have been found which were most likely intended to symbolize the ladder to the sky (Griffiths 1966); so that the deceased could have had the choice between a stairway and a ladder.

The pharaoh could fly to the after-life by assuming the form of a bird such as a goose or a heron; or by being carried on the wing of a falcon or of Thoth (represented as an Ibis). He could also reach the after-life by travelling along the sun's rays; by the smoke of burning incense; or by other methods mentioned in the Pyramid Texts. Unfortunately some of these are unlikely to have left any archaeological evidence.

During the Middle Kingdom wooden models of boats (some funerary) were often buried with the dead, especially in the cemeteries at Beni Hasan, Meir, and elsewhere in Middle Egypt. The *Coffin Texts* (which now replace the Pyramid Texts) continue to mention the ferryman.

During the New Kingdom the Coffin Texts are replaced by the so-called *Book of the Dead*. One of the most complete versions, the *Papyrus of Ani* in the British Museum, illustrates the ferryman in the vignette to chapter 93. The tomb of Tutankhamun (*c.* 1336 BC)

52 Funerary stela with boat from
Terenuthis, Egypt. (After
Bonner)

contained a set of oars placed on the floor between the gold-covered shrines and the north wall of the burial chamber. Eleven wooden model boats, from the room called by Howard Carter the Treasury, may have been replicas of those used at the pharaoh's funeral for his journey to the after-life or for pilgrimages to sacred places.

The idea of the ship of the dead was present in Egypt at later periods. An early Christian cemetery (*c.* AD 350–450) at Terenuthis in Middle Egypt contained four funerary stelae showing the deceased in a boat or about to enter one (Bonner 1941).

The eastern Mediterranean

The stone sarcophagus (*c.* 1400 BC) from Hagia Triada in Crete is generally considered to show Egyptian influence (Chapter Eight). One long side shows the deceased kneeling in front of his tomb to receive gifts brought by three offering-bearers; the first brings an object usually interpreted as a model boat and similar to two model boats found at Hagia Triada. Each of the short sides shows a chariot with two female riders (perhaps goddesses); one is drawn by a pair of goats (often erroneously described as horses); the other is drawn by a pair of winged griffins. Both scenes are plausibly interpreted as symbolic of journeys to the after-life (Nilsson 1950, 426–43; Nauert, 1965). The person interred in this sarcophagus was probably a deified chief (Mylonas 1966, 176–7).

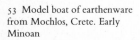

53 Model boat of earthenware from Mochlos, Crete. Early Minoan

Model boats occur in Cretan tombs from the Early Minoan onwards (Hood 1971, 126). Evans found a Late Minoan ivory boat model with an inhumation in the cemetery at Zafer Papoura near Knossos (A.J. Evans 1906, 25–7). Nonetheless, the occurrence of boats or representations of them in Minoan tombs seems to have been exceptional unless boat models of wood or other perishable material were deposited. Rather later in date is a small Geometric period (ninth to eighth centuries BC) terracotta boat-model with a bearded helmsman seated at the stern, from tomb D north of the palace at Knossos.

The Mycenaean archaeological record provides little evidence of the deposit in tombs of any objects which might have been intended as vehicles for a journey to the after-life. We may, however, note clay models of a chariot and a ship from chamber tombs at Mycenae (Inv. 2262 and 3099, Athens Archaeological Museum), and terracotta models of chariots from a tomb at Nauplia (Inv. 3493 in the same museum). Unless they were toys accompanying the burials of children they might have been intended to symbolize journeys to the other world. The idea of an after-life across the sea tends to be more frequent among islanders than mainlanders, but even in Crete it may have been inspired from Egypt.

The idea of Charon ferrying the dead across the river Styx or other watercourses to the after-life is first mentioned in a play by Aeschylus (*c.* 525–456 BC). Charon is depicted on a terracotta perhaps of the late sixth century BC, and during the following century on many white-ground *lekythoi* (small funerary vases)

54 The barque of Charon with Charon sitting on the left. Kerameikos cemetery, Athens, *c.* 320 BC

made in Athens. The scene is also shown on a fine tombstone (*c.* 320 BC) in the Kerameikos cemetery in Athens (Karo 1943, 32). One of the best-known descriptions is in the *Aeneid* (Book 6, xli) of Virgil (70–19 BC):

> *Charon there,*
> *Grim ferryman, stands sentry. Mean his guise,*
> *His chin a wilderness of hoary hair,*
> *And like a flaming furnace stare his eyes.*
> *Hung in a loop around his shoulder lies*
> *A filthy gaberdine. He trims the sail,*
> *And, pole in hand, across the waters plies*
> *His steel-grey shallop with the corpses pale,*
> *Old, but a God's old age has left him green and hale.*

The coin known as an *obol*, with which the dead were required to pay Charon, occurs in graves from *c.* 470 BC onwards. At first it was placed in the grave, or in the hand of the dead; but from the fourth century BC it was usual to place the coin in the mouth (where the Athenians normally carried their small change wrapped up). Sometimes two or more obols were placed with the dead in the hope of securing a special place in Charon's boat; on other occasions coins of smaller denominations were considered good enough for Charon. 'Ghost-coins' of gold leaf or other material were also sometimes used (Grinsell 1957*b*; Kurtz and Boardman 1971, 211).

During the Geometric period (ninth to eighth centuries BC) several instances are known of clay model boots or shoes placed with the dead (Kurtz and Boardman 1971, 63, 211–12). It seems reasonable to believe that these objects were deposited to cover that part of the last journey which had to be done on foot.

Italy and the central Mediterranean

In parts of Etruscan Italy, notably Bologna and Volterra, Etruscan tombstones and cremation urns are sometimes decorated with reliefs showing the deceased travelling in a carriage to the after-life. Carriages or remains of them have also been found in the richer Etruscan tombs, the best known being the Regolini-Galassi tomb at Cerveteri, the vehicles from which are in the Gregorian Museum in the Vatican. In some instances these vehicles may be the remains of funerary hearses with or without the added idea of the final journey to the after-life (Von Vacano, 1960, 89–94).

From *c.* 400 BC onwards Etruscan funerary ritual underwent a change. The Greek Charon became the Etruscan Charun, still closely associated with the dead but with different attributes possibly derived from a native god of the dead. He is usually depicted carrying a hammer with which to inflict the final blow if necessary. In the tomb of the Orco at Tarquinia he is shown bearded and with wings. Charun is normally shown that way, and with snaky hair, guiding the dead on the road to Hades or through its doorway.

As early as the Archaic period (*c.* 600–470 BC) a journey to the underworld is carved on a funerary monument from Chiusi (Richardson 1964, pl. XIX). During the fourth century BC funerary urns and sarcophagi often show the dead journeying to the underworld in a horse-drawn chariot or other vehicle, on horseback, or on foot.

Painted tombs at Paestum, dated to the fourth century BC, discovered during the last two decades, show the deceased as a warrior on horseback journeying to the hereafter, or riding there in a chariot preceded by a warrior with two spears (Sestieri 1959).

Central Europe

To the best of the writer's knowledge the archaeological record provides no certain evidence for any belief in a journey to an after-life in later prehistoric times in central Europe. Remains of various four-wheeled wagons, two-wheeled carts, and wheeled metal cinerary urns found in Late Bronze Age and Early Iron Age graves in various parts of mainland Europe are all believed to be royal or semi-royal hearses. The inevitable absence of contemporary written sources makes it unwise to offer any other explanation of these finds. The belief in a voyage to the otherworld is not to be expected among those dwelling in the middle of a continent; and the evidence for a belief in a land journey to the after-life seems inadequate.

Scandinavia

The sea-girt lands of southern Scandinavia provide convincing evidence of a belief in a journey to the after-life from at least the Early Bronze Age onwards.

The best-known evidence is from the series of carved slabs in the long stone cist in the great round cairn of Bredarör near Kivik in Scania. At least seven of the eight slabs comprising the two long sides of this cist bear carvings of subjects most likely connected with the funerary ritual of the chief buried in it (Chapter Eight). Two sun-symbols, a boat with six people on board, and indications of a second boat are relevant here. As these scenes have to be considered as a whole their interpretation presents many difficulties, because taken as a group they are without parallel in Scandinavia. Carvings of three boats and three sun-symbols are, however, known from the cover-slab of a (Neolithic ?) burial-chamber at Grevinge in Zealand, and a slab from a barrow at Villfara, about 6 km south of Kivik, was incised with three boats and a chariot drawn by two horses or ponies. Slabs from a cairn called Mjeltehaug in Giske parish, Romsdal district in southern Norway, were decorated with sun-symbols and ships (Grinsell 1941). It seems not unreasonable to interpret these as symbolic of a journey to an after-life in either a boat or a wheeled vehicle. Indeed the journey by day might have been across the sky in a chariot, and the journey by night beneath the earth in a boat.

The Kivik carvings have been compared with the paintings on the sarcophagus of Hagia Triada in Crete (Chapter Eight).

In a Late Bronze Age urn from a barrow in Denmark the cremated bones of a young adult had been placed along with the wings of four birds – three pairs from jackdaws and one from a crow or rook – presumably to assist the soul of the dead to fly to the hereafter (Klindt-Jensen 1957, 72, 145).

Of the south Scandinavian ship-graves edged with standing stones arranged in the form of a ship (*skeppssattningar*), some on the island of Gotland date from the Late Bronze Age, but over southern Scandinavia they were mostly built between the Iron Age and the Viking period. Among the best groups is that at Lindholm Høje in Jutland, where a cemetery of about seven hundred graves includes a ship-setting 23 m long and numerous others up to 8 m long, all of Viking age (Ramskou 1960).

Merovingian and Viking ship-graves have now to be considered. They date from about the end of the sixth century onwards and were normally beneath round or oval barrows. The best-known examples are at Oseberg and Gokstad in Norway but there are many others in Norway and Sweden and one at Ladby in Denmark. Whether this custom of interring the dead with a ship or boat was practised from a belief in a journey by sea to the after-life is a matter to be considered in the light of the evidence from each burial. The ship at Ladby, dated *c.* AD 950, was buried with its prow pointing south towards the supposed location of Valhalla, and the ship's anchor was stowed in the bows ready to be dropped when the destination had been reached. In this instance therefore there can be no doubt that the voyage to the after-life was in the minds of those concerned. As most of the Norwegian ship-burials have the ship pointing to the south it seems reasonable to assume that these burials were inspired by a similar belief. In some instances, such as Hedeby in Jutland and Hegge in Trondhjem, the ship was inverted over the burial-chamber, a practice suggesting that the idea of a voyage to the after-life was no longer seriously entertained.

France

Of the chamber tombs of Armorica, Mané-Lud (Locmariaquer) has two slabs decorated with 'boat' symbols – about four on one and one on the other (Péquart and Le Rouzic 1927, 66 and pls. 44–51; L'Helgouach 1965, 82–3). Beneath one of the 'boat' symbols on the better-preserved slab there is a dot-in-circle, perhaps a sun-symbol.

On the Ile-de-Groix (Morbihan) a Viking ship-burial of the late ninth or tenth century, excavated early this century, was found to contain a cremation of a male adult and a younger person with rich grave furniture (Davidson 1967, 117).

The British Isles

Among the decorations in New Grange in the Boyne valley is a pattern resembling a ship with a circle (sun-symbol?) on slab C4 of the cruciform burial chamber, but the date and interpretation of this carving are doubtful (Ó Ríordáin and Daniel 1964, 59 and pl. 25). A similar but even more doubtful 'ship' carving was noted by Coffey on the underside of the lintel of the entrance to the side-chamber of the south tomb at Dowth (Ó Ríordáin and Daniel 1964, 71–2 and fig. 14).

A rake-like carving on a free-standing slab (since destroyed) in a stone cist in a Bronze Age round barrow at Ri Cruin near Kilmartin (Argyllshire) formerly interpreted as a boat with rowers, may represent a halberd with streamers hanging from its handle, but even this is only conjecture (Atkinson 1954, 13).

Various Early Bronze Age round barrows in England and Wales have yielded interments placed in wooden coffins of a shape somewhat resembling a boat. In one or two instances (as at Loose Howe in Yorkshire) it is even possible that an old boat might have been used as a coffin; but it is an open question whether those concerned were thinking of a voyage to the after-life (Grinsell 1941, 365–6; Elgee 1949). There is, however, a hint that some of these coffins contained the remains of maritime adventurers concerned with the amber trade and the tendency to a coastal distribution of such burials may support this.

The Iron Age chariot burials, usually beneath round barrows in Yorkshire and other areas influenced by the 'Marnian' culture of France, do not seem to indicate any belief in a journey to the hereafter. Like the more elaborate chariot burials and wagon burials (*c.* 700–400 BC) beneath large round barrows in central Europe and France, they are normally chieftains' graves in which the wagon may have been a hearse and both vehicles were probably status symbols (Filip 1962; Stead 1965).

In Roman Britain, numerous instances of people buried in their boots, normally evidenced archaeologically by their hobnails, are usually interpreted as burials of poor people who have to make their journey to the after-life on foot.

Instances of Roman coins, usually of bronze, placed with cremations (*c.* AD 43–200) and inhumations (*c.* AD 200–410) in England have been listed and discussed (Grinsell 1957b, 264–7). The purpose of those with cremations is not always clear; but those with inhumations, usually placed in the mouth and often leaving a bronze stain on the jawbone, were certainly fees for Charon. Charon's boat is depicted on some examples of funeral sculpture on the continent (Cumont 1922, 155) but no instances from Britain are known to the writer. The large collection of Roman tombstones found locally and in the Grosvenor Museum, Chester, includes two of females, incorporating a huge shell design, possibly alluding to the voyage to the Isles of the Blest. Another depicts two opposed Tritons blowing shell-trumpets for the same purpose (Wright 1955, 44–5).

From the Sutton Hoo ship-burial (*c.* AD 630–40) comes a purse containing thirty-seven Merovingian gold coins and three blanks. It has been suggested by Grierson (1970) that these coins were for each of the forty rowers to pay their 'ferryman's fee' to Charon. The idea of a voyage to the after-life is also present in the description in the introduction to *Beowulf* of the disposal of the body of Scyld by sending it out to sea in a ship laden with treasure.

More than a dozen Viking ship-graves have been found in various parts of the British Isles, mostly in Scotland, Northumbria and the Isle of Man. It is uncertain whether these were symbolic of a voyage to the after-life or merely status symbols for the burials of Viking aristocrats.

Medieval and later survivals and recurrences

The custom of depositing a coin with the dead was practised in medieval times in Hungary and spread from Hungary to Moravia around 1010–30 and from there to Bohemia, ending by about 1100. The coin placed in the grave was usually a freshly struck denarius. Radomersky (1955) has listed and mapped seventy-one sites where this practice is known to have occurred. It seems uncertain whether the purpose of these coins was to pay a ferryman's fee.

Writing before 1688, John Aubrey (1881) stated that in his youth it was the custom in some country places to put a 'Peter penny' in the hand of the dead man to pay his passage to heaven. There are in fact instances of the survival or recurrence of this custom in several parts of Europe (Grinsell 1957b, 265–9).

Chapter Ten

Later usage of the tomb

If, however, you are determined upon bloodshed with the least possible delay, one thing there is for which we will fight – the tombs of our forefathers. Find those tombs and try to wreck them, and you will soon know whether or not we are willing to stand up to you. King Idanthyrsus of Scythia to King Darius of Persia, quoted by Herodotus. *History* IV, 127.

The official Scythian attitude to their illustrious dead is shown by the notable challenge quoted above. The reverence for the dead which inspired it is paralleled among other peoples and at other periods. The ancient Scandinavian custom of the chief 'sitting on a howe' (barrow) seems to enshrine the idea of receiving inspiration from the spirit of the great person buried therein, and may have Bronze Age origins (Ellis 1943, 105–111). The occasional association of barrows and burials with popular assemblies, fairs and races in ancient Ireland has been collected by Ettlinger (1952), and this also may date from the Bronze Age. In England there are several instances of the holding of hundred moots or other assemblies of distinction at barrows. Dorset alone provides at least four instances: Hundred Barrow in Bere Regis, Mot or Moot Barrow in Portesham, the Pimperne Long Barrow where Longbarrow Hundred used to meet, and Culliford Tree Barrow where Culliford Tree Hundred met. Other instances include Gemot Barrow (Isle of Wight), Brightwell's Barrow hundred in Gloucestershire, and Swanborough hundred in Wiltshire. A few instances of witches of the seventeenth and eighteenth centuries repairing to barrows to derive their powers from the dead are an odd recurrence of this idea (Grinsell 1973*b*).

The main purpose of this chapter, however, is to consider for how long the tomb continued to be used for burial after it was built; and whether, and if so for how long, it was the location of a cult originating with ritual for the dead. The answer inevitably differs for each site.

Egypt

It is known that the pyramid complex of each pharaoh, at least during the Old Kingdom, was endowed with funds for maintaining a priesthood whose duty it was to make offerings and perform suitable ritual for the dead pharaoh at frequent intervals. Many of these pyramid endowments probably lapsed during the First Intermediate Period though they may have been resumed later. Others, including those of Snefru, Kheops, Djedefre, and Khephren, continued at all events nominally until the Ptolemaic period (Fakhry 1969, 19). The pharaoh's wives and relatives were normally interred in tombs surrounding his own.

The tombs of the aristocracy of the Old Kingdom were often of husband and wife (as Rahotep and Nefert, Dynasty IV, at Maidum); occasionally of brothers (as Kawab and Hardedef, Dynasty IV, at Giza); or of father and son (as Akhet-hotep and Ptah-hotep II, Dynasty V, at Sakkara); or of husband and wife and son (as Mere-ruka and others, Dynasty V, at Sakkara). In such instances the tomb and tomb chapels were often enlarged. Exceptionally a tomb was re-used by someone whose relationship to the original owner is unknown (as Meruka's re-use of the tomb of Nekaukhenemu at Giza). In general, however, it seems that in the spacious days of the Old Kingdom it was customary for the head of each family to found his own tomb, which may have been an affair of one or at most two generations only, apart from the possibility of the continuance of offerings and ritual in the adjoining tomb chapel. There are several instances of Old Kingdom tombs being either built or completed by the children of the deceased (Pirenne 1936, 921). There is at least one instance, from Dynasty XI, of the owner of a tomb arranging for the upkeep of a priesthood to make periodical offerings in the tomb chapel (Peet 1916).

Occasionally there is a hint of an astonishing survival or recurrence from the past. Thus the tomb of Debehen (Dynasty IV) at Giza is still visited on Fridays by villagers from Giza who perform a *zikr* comprising incantations and folk-music, the content and instruments with which it is performed being both strikingly similar to those of Pharaonic Egypt (Hickmann 1957).

The Minoan-Mycenaean world

Many of the Minoan circular 'vaulted' tombs are thought by Branigan (1970, 128–30) to have been for clans. They often contain the remains of several hundred burials each and some of them may have been in use for a few centuries. The tholos tomb at Kephala, near Knossos, constructed in Late Minoan Ia (*c.* 1550 BC), contained later burials with pottery of Late Minoan IIIc, *c.* 1150 BC (Cadogan 1967).

The shaft-graves in Grave Circles A and B at Mycenae each contained between one and five burials, and it is generally believed that those with more than one interment were family tombs. The earlier burials and their grave-goods tended to be brushed aside to make way for the later ones, and in some instances a shaft-grave was evidently used by more than one generation.

At least two of the tholos tombs in Messenia were used for two or considerably more generations. The undisturbed example near the Palace of Nestor at Pylos contained about twenty-three interments, and the associated grave-goods indicate that it was in use for funerary purposes for about 150 years (Blegen 1954). That at Myrsinochorion, excavated by Marinatos in 1956, contained six successive burials, the earlier ones slighted to provide accommodation for the later. On the other hand the tholos tombs at and around Mycenae seem to have been the tombs of individual kings or chiefs; but they have been so badly robbed that this conclusion could be upset by the discovery of an undisturbed example in that region.

The chamber tombs were family graves and were used over and over again in the course of the centuries, possibly by descendants of the head of the family for whom it was originally built (Mylonas 1966, 112).

A chamber tomb with two dromoi beneath the Temple of Ares in Athens contained at least fourteen burials, and was in use continuously from *c.* 1450 to *c.* 1200 BC or later. A deposit of seven *lekythoi* of the fifth century BC in a pit above this tomb may have been a propitiatory offering by the builders of the Temple for having disturbed the ancient dead (Townsend 1955, 196).

It has for many years been discussed whether a cult of the dead, in the sense of a cult continuing for many years after the tomb ceased to be used for burial, was practised in Minoan and Mycenaean contexts. Many of the Minoan circular tombs have additional rectangular outer chambers which were certainly used for ritual purposes, but whether immediately after or long subsequent to the funeral is uncertain. On balance there seems no conclusive evidence of a cult of the dead in Minoan Crete (Branigan 1970, 113–20). Mylonas has presented convincing arguments that no such cult was practised at Grave Circle B which had most likely been forgotten by the time the tholos tomb of Clytemnestra was built partly over it about a century later; and he maintains that no such cult was practised at Grave Circle A (Mylonas 1966, 178–9).

Some have believed that a cult of the dead, or a hero-cult, existed at some of the tholos and chamber tombs. After a critical examination of the evidence, Mylonas (1966, 181–4) has concluded that such a cult can be demonstrated to have existed at only one tholos tomb so far explored – at Menidi (Acharnai) just north of Athens. Even there, the cult did not immediately follow the burial, but began in the early Geometric period (perhaps *c.* 1075 BC) and continued until Classical times, as suggested by a detailed study of the pottery and other material from the dromos.

The rest of the Mediterranean

Tomb 50 at Salamis in Cyprus, popularly known as the *Tomb* or *Prison of St Catherine*, a name which has been traced back to about 1340, originated in the seventh century BC as a normal chamber tomb approached by a dromos (Chapter Sixteen). In early Roman times major structural alterations were made, of which the chief was the conversion of the entrance portal into the barrel-vaulted structure seen today. The purpose for which it was built is unknown, but it has been suggested that it might have been a sanctuary or *heroon* for performing ritual connected with a hero-cult or cult of the dead. From the fourth until the seventh century the surroundings were used as a cemetery. Since the fourteenth century, if not earlier, it has been known by its present name, implying a tradition that either the great St Catherine or a minor saint of the same name was martyred there. 'It is interesting to see how the site . . . never lost its sanctity from the seventh century BC onwards' (Karageorghis 1969, 63).

In Sardinia recent excavation of four 'Giants' Graves' has shown that they had been rebuilt several times, and most likely used for burial for some centuries (Castaldi 1969, 155–6). In Sicily the Iron Age cemetery of Sant'Angelo Muxaro, 30 km north of Agrigento, includes a tomb about 8·5 m in diameter, with 'tholos' roof, probably used for interment from the eighth until the mid-fifth century BC; its interior was in the Byzantine age converted into a chapel dedicated to Sant'Angelo (Guido 1967, 129–30).

Many, perhaps most, Etruscan tombs were family tombs. For earlier tombs this is evident from the number of funerary beds, which in the Tomb of Reliefs at Cerveteri reaches forty-five and must represent several generations. For later tombs this is shown by the inscriptions giving the names and relationships of those interred. The Tomb of Inscriptions at the same site is known from its texts to have been used for eight generations of families, some named Tarchna. The Volumnia Tomb near Perugia, used by at least four generations, is notable for the pictorial urn of the head of the family, given the place of honour in the central chamber lit by an oil lamp and probably used as a chapel. In that limited sense only does there seem to have been anything approaching a cult of the dead among the Etruscans (Von Vacano 1960, 86).

At Carthage the tomb of Himilkat contains an epitaph mentioning five generations buried therein (Harden 1962, 102). When considered with the evidence from other periods and regions, one gets the impression that during the later prehistoric periods a family tomb could accommodate anything up to eight generations.

In discussing Christianized megalithic tombs in the Iberian peninsula and France one must bear in mind that Christianization of a prehistoric site does not necessarily date from the beginning of Christianity. Just southwest of Mahon in Minorca is the naveta of Cudia Cremada, containing a beautiful statue of St Mary Magdalene; as it was placed there sometime during the last century this statue is, however, of no particular historical interest.

55 The shrine of St Catherine in Tomb 50, Salamis, Cyprus. This tomb has been used since at least the fourteenth century as a chapel to St Catherine

The Iberian peninsula, France, and the Channel Islands

Our knowledge of the veneration of megalithic monuments in these countries from Merovingian times onwards is derived from two main sources – edicts issued between the fifth and ninth centuries, and megalithic monuments Christianized by having a cross carved or placed on them.

The chief edicts directed against the veneration of (and lighting of torches at) trees, stones, and springs are the 23rd canon of the Council of Arles (443–52), the 23rd canon of the Council of Tours (567), evidently based on the former, and the Councils of Toledo (681 and 693). In addition, an edict of King Childebert I (511–58), though not very clear, seems to have been directed more specifically against the veneration of stone alignments, statue-menhirs, and standing stones in Brittany. It would not be justifiable to assume that the stones of the other edicts were always megalithic monuments; sometimes a natural stone of unusual size or shape was the subject of veneration. The Council of Nantes (late ninth century) referred to the veneration of stones among ruins, which can scarcely be other than megalithic (Guenin 1934).

56 Christianized megalithic tomb: the dolmen de la Belle-Vue, Carnac, Morbihan, Brittany

The veneration of stones, particularly megalithic, was often 'regularized' by Christianizing them, a Christian cross being either carved on or added to the monument. In some instances an entire megalithic tomb was incorporated into a church, as at Alcobertas and San Dionisio in Portugal, Gangas de Onis near Oviedo in Spain, and the Chapelle des Sept Saints at Plouaret in Brittany (Daniel 1972, 26–31). At Saint Michel at Carnac, and La Hougue Bie in Jersey, churches have been built on top of a megalithic tomb; and it may be no accident that two statue-menhirs in Guernsey stand in churchyards.

It is likely that only a small proportion of 'venerated' stones were natural; the proportion could in fact be roughly calculated by working out the percentage of Christianized natural stones to Christianized megalithic monuments. Large natural stones resembling a megalithic tomb were incorporated into the church of Arrichinaga in Spain (Daniel 1972, 28 and fig. 19).

From what period dates the Christianization of a megalithic site bearing a cross? In some instances, where a megalithic slab is inscribed with a cross and a hafted axe of Early Bronze Age type (as at Confolens in France), there may be a strong case for a cult of the dead or a hero-cult dating from the Bronze Age becoming adapted to later needs. Many metal crosses added to French megaliths are clearly modern but they may have replaced earlier ones. In other instances a cross has doubtless been added to a standing stone in recent times merely because it was convenient to do so, without any thought of Christianizing a pagan site.

The British Isles

The fairly recent excavation of the chambered long barrow at West Kennet (Wiltshire) showed that its construction, probably well before 3000 BC, was followed by at least a thousand years' use for burials, although the number of individuals represented by the surviving skeletal material is perhaps less than forty. After the last burial had been inserted, the barrow was closed by filling the interior with chalk rubble, blocking the entrance forecourt with large sarsens, and constructing across it an arrangement of large sarsens (Piggott 1962a, 68–71, 78). The history of the use of other chamber tombs in Britain varies from site to site, but an important detail is that while some had their interior filled with rubble after the final burial had been made, others were left open and readily accessible to the plunderer. There is growing evidence that many of the British chamber tombs underwent several reconstructions during the Neolithic period and perhaps later, implying use for burial over several centuries (Corcoran 1972).

Some continuity of site sanctity from the Neolithic into the Bronze Age is suggested by the siting of certain round barrows in relation to long ones. At the Winterbourne Stoke cross-roads group (Wiltshire), a row of round barrows is aligned on the axis of the long barrow, which would seem to have been of the founder of this cemetery. Similar relationships of round to long barrows occur elsewhere, notably in Dorset and especially on the Cotswolds (O'Neil and Grinsell 1961, 15, 31).

The introduction of the round barrow from the Copper Age (Beaker cultures) onwards, essentially for individual burial, but often in fact containing several interments in different parts of the mound, poses the problem of what relationship, if any, there was between the primary, subsidiary and secondary interments. The Homeric description of the enlargement of the barrow of Patroclus to accommodate the body of his friend Achilles (*Iliad*, Book XXIII) has many parallels among the Copper and Bronze Age round barrows of Britain, and it can be safely assumed that many more such enlargements of round barrows missed detection by the nineteenth-century and earlier antiquaries even when they succeeded in locating the later interments. The fourfold circles on Shuggledown and Yellowmead Down, Dartmoor, may be the remains of circular cairns with four retaining circles, indicating three successive enlargements (Worth 1953, 187–90).

It seems possible that the rite of cremation became prevalent within three or four generations, at most, of the arrival of the normally inhuming Beaker peoples from various directions as indicated by Clarke (1970). The frequency with which primary inhumations are followed, in the same barrow, by cremations, causes the question to be asked whether those cremated were sometimes the direct descendants of those inhumed.

The insertion of Deverel-Rimbury cremation cemeteries or urnfields into the south or southeastern sector of several Copper Age and Early Bronze Age round barrows in Wessex suggests in these instances a degree of continuity enduring for several centuries. Sometimes each cremation inserted was marked by a stake or post to eliminate risk of disturbance by a later deposit (Holden 1972, 80). One wonders whether the presence of pagan Saxon intrusive burials in Neolithic and Bronze Age barrows may have been merely a labour-saving device; it is doubtful whether it should be interpreted as evidence of any funerary cult continuing from prehistoric times.

Other regions

The Copper Age cemetery at Basatanya (Yugoslavia) is estimated to have covered about two hundred years and to have been used by eight or nine generations, with their average age at death 27·5 years (Bognár-Kutzián 1963). A family relationship has been demonstrated from instances of two or three or more burials in oak bole-coffins in Danish Early Bronze Age barrows. This is supported by resemblances in skull form and by the date of the finds associated (Broholm and Hald, 1940, 12).

Chapter Eleven

Protection of the tomb

Do not open my tomb and do not disturb me, because it contains no silver, no gold, and no vases of any kind. Do not violate my tomb, because it is an act abominable to Ashtarte, and if you dare to disturb me you will have no descendants among the living under the sun. . . . (Translation of) inscription on sarcophagus of Tabnit (fifth or fourth century BC). André Parrot. *Malédictions et Violations des Tombes* 1939, 36–7.

Architectural devices to protect the tomb against the plunderer will be considered in the regional chapters in Part Two and will be discussed only briefly in the present chapter, the main concern of which is with various other methods used to protect the tomb. They include arrangements made to maintain it in good condition; to have ritual performed before it at intervals; to substitute wall-pictures for real offerings thereby reducing the temptation to the robber; to employ magic devices such as spells and representations of fierce animals or serpents guarding the tomb, or pictures of arrows being shot in the direction of the would-be marauder; to provide written imprecations warning the tomb robber, and to impose heavy fines on the plunderer.

Egypt

Throughout the Dynastic period the fear of looting provided the chief stimulus to the architectural development of the royal tomb and of any other tombs likely to be worth robbing. The Early Dynastic tomb 3477 at Sakkara was thought by Emery (1962) to have escaped plunder only because it was known to contemporaries that it contained nothing of intrinsic value. Emery believed that most of the Early Dynastic tombs at Sakkara were broken into by those who were well aware of their contents. Occasionally, as with the tomb of Hetepheres at Giza, the tomb escaped plunder as there was no 'give-away' superstructure to attract attention. The endowments arranged by each pharaoh for the continued maintenance of his pyramid from the Old Kingdom onwards should have resulted in the achievement of adequate security for a few decades, until those funds were appropriated by later pharaohs for other purposes.

The Pyramid Texts (Dynasties V and VI but incorporating earlier elements) already contain an imprecation against anyone damaging the pyramid and its associated mortuary temples (§§ 1278–9):

'As for anyone who shall lay a finger on this pyramid and this temple which belong to me and to my double, he will have . . . offended . . . Geb; his affair will be judged by the Ennead and he

will be nowhere and his will be nowhere; he will be one pro-
scribed, one who eats himself.'

Blessings, on the other hand, are showered on those who protect
the pyramid (§§ 1650–1). Similar imprecations sometimes occur
outside private tombs of the Old Kingdom (Parrot 1939, 98).

   The introduction into the pyramids, from that of Unas onwards, of Pyramid Texts with their hieroglyphs often in the form
of human beings, animals and snakes, brought with it fresh
problems. Fearful lest the creatures represented might come alive
and foul the tomb, the priestly scribes gradually developed methods of rendering these signs innocuous by one or other of the
following means:

 (i) replacing them by alphabetic signs
 (ii) representing part only of the living creature
 (iii) bisecting the sign for the living creature

This system was further developed on the *Coffin Texts* of the
Middle Kingdom, which often have in addition the signs for birds
mutilated (Lacau 1914).

   During this period the revival of pyramid-building was accompanied by the introduction of fresh architectural devices against
the plunderer: varying the position of the entrance; increasing the
complexity of the substructure; and building a large monolithic
burial chamber. During the Middle Kingdom also some of the

57 Suppressions and
modifications of hieroglyphic
signs in Egyptian funerary texts

Period	Human Beings				Animals	Birds	Reptiles	Fishes
	People	Hungry	To invest	Enemy	Lion	Owl	Viper	
Non-funerary texts								
Funerary texts								
Dynasty V Unis								
Dynasty VI Teti								
Pepy I								
Mernere								
Pepy II								
Dynasty XII								
Dynasty XVIII								

95

Restoration inscription of
Khaemwese, a son of Ramesses
II (Dynasty XIX), who caused
this inscription to be placed on
the casing blocks of the pyramid
of Unas (Dynasty V) at
Sakkara, stating that he had
restored it

earlier tombs were restored. In Dynasty XI, a tomb at Thebes was
restored by Intef, son of Mayet (Badawy 1966, 92); and during
Dynasty XII tombs at Beni Hasan and Sheikh Said were restored
(Badawy 1966, 123–4). The probable motive behind this was that
by respecting the tombs of one's predecessors one earned the right
to similar treatment by one's successors.

During the New Kingdom, the establishment of the royal
necropolis in the Valley of the Kings at Thebes was dictated almost
entirely by previous experience of the futility of burying royalty,
with their rich grave-furniture and offerings, in any tomb that
was not concealed. It is curious that imprecations against the tomb
robber, so frequent during the Old Kingdom, are almost non-
existent during the New Kingdom, even in the Valley of the
Kings, despite the popular myth of the 'Pharaoh's Curse' following the death of the fifth Lord Carnarvon in 1923.

The burial chambers of tomb 39 (Puimre) at Thebes contain
niches high up in the walls, to contain magic clay tablets inscribed
with spells to protect the tomb from thieves, sand, and other
enemies of the dead (Monnet 1951).

During Dynasty XIX Ramesses II's eldest son Khaemwese,
who took a great interest in the monuments of the Old Kingdom,
restored the tomb of Shepseskaf at south Sakkara, the pyramids of
Userkaf and Unas at north Sakkara and possibly other pyramids.
He placed on them inscriptions commemorating his work
(Fakhry 1969, 182, 184, 229).

During Dynasty XXI the evidence presents a picture of the
panic-stricken priests of Amun at Thebes endeavouring to
recover the mummified bodies of the pharaohs of the New Kingdom from their recently looted tombs, and placing them for better

security in the secluded tomb of Amenophis II where they were found in 1898, and in the cache at Deir el-Bahri where they were rediscovered by natives from 1875 onwards and acquired by Cairo Museum in 1881.

During Dynasty XXVI (the Saite period) there was a great revival of interest in the arts and architecture of the Old Kingdom and this sometimes found expression in the restoration of tombs. A good illustration is the pyramid of Mycerinus at Giza, in which the body of the pharaoh was apparently placed in a newly-made wooden coffin bearing his titles (fragments now in the British Museum), while on the east side of the entrance to the pyramid an inscription was carved stating that it was the pyramid of Mycerinus (Chapter Thirteen).

Syria and Asia Minor

Among devices against the tomb robber may be mentioned a sarcophagus too large to be taken through the door of a tomb at Labraynda in Turkey (Bean 1971, 68). The sarcophagus of Ahiram, King of Byblos, probably dated sometime between 1100 and 1000 BC, is of interest because its lid bears an 'imprecation' inscription translated as follows (Jidejian 1968, 31):

'The coffin which (It)tobaal son of Ahiram, King of Byblos, made for his father as his abode in eternity. And if any king or any governor or any army commander attacks Byblos and exposes this coffin, let his judicial sceptre be broken, let his royal throne be overthrown, and let peace flee from Byblos; and as for him, let a vagabond (?) efface his inscriptions.'

The 'lion couchant' carved on each corner of the sarcophagus was doubtless to symbolize additional protection.

The black basalt sarcophagus of Eshmunazar, King of Sidon in the fifth century BC, has an inscription in Phoenician which is translated thus (Jidejian 1971, 111):

'Whoever you are, ruler and (ordinary) man, (do) not open this resting-place and (do) not search in it for anything, for nothing whatever has been placed in it.'

At Palmyra the tomb of Shamshigeram, son of Nurbal, bears an inscription of which a translation follows (Parrot 1939, 43):

'There is no fortune for the violator; he will enjoy no prosperity and he will never be supplied with bread and water.'

In Asia Minor there are numerous tombs, mostly and perhaps all dated to between the first and third centuries AD, bearing 'imprecation' inscriptions including the imposition of fines on tomb robbers. At Aphrodisias, the centre for a cult of Aphrodite, the fines imposed reach a maximum of 50,000 denarii (Bean 1971, 231). From Termessos 650 tomb inscriptions have been published and many of them include the imposition on tomb robbers of fines usually payable to Solymion Zeus, the Imperial Chest or the City Treasury; they vary in amount from 300 to 100,000 denarii.

There is sometimes a provision for the informer to receive one-half or one-third of the amount of the fine (Bean 1968, 135).

From the Nabataean region centred on Petra comes a tomb inscription translated as follows (Parrot 1939, 81):

'Whoever (destroys this monument) will pay a fine of double the cost of constructing the entire monument and will incur in addition the malediction of Dushara and Manutu.'

An inscribed marble slab, acquired in Nazareth in 1878 and now in the Bibliothèque Nationale in Paris, carries a text translated as follows:

'Ordinance of Caesar. It is my pleasure that graves and tombs remain undisturbed in perpetuity for those who have made them for the cult of their ancestors or children or members of their house. If however any man lay information that another has either demolished them, or has in any other way extracted the buried . . . against such a one I order that a trial be instituted. . . . In case of contravention I desire that the offender be sentenced to capital punishment on charge of violation of sepulture.'

This is believed to be a rescript from an emperor (it is not certain who, but he was probably in power between 50 BC and AD 50) to a provincial governor (De Zulueta 1932).

Continental Europe

When one moves from the literate to the non-literate civilizations, or those whose literature has not yet been deciphered, the evidence for tomb protection becomes mainly architectural, sculptural, and pictorial. The architects of the tholos, chamber and other tombs of the Minoan-Mycenaean world seem to have been content with normal security measures such as covering the doorway with a sealing-slab, filling the dromos with rubble after each interment had been made, and continuing the retaining wall of the tumulus across the entrance to the dromos as an extra safeguard.

Some of the more notable Etruscan tombs have (or originally had) statues of lions at their entrance, presumably intended to symbolize protection against the marauder. At Veii the Campana Tomb was protected in this way by a statue of a lion on each side of its entrance and on each side of its inner door; the outer pair at least had been removed before 1909. At Cerveteri the Tomb of Reliefs had its entrance guarded on each side by a life-size statue of a lion; only the head of that on the right is still in position. There are similar instances of tombs in Lycia and Phrygia protected by statues or reliefs of lions (Dennis 1883, i, 33).

In Majorca slots for a closing slab are present on both sides of the entrance-ramp of several Bronze Age sepulchral caves, perhaps the best being at Son Boscana, northeast of Capicorb Vey.

Some of the megalithic tombs of Brittany have wall-decoration suggesting the use of magic against the tomb robber. Passage grave H at the great tumulus of Barnenez (Finistère) has on one of its walls a carving of a bow 'placed so that it appears to shoot towards the passage, the only normal approach to the tomb' (Giot

1958, 149–53; 1960, 52). A few carvings of sinuous lines, interpreted as serpents, can be considered, perhaps with some reserve, as symbolic guardians of the tomb, as for example the Menhir des Serpents du Manio at Carnac, probably part of a megalithic tomb despite its name. A wall of the passage grave at Gavrinis is carved with representations of eighteen polished jadeite axes, most likely a substitute for the deposit of real axes to defeat the tomb robber.

Some of the Danish Early Bronze Age oak bole-coffins have a locking device embodying the use of wooden stakes, in the hope of deterring the robber (Broholm and Hald 1940, 10).

The British Isles

The theory that chamber tombs with false or blind entrances were the funerary architects' answer to the activities of the tomb robber was generally accepted until it was called in question by Corcoran (1969). The writer still follows the traditional view that the false entrance (as at Belas Knap long barrow on the Cotswolds) developed because experience showed that chamber tombs with a true entrance could be too easily entered by those with sinister purposes in mind. These purposes are unlikely to have been treasure-searching since nothing of intrinsic value was normally placed in these tombs by those who built them; it was desirable to secure the tomb against the attentions of personal enemies and unruly youths attracted to the tomb by morbid curiosity or other idle motives.

From time to time it is noticed that what would appear to be primary interments have been placed away from the centre of a round barrow of Beaker culture or Bronze Age. It is possible that in some instances the siting of a primary grave or cist off centre might have been to cause the tomb robber to miss his objective. Otherwise the round barrows of this period seem to contain little or no evidence that any precautions against the tomb robbers were normally taken, apart from covering the interment with a circular mound of earth or stones, often constructed with great care to satisfy the requirements of tradition and funerary ritual. The covering of interments with enormous cairns, such as Flint Barrow (Kingston Deverill II, Wiltshire), could have been to discourage the tomb robber but other reasons are possible, namely the importance of the person interred; the availability of cairn material ready to hand and of a labour force to use it. The deposit of grave-goods of intrinsic value in round barrows of the Bronze Age was exceptional and confined mainly to special areas, including the environs of Stonehenge and one or two localities in Cornwall and Dorset. It was probably considered unlikely that looting would occur until after the ruling dynasty had passed.

The idea of looting British barrows for treasure may well have received a stimulus from the pagan Saxon period when the custom of depositing the most treasured possessions with the dead was resumed in a big way. This has been emphasized by the discovery of the treasure in the barrow at Sutton Hoo, Suffolk, and led to a reconsideration of the descriptions of barrow treasure in *Beowulf*. Traditions of treasure concealed in barrows in Britain are unlikely

59 Dragon-like figure in Maes Howe, Orkney

to have originated earlier than this period; if they did they would have normally had little or no factual basis.

It is a question whether the legend of treasure in a barrow guarded by a dragon, narrated in *Beowulf*, related to a prehistoric chambered barrow perhaps re-used by the pagan Saxons, or to a barrow constructed for a pagan Saxon interment with its treasure. In any case the dragon was there to protect the treasure as much as (perhaps more than) the interment. The great chamber tomb of Maes Howe, Orkney, is undoubtedly prehistoric in origin, but has its interior walls carved with a dragon-like figure and Viking inscriptions in Runic of the mid-twelfth century relating to treasure placed in the barrow, evidently symbolically guarded by the dragon represented on the wall. These wall decorations must have been carved by a Viking who was versed in northern mythology.

The influence of later superstition

Superstitions connected with early burial sites are fairly well documented in the British Isles, France, and Scandinavia from Saxon and Viking times onwards. From the Middle Ages until the early nineteenth century there is no doubt that in some regions barrow-opening was discouraged by local beliefs that such acts would be followed by some calamity or by a death. The belief that barrows are inhabited by fairies, elves, hobgoblins, pixies and the like, and that if a barrow were destroyed these creatures would have to make a home elsewhere and that in the meantime their acts would be unpredictable, undoubtedly induced some would-be barrow diggers to desist. In this context it is unfortunate that during the last century most British people have been becoming less superstitious.

Chapter Twelve

Tomb robbing

The graves of their former (and) later kings, who had not feared Ashur and Ishtar, my sovereigns, (and) who had harassed the kings my fathers, I ravaged, destroyed, (and) exposed to the sun. Their bones I took to Assyria. Upon their spirits I imposed restlessness (and) cut them off from food offerings (and) libations of water. Inscription of Ashurbanipal (668–627 BC), quoted from H. C. Rawlinson. *The Cuneiform Inscriptions of Western Asia* 1884, V, pl. 6, col. vi, 70–6.

As long as objects of intrinsic value have been placed with the dead, and human nature (including that of kings) has been what it is, there have been tomb robbers. Among motives influencing the tomb robber have been the desire for treasure, the search for building materials, the wish to harm the after-life of an enemy, plain vandalism, mere curiosity, and occasionally religious fanaticism.

By no means every tomb robber in antiquity was considerate enough to leave enough potsherds or other artifacts in his robber's hole to enable the date of his intrusion to be ascertained within reasonable limits by future archaeologists. It will hereafter be noted that tomb robberies have been made at all periods since tombs were constructed: indeed some were made before the tomb was completed and occasionally with the connivance of the funerary architects, as for instance in Egypt and in Germany during the Hallstatt period.

Most of the earlier Neolithic ceremonial burials were beneath the floors of houses, as in the Pre-Pottery Neolithic at Jericho (Anati 1963, 254); at Khirokitia in Cyprus (Dikaios 1953, 214–21, 228–31); and at Çatal Hüyük in Anatolia (Mellaart 1967, 204–9). In such instances the problem of tomb robbery was virtually non-existent as the family had complete control of the situation so long as they continued to dwell there.

Egypt

The most comprehensive evidence of the handiwork of the tomb robber has come from Egypt. The written sources so far discovered are only a minute fraction of those originally made, but they provide an adequate cross-section of the extent of the pillage and also of the apprehension and trial of the offenders.

A tomb could be violated without necessarily being robbed. To deny the dead the pleasures of the after-life was among the most spiteful acts that an enemy could perform, and to achieve this it was merely necessary to delete the name of the deceased from wherever it occurred in his tomb. An instance of this is provided by the false door of Re-wer southeast of the pyramid temple of Teti at Sakkara.

60 Erasure of name of tomb owner (Re-wer) on false door of tomb at Sakkara. The name has been erased by an enemy from the upper and lower lintels, door drum and vertically inscribed jambs. Late Dynasty VI

After the collapse of the Old Kingdom at the end of Dynasty VI, the mob let themselves loose on the pyramids with their associated temples, all of which were probably looted during the First Intermediate Period. Early in the Middle Kingdom the pyramid of Amenemhet I at Lisht was being built partly of sculptured slabs pillaged from the Giza pyramids and from other tombs at Giza and Sakkara (Fakhry 1969, 99, 213). From the same period date some wooden coffins made to include a concealed aperture for the benefit of the tomb robber, thereby showing that the maker of funerary equipment was sometimes in league with the tomb robber (Badawy 1966, 91). The pyramids of the Middle Kingdom were probably all or nearly all broken into during the Second Intermediate Period. The pyramidal superstructure of the funerary monument of Nebhepetre Mentuhotep at Thebes was pillaged for materials which were used in the building of the neighbouring Temple of Queen Hatshepsut (Fakhry 1969, 209).

From the beginning of the New Kingdom it was hoped that the cutting of royal tombs in the rock faces of the Valley of the

Kings at Thebes, the concealment of their entrance, and the placing of their mortuary temple well away from the tomb and between the Theban Hills and the Nile valley, would go far to minimize risk of disturbance by the plunderer. The great prosperity of Dynasties XVIII and early XIX, arising from the receipt of vast booty from foreign wars and expeditions, led to the deposit of immense treasure to accompany the pharaohs to their tombs. This could not have been done without the knowledge of where it was hidden being handed down from one generation to the next until advantage could be taken of a period when discipline was sufficiently relaxed to enable the tomb robber to resume his activities. Indeed it is likely that tomb plundering continued to a limited extent throughout the earlier part of the New Kingdom even under the fairly strong administration of most of that period. There was probably a more active revival of it during the Amarna period. There is evidence that the tomb of Tuthmosis IV was broken into probably at this time, as it was restored and some of the funerary furniture mended by Meya

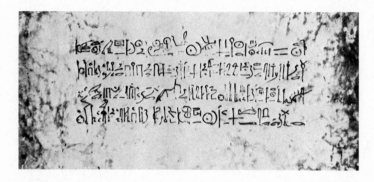

61 Restoration inscription of Meya, Chief of Works in the necropolis at Thebes, who restored the burial of Tuthmosis IV in his tomb in the Valley of the Kings

during the eighth year of the reign of Horemheb. Two incursions were made into the tomb of Tutankhamun within a few years of his burial (see below).

The available evidence suggests, however, that some looting in the Valley of the Kings occurred during the reign of Ramesses III, and looting on an exceptionally large scale occurred during the reigns of Ramesses IX and XI. Needless to say, most of the tombs in the Valley of the Queens were also broken into. As Dynasty XX proceeded under the Ramesside pharaohs III to XI, each perhaps weaker than his predecessor, infiltrations by Libyans and other foreigners increased and even reached Thebes. The administration of the Theban necropolis accordingly became more and more difficult. Its defence became inadequate; clothes and food for the necropolis workmen were distributed with increasing irregularity; complaints of non-delivery were made by officials of the necropolis to their superiors, often to little or no purpose. The workers in the royal necropolis, many perhaps reduced to a state of dire necessity, may have had no option but to yield to the temptation to break into the royal tombs and also to plunder the royal mortuary temples. The circumstances leading to the apprehension of the miscreants and details of their trial are described in a series of papyri from the temple of Ramesses III at Medinet Habu from which the royal necropolis was administered. These papyri are mostly in the museums at Cairo, Liverpool, London, and Turin. They provide much information on the names of the defendants, on criminal procedure and, among other matters, on the forms of corporal punishment used to extract confessions from the defendants. They also give information on which tombs had been entered, and the quantities of gold, silver, copper, and bronze taken from them; sometimes indeed it is stated that the metal was wrenched from specific items of funerary furniture. Other papyri supply information on vases, oils, and clothing taken from the tombs or temples (Peet 1930). In this connection it will be recalled that the tomb of Tutankhamun was subjected to two minor robberies soon after the king's burial; on the first occasion the easily portable objects of precious metals were removed; on the second occasion the robbers emptied the oils and unguents from the various vases. (Desroches-Noblecourt 1963, 280).

Ramesses XI, with whom Dynasty XX ended, was probably the last pharaoh to have a tomb in the Valley of the Kings. The only known Egyptian royal tombs of the two following dynasties are at Tanis in the Delta. During Dynasty XXI the priests of Amun decided to remove the robbed mummies of the pharaohs from their original tombs and place them in locations where adequate security was considered possible (p. 88).

Other regions in the Near East

Of the nine tombs of the client-kings at Byblos, of the Egyptian Middle Kingdom, five had been robbed in ancient times and one in more recent times (Jidejian 1968, 26). Amongst the tombs of the Persian period at the same site that of Batno'am bore an inscription, translated as follows (Parrot 1939, 35–6):

'I Batno'am, mother of the King Ozbaal, King of Byblos, son of Pillet-baal, priest of Baalat, I rest in this sarcophagus in clothes, wearing a diadem and with a gold mouth-mask, like that which has been done for royalty before me.'

It is hardly necessary to add that her tomb was robbed in antiquity.

At Ur the tomb of King Abargi was looted by those making the tomb of Queen Shubad, probably his widow, whose tomb lay immediately above his. Elsewhere in the royal cemetery Woolley found a robbers' hole dated by potsherds to the time of Sargon of Akkad, *c.* 2350 BC (Woolley 1954, 57, 62–8).

Cyprus

The great necropolis at Salamis was being plundered and re-used in Hellenistic and Roman times. Later plundering is recorded by a Swiss traveller, Joseph de Meggen, who in 1542 saw tombs being looted, and indeed purchased various items of jewellery from the robbers then at work. The necropolis owes its rediscovery about 1956 largely to the activities of modern clandestine diggers. Tomb no. 3 in that group is known as the Goldsmith's Mound, perhaps from treasure sometime found there (Karageorghis 1967, I, 4).

The Minoan-Mycenaean world

In the Cretan Mesara are numerous circular stone-built tombs (*c.* 2800–1700 BC) with entrance usually to E, NE, or SE. They were often used for centuries for successive burials, access being obtained merely by moving back the closing slab. When the tomb was reopened for a fresh burial it was normal practice to fumigate the interior. During this process the temptation to relieve earlier burials of any grave-goods of value must often have been irresistible, and there is unlikely to have been any shortage of fumigators. After all, the grave-goods had served their purpose for long enough with the occupant for whom they had originally been placed; and they may have been re-appropriated to form part of the funerary equipment of the next occupant, who might well have been a relative or descendant. Plundering during fumigation seems to have been standard practice even when later burials were added several centuries after the earlier ones, so that the tendency is for rich grave-goods to be associated (now) with the most recent burials; but there are strong reasons for believing that the earlier burials were often accompanied by rich grave-goods. This is shown by the excavation of a very few tombs which escaped plundering during successive fumigations (Xanthoudides 1971 reprint, 8; Branigan 1970, 107–10). It is of course likely that for every instance of objects of high value being transferred from an earlier to a later burial, there were a hundred of plain theft by the fumigators.

'After the end of the Bronze Age, there is little evidence of looting and disturbance until relatively modern times' (Branigan 1970, 13). During the last century the purpose of such activities would usually have been to obtain suitable building materials, and the sepulchral nature of the site would often not at first have been evident. During the last decades the increasing market value of antiquities has led to a great increase of looting.

Once the Mycenaean tholos tomb had reached a stage in development involving the construction of a relieving triangle above the doorway lintel (Wace's Groups II and III), the security of the tomb was reduced, as it was easy to remove the masonry which filled the relieving triangle and so gain entry. The Tomb of the Genii at Mycenae must have been entered by this means as its tholos is intact. The tholos tomb just northeast of the Palace of Nestor at Pylos had probably been robbed before the end of the Mycenaean period. It has been suggested that the tholos tomb at Tiryns was plundered within a century or so of 1000 BC and some of its treasure may be included in the 'Tiryns Treasure' found in 1915 in the probable site of the robber's house near by. The Tomb of Clytemnestra, the Lion Tomb at Mycenae, and many of the other tholos tombs on the Greek mainland may have been plundered by the Dorian conquerors. The Tomb of Aegisthus was most likely robbed in Hellenistic times. By that time the Treasury of Minyas at Orchomenos had most probably been plundered as it was then in use as a sanctuary. The Treasury of Atreus was broken into before the time of Pausanias (late second century AD). On the other hand a few tholos tombs, including examples at Dendra, Menidi (Acharnai) near Athens, and Vaphio were still virtually intact until archaeologically investigated within the last century.

Etruria

The rather accessible character of most of the Etruscan tombs, and the rich contents of many of them in jewellery, vases and other objects, tended to encourage the tomb robber. The official attitude of their Roman successors on this subject is not very clear but Dennis (1883, xcvii) found little or no evidence that Etruscan tombs were looted on any appreciable scale during the Roman period. Theodoric the Goth (AD 489–526) did, however, sanction the robbing of ancient tombs for the recovery of precious metal objects on the ground that those objects are of more use to the living than to the dead. Dennis remarks on the curious manner in which many of the Etruscan tombs had been robbed in antiquity of their precious metals but not of their vases, and this fits in with Theodoric's policy to encourage the removal of only the former from the tombs (Cassiodorus, *Variar* IV, 34). Therefore large-scale robbing of Etruscan tombs may well date from this period and has probably continued intermittently ever since. Dennis noted that at Vulci not one tomb in a hundred remained intact by 1883. Of the very large number of tombs explored by the C.M. Lerici Foundation in the Banditaccia necropolis at Cerveteri between 1955 and 1965, only one (no. 43) was found intact. From the mid-nineteenth century onwards (and probably earlier) tomb looting has tended to increase as the market value of Etruscan antiquities has risen. This problem has reached alarming proportions during the last few years, the products looted by the *tombaroli* (as the professional tomb robbers are called) and their part time associates finding a ready market through dealers in Switzerland, the USA and elsewhere to the rest of the world. Lerici estimated in 1961 that the market value of objects stolen from Etruscan tombs was then of the order of three million dollars a year.

The rest of Europe

Many graves of the Bronze Age Usatova and Catacomb cultures in Russia were robbed soon after the funeral, probably by lower-class natives (Sulimirski 1970, 184, 223). This is indeed likely to have happened in any areas where an immigrant ruling aristocracy was accorded burial with rich grave-goods. The Únětice cemetery of about sixty-four graves at Rebešovice, Moravia, was plundered later in the Únetice period by invaders of a neighbouring tribe (Filip 1966, 120). There are at least two instances of rich Hallstatt tombs in Germany having been robbed of some of their contents before the tombs had been completed after the burial (Riek and Hundt 1962; Zurn 1970). One of the most flagrant instances of large-scale tomb robbery occurred at the great Punic cemetery of about four thousand tombs, many of them easy of access, on the Puig des Molins, Ibiza. Collections of finds from this cemetery are to be seen in the museums at Barcelona, Ibiza, Madrid, Valencia, and in several other countries, as well as in many private collections (Pericot 1972, 119–24).

In France a society was formed in 1811 at Auray for the express purpose of finding gold in megalithic monuments and it is said that its members found no less than thirty gold armbands. The finding of two gold armlets in the Roch-Guyon megalithic tomb near Plouharnel led to another outbreak of violation which included the use of gunpowder to blast away cover-slabs (Le Rouzic 1939). Other megalithic tombs and barrows were used as quarries for obtaining road material during the last century when roadmaking was rampant (Daniel 1960, 18). The great group of passage graves at Barnenez South (Brittany) was discovered while being used as a quarry for road material (Giot 1958).

The subject of tomb robbing in Scandinavia is of special interest because of its bearing on the early laws of Treasure Trove. The

62 Tomb robbing in Scandinavia, *c.* 1713. The illustration seems to suggest the beginnings of a spirit of scientific enquiry

Code of King Valdemar II of Denmark (1202–41), completed in 1241, included a statement that 'if anyone finds silver or gold in a howe [barrow] . . . then shall the King have it'. This may have been a reaffirmation of an earlier code; it was itself reaffirmed by King Christian V of Denmark (1670–99) and was still in force in 1936 (Hill 1936, 182). In Norway the law decreed that treasure from howes be divided between the King, the finder and the landowner, in proportions varying according to the circumstances. There is reason to believe that the English Law of Treasure Trove is partly based on those of Scandinavia.

The British Isles

So far there seems little evidence that many of the Neolithic long barrows and Bronze Age round barrows and cairns were plundered before the Roman period, but such evidence should always in future be looked for. Analysis of recent excavation records suggests that several of the chambered long barrows on the Cotswolds, and one or two long barrows and several round barrows on and around Mendip, were dug into during the Roman period. Roman interest in British prehistoric tombs appears, however, to have been limited to curio-hunting.

From the Anglo-Saxon period comes a curious reference to St Guthlac making his home *c.* AD 699 in a chamber revealed by treasure-seekers in the side of a barrow near Crowland in Lincolnshire. This is not an area for prehistoric chambered barrows but this barrow might have been Roman. Early Irish texts suggest that 'St Patric and Caeilte were not slack themselves in unearthing grave treasures'. The Councils of Arles and Nantes were directed (*inter alia*) against anyone *omitting* to destroy places of pagan ritual, which must sometimes have included earlier tombs. From the period of the Viking invasions comes further documentary evidence of tomb robbing in Britain. The *Annals of Ulster* and the *Annals of the Kingdom of Ireland* contain entries *c.* AD 860–2 strongly suggesting that New Grange and perhaps other megalithic tombs in the Boyne valley were plundered by Norsemen at that time (O'Kelly 1967, 63–5). The great chamber tomb of Maes Howe in Orkney was entered about 1150 and 1153 by two parties of Vikings who left Runic inscriptions on the walls concerning the treasure removed (Dickins 1930).

From the Norman period comes evidence of barrow-digging for another purpose. About 1178 monks from St Albans, bent on acquiring saints' bones to work miracles in their Abbey, dug into a group of barrows known as the Hills of the Banners near Redbourn and found human bones which they confidently hailed as those of the holy martyr Amphibalus. In 1199 a barrow at Ludlow was opened and three human skeletons found therein were indentified as those of Irish saints. It is possible that a thorough search of monastic archives might reveal further evidence of digging into prehistoric barrows to acquire saints' bones.

The concept of royal authorization for treasure-seeking in ancient tombs in western Europe is of considerable antiquity. In the words of Sir Thomas Browne, 'what was unreasonably committed to the ground is reasonably resumed from it: Let Monuments and rich Fabricks, not Riches adorn mens ashes'. The Goth king Theodoric inaugurated a Commission for finding sepulchral treasure. This was one of perhaps several precedents for the issue in southern Britain between 1237 and 1680 of Authorizations to dig into barrows for treasure. The Authorizations were usually addressed by the king to the sheriff or other senior official of the county or district, and they have survived for Cornwall and the Isle of Wight (1237) and Devon (1324), and closely related documents have been published concerning barrows near Dunstable in Bedfordshire (1290), at Upwey in Dorset (1621) and at Cocklow in Staffordshire (1680).

Fragments of a tigerware jug from the robbers' hole of the ship-barrow at Sutton Hoo have been dated *c*. 1600. This accords fairly well with the suggestion that the incursion might have been made by or at the instigation of Queen Elizabeth's astrologer and alchemist Dr John Dee, 1527–1608 (Green 1963, 31).

One of the most unusual of recorded motives for digging into prehistoric tombs is to obtain bones from which to concoct medicines. In the late seventeenth century Dr R. Toope of Marlborough dug in and around barrows near the Sanctuary southeast of Avebury for human bones 'of which I made a noble medicine that relieved many of my distressed neighbours'. He also dug into the West Kennet long barrow, almost certainly for the same purpose. Human bones are known to have been part of the druggists' *pharmacopoeia* until sometime after that date.

In Britain as in France and elsewhere, the construction of turnpikes and other roads in the late eighteenth and early nineteenth centuries was indirectly responsible for the plundering of many prehistoric monuments in their vicinity for stone and other materials for roadmaking. This plundering was encouraged by a clause in the Highway Act of William IV authorizing the removal of surface stones for road construction or road mending. Many of the cairns on Dartmoor were despoiled on the authority of this Act (Burnard 1902). On the other hand the gathering of stones from any likely spots for road mending occasionally led to the discovery of a hitherto unknown prehistoric tomb; Hetty Pegler's Tump on the Cotswolds was found this way.

PART TWO   REGIONAL

Chapter Thirteen

Egyptian pyramids

Various writers have in the past tried to arrange the pyramids chronologically and work out a scheme of development from the primitive mastaba (rectangular flattish-topped tomb) of the first two dynasties. This approach has been rightly criticized by J. P. Lauer on the ground that the work of architects of genius should not be forced into a sort of developmental straitjacket (Lauer 1962, 6–7). The material of each pyramid to be described is limestone except where otherwise indicated.

Dynasty III (c. 2686–2613 BC)

The first pharaoh of this dynasty was probably Sanakht. At Sakkara the original flat or slightly cambered topped mastaba (later slightly enlarged) which forms most of the first step of the Step Pyramid of Zoser, successor and probably younger brother of Sanakht, may have been built by Sanakht. The outline of both stages of this mastaba, which was square-based, is visible on the south side of the Step Pyramid where the later masonry has disappeared.

The Step Pyramid of Zoser was added to this mastaba at first in four steps and later extended to the north and west and the height increased by adding another two steps. The resulting structure is rectangular with the longer axis east–west. The interior, being unsafe, is normally inaccessible to visitors. From the funerary temple on the north side a ramp leads to a probably slightly earlier stairway descending to the bottom of a shaft, 28 m deep and 7 m square, where there is a red granite sepulchral chamber whose roof is closed by a granite plug block which was housed in a niche a few metres up the stairway until required for use after the pharaoh had been buried. A mummified foot found in this chamber in 1934 may have belonged to Zoser. From the sepulchral chamber extend subterranean galleries, some decorated with reproductions in blue faience tiles of hangings of reed matting, and with full-length limestone reliefs of Zoser performing ritual acts. Within the east side of the pyramid is a row of eleven tombs for members of the royal family which have already yielded two alabaster sarcophagi, one originally containing the body of a child aged eight in a gold-covered coffin.

The structures outside the Step Pyramid but within its rectangular enclosure are complex. East of the funerary temple on the north side is the serdab enclosing a replica of the seated painted limestone statue of Zoser (original in Cairo Museum). Opposite the eyes of the statue the wall of the serdab is pierced by two holes, perhaps for burning incense before the statue. East of the serdab are

63 (*Opposite, upper*) Plan of north Sakkara showing the Step Pyramid of Zoser (Dynasty III, c. 2650 BC) and surroundings.

64 (*Opposite, lower*) Step Pyramid of Zoser, Sakkara. View from the south showing the profile of the original mastaba (of Sanakht?)

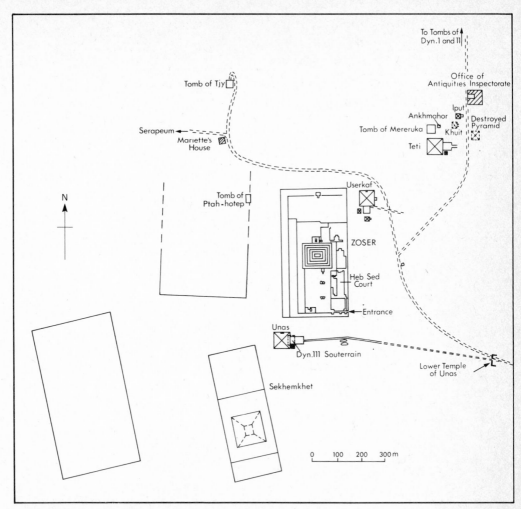

To Tombs of
Dyn.1 and 11

Office of
Antiquities Inspectorate

Tomb of Tjy

Iput

Ankhmahor

Destroyed
Pyramid

Tomb of Mereruka

Khuit

Serapeum

Teti

Mariette's
House

N

Tomb of
Ptah-hotep

Userkaf

ZOSER

Heb Sed
Court

Entrance

Unas

Dyn.III Souterrain

Lower Temple
of Unas

Sekhemkhet

0   100   200   300 m

65 Enclosure and Step Pyramid of Zoser, Sakkara. Reconstruction by J. P. Lauer

the North and South Buildings, south of which is a court containing two D-shaped structures. South of this court is the Heb Sed court, with numerous chapels on its east and west sides, where the king enacted the ritual of re-dedication for a further term. West of this is a Temple with three engaged fluted columns. Near the south end of the east side of the enclosure wall are the entrance and colonnade, restored by Lauer, who has been studying the funerary monument of Zoser since 1927. Between the west end of the colonnade and the south side of the pyramid is the great court with its two B-shaped ritual structures. South of this court is the 'South Tomb', 28 m deep and 7 m square, made of granite and similar to that beneath the Step Pyramid; branching from it are galleries walled with blue faience tiles and on its north side is a small funerary chapel. Beneath the Step Pyramid two storerooms yielded more than thirty thousand stone vases of many types, and many thousands more remain to be recovered from the other storerooms. Most of these vases did not contain food or drink; these were doubtless intended to be provided by magic.

It remains to emphasize the extent to which this, the world's earliest known major stone-built tomb, reproduces in stone the architectural forms previously developed in mud-brick (for example the bastioned enclosure wall with imitation double gates), wood and reed bundles (columns and 'palm-log' roofing). Zoser was known in his lifetime as Neterikhet (Divine of Body) and was not called Zoser until Dynasty XII. The architect of his funerary monument was Imhotep, whose name occurs with that of Neterikhet on a statue-base found in the enclosure.

Southwest of the funerary monument of Zoser are the remains of the unfinished tomb of Sekhemkhet who was probably Zoser's successor. Being square-based it would, if completed as a pyramid, have been nearer the form of the true pyramid than that of Zoser. The tomb stands within an enclosure as long as that of Zoser but about two-thirds of its width. Sekhemkhet probably reigned for only six years and his monument was used as a quarry for many centuries. The maximum height of the surviving structure therefore seldom exceeds 6 m. The interior is not normally accessible. A ramp from the north side descends to the burial chamber with its alabaster sarcophagus, still covered with the remains of a funerary garland when the tomb was explored in 1954. Although the sarcophagus appeared intact before being opened that year, it was empty. It might have been a dummy or thieves might have been in league with those concerned with the pharaoh's burial. Finds from the passage beneath the tomb included twenty-one gold bangles, a gold necklace, and a gold box with a lid in the form of a cockle-shell: perhaps offerings dropped in the passage by plunderers during a hurried getaway. Near by were storerooms containing stone vases, seven with mud sealings of Sekhemkhet. A corridor, with compartments along the north side and with branches at right angles covering the northern parts of the west and east sides, resembles that at the Southern ('Layer') pyramid of Zawyet el-Aryan so closely as to leave little doubt that the latter is also Dynasty III, and probably the tomb of Khaba who may have followed Sekhemkhet.

West and north of the funerary monument of Sekhemkhet are the remains of two other vast rectangular walled enclosures, probably also royal tombs of Dynasty III, not yet excavated. Their examination should lead to a revision of our knowledge of the sequence of pharaohs of this dynasty for which the extant kinglists may not be complete.

Dynasties III-IV

The layout of the pyramid complex at Maidum, near the Faiyum oasis, initiated those of Dynasties IV to VI. It comprises a valley temple near the desert edge; a causeway extending westwards from this temple to the walled enclosure containing the main pyramid; the pyramid, on the east side of which is a shrine containing an offering-table between two uninscribed round-topped stelae; and between the south side of the pyramid and the walled enclosure was a subsidiary pyramid, in much the same position as the 'South Tomb' of the funerary monument of Zoser. The lower temple has not yet been explored, being now below flood level.

The structure of the pyramid originally comprised a central core flanked by six accretion faces producing a stepped pyramid of seven steps. This was enlarged to one of eight slightly higher steps. The outer faces of both flights of steps, as with the earlier stepped pyramids, were in Tura limestone dressed to a finished surface. The masonry of the steps was similarly inclined downwards towards the centre to discourage the stone robber. Yet the steps were soon filled with masonry and casing blocks were added to form the first known true pyramid. A plausible explanation of this building sequence is to attribute the first phase of the stepped

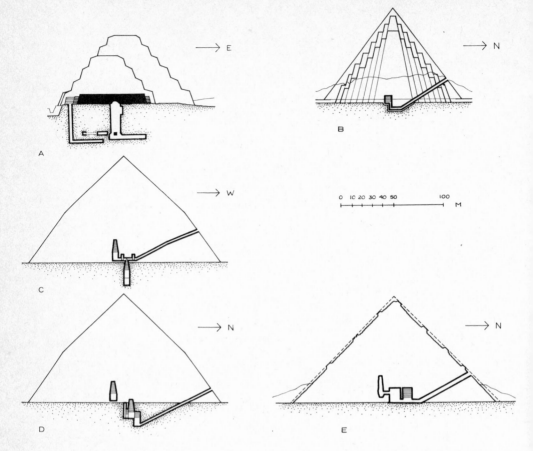

66 Sections of pyramids of
Dynasties III and IV. (After
Aldred)

A Step Pyramid of Zoser,
   Sakkara
B Pyramid of Huni (?),
   Maidum

C and D Bent Pyramid of
   Snefru, Dahshur
E North pyramid of Snefru,
   Dahshur

pyramid to Huni, last pharaoh of Dynasty III, and the second
stepped phase and also the finished true pyramid to Snefru. This
would explain why the inscriptions of New Kingdom visitors on
the walls of the funerary shrine attribute the pyramid to Snefru.
The difficulty of considering the Maidum pyramid in its entirety as
the work of Snefru is that it is almost certain that the North and
South stone pyramids at Dahshur were also his; and it seems most
unlikely that yet another pyramid could have been built during his
reign. A study of the architectural features of these pyramids has
led Maragioglio and Rinaldi (1964, 6–8) to believe that the Maidum
pyramid is earlier than the two stone pyramids at Dahshur which
have close affinities with that of Kheops; and they accept, provisionally, the attribution of at least the first phase of the Maidum
pyramid to Huni.

The entrance is in the middle of the north side at a height of 30 m.
A ramp descends through the masonry into the bedrock, and a
horizontal passage leads from the bottom of the ramp to the base

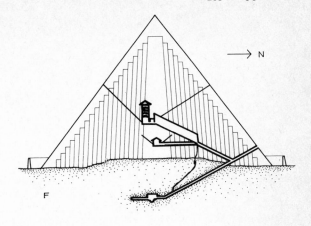

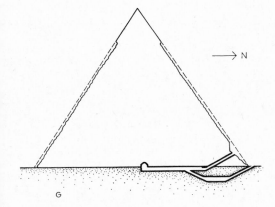

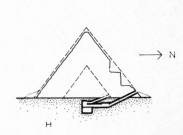

F Pyramid of Kheops. Giza
G Pyramid of Khephren, Giza
H Pyramid of Mycerinus, Giza

of a vertical shaft. A modern wooden ladder ascends this shaft to
the burial chamber with its corbelled ceiling of seven stages. In
this chamber Petrie found parts of a wooden coffin of uncertain
attribution. Snefru's title as founder of Dynasty IV derived
from his marriage to Huni's daughter Hetepheres, famous for the
funerary furniture from her shaft at Giza, now in Cairo Museum.
Regard for his father-in-law may have induced Snefru to convert
Huni's step pyramid into a true pyramid. In this he may have been
influenced by a change in religious belief, from a step pyramid as a
'stairway to the sky' to a true pyramid as conferring the sun-god's
protection on the deceased pharaoh.

Dynasty IV: the Dahshur pyramids of Snefru (c. 2613–2589 BC)

The South stone pyramid at Dahshur is unique in having its lower
and upper portions at different angles of inclination, resulting in its

being called the Bent Pyramid. Excavation from 1945 onwards has shown that it is almost certainly the southern of two pyramids attributed to Snefru in the Dahshur Decree of Dynasty VI.

The southern pyramid complex of Snefru comprises a rectangular valley temple; a causeway extending from it for *c.* 700 m west–southwest to a point near the northeast corner of the walled enclosure of the pyramid; within this walled enclosure is the pyramid with a small temple in the middle of its east side; in the centre

67 South pyramid of Snefru, Dahshur, from the air. Early Dynasty IV. The causeway, lower temple and temenos wall of the pyramid are clearly seen

of the south side of the enclosure is a subsidiary pyramid, with traces of a funerary chapel on its north side. The valley temple was excavated by Fakhry and produced about 1400 fragments of reliefs of Snefru performing various ceremonies and processions of offering-bearers from the Egyptian nomes. Along the northern wall were six shrines, each originally containing a statue of Snefru. Fragments recovered from three of these statues show that they were life-size or larger. The walls of the causeway from valley temple to pyramid enclosure were nearly destroyed, but the curved top of surviving parts of these shows that it was not roofed. The funerary temple on the east side of the pyramid resembled that of the pyramid of Maidum in size and plan, and it too contained an offering-table and two stelae. It had been reconstructed three times and a cult of Snefru had continued there for several centuries.

The decision of the architects to change the slope angle of the pyramid was caused by the appearance in the lower part of cracks which they had filled with gypsum mortar. The upper part is of smaller blocks and coarser workmanship than the lower. Being inclined, the casing is nearly all in place except at the northeast corner.

In the middle of the north side of the pyramid is the vestige of an offering-shrine originally containing a small offering-table. The northern of the two entrances to the pyramid is 11·8 m above this shrine at its base. A rather steep ramp descends through the super-structure into the substructure to an antechamber and a chamber with corbelled roof of fifteen stages. The western entrance is 33·2 m above the base and is slightly south of the centre of the western face. From it extends a steep ramp to a horizontal passage just above the level of the base of the superstructure. Along this passage are two oblique slots for portcullises, and at the end of the passage is a chamber with corbelled roof of thirteen stages. One of the slabs in this chamber was inscribed in red with the cartouche of Snefru, placed upside-down. An inclined passage, believed to be of the period of Snefru, leads from the upper part of the lower chamber to the horizontal passage of the upper chamber otherwise reached by the western entrance. This chamber was lined with a framework of cedar logs.

The subsidiary pyramid has its entrance in the middle of the north side at ground level. This leads to a V-shaped ramp (first descending and then ascending) leading to a central corbelled chamber of eight stages. East of the pyramid were two stelae, originally *c.* 5 m high, bearing the titles of Snefru and a relief of the king seated and in the robes of the Heb Sed festival. It is there-fore certain that this subsidiary pyramid was connected with Snefru's burial ritual.

The North stone pyramid complex at Dahshur has not yet been explored, but aerial photographs show a causeway leading (from a valley temple ?) westwards to the northeast angle of the pyramid. Excavation in front of its eastern face in 1953 was too slight to reveal the funerary temple. The slope-angle of the pyramid, *c.* 43° 31′ (the lowest of any Egyptian pyramid), is nearly equal to that of the upper part of the Bent Pyramid and could suggest that it was built after that pyramid had been completed. The entrance, near the middle of the north side, is 28 m above the base. From the entrance a ramp descends through the masonry to a horizontal passage on the natural level, leading through two corbelled ante-chambers to a corbelled end-chamber at a higher level. These three chambers are now difficult of access. To the southwest are cause-

68 North pyramid of Snefru, Dahshur, from the air. Early Dynasty IV. Note the two construction ramps, or causeways, to the southwest

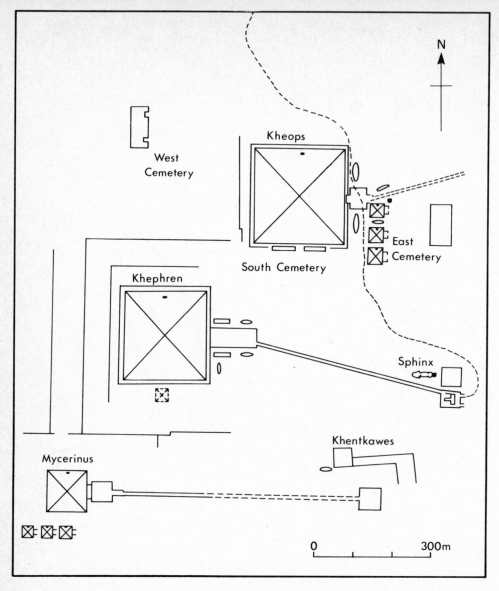

ways presumably leading to the quarries whence the coarse local
limestone was obtained for the main body of the pyramid. As this
pyramid has tombs of Snefru's period in its vicinity, and a casing
block from its northeast corner bears Snefru's Horus name (Neb
Maat) in red ochre, it is almost certainly the North pyramid of
Snefru mentioned in the Dahshur Decree of Dynasty VI.

Dynasty IV: the pyramids of Giza and Abu Rauwash (c. 2589–2494 BC)

Snefru was succeeded by his son Kheops, whose Great Pyramid is
the earliest major element in the royal necropolis at Giza. His
immediate successor Djedefre had his pyramid at Abu Rauwash c.
8 km to the north; but his other successors Khephren and Mycerinus added their pyramids on the Giza plateau to the southwest of
that of Kheops. The pyramids of Giza and their associated monuments constitute perhaps the world's largest royal necropolis.

The valley temple of the *Pyramid of Kheops* is not visible, being beneath the village of Nazlet es-Samman. From here to the funerary temple extends a largely destroyed causeway, whose wall reliefs were noted by Herodotus (*c.* 450 BC). Of the funerary temple east of the pyramid little remains but the basalt floor of an open court surrounded by sockets for granite pillars. The pyramid is enclosed by a platform of limestone slabs; a gap near the entrance on the north side may indicate the site of a North Chapel. The pyramid is the largest of all and was originally 146 m high and 230 m square. Its present height is 137 m, the uppermost courses having been removed. The top-stone (pyramidion) was probably of granite. The slope-angle is about 51° 50′. Nearly all the Tura limestone casing has been stripped except for parts of the lowest course on the north and south sides. As the earliest dated inscription on the backing-blocks is AD 1441, most of the casing must have been robbed before that date, probably to build medieval Cairo. On those backing-blocks, from which sand has been cleared within the last few decades, builders' inscriptions in red ochre are visible, including the name Khnmwkhuf and other names of Kheops.

70 Pyramids of Giza, from the air, *c.* 1944

The more accessible parts of the interior are now electrically lit. The original entrance, access to which is now (1972) being prepared, is *c.* 17 m above the base and just east of centre on the north side and has a pitched roof inscribed in hieroglyphs by the German Egyptologist Lepsius in 1843. From it a ramp descends through the masonry and the bedrock to a horizontal passage and an unfinished chamber slightly south of the apex of the pyramid. Beyond this chamber is a blind passage. The present tourists' entrance is said to have been cut through the masonry into this ramp by the Caliph El-Mamun (AD 813–33). Just below the point of junction of this forced passage with the original descending

71 Devices for closing Old
   Kingdom pyramids

A Sliding the lid on the
  sarcophagus. (After
  Hölscher)

B Lowering the portcullis
  slabs. (After Borchardt and
  Ricke)

C Blocking the ramp. (After
  Gautier and Jéquier)

D Sealing the entrance.
  (After Borchardt)

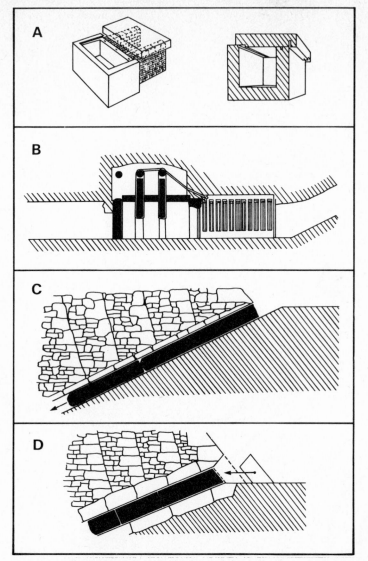

ramp, another ramp ascends southwards to a horizontal passage
ending in the 'Queen's Chamber', almost directly beneath the apex
of the pyramid. This chamber is rectangular, with a pointed roof,
and has a corbelled recess at its eastern end probably for a statue.
The irregular floor of this chamber suggests that it is unfinished.
To the north and south extend narrow oblique shafts to what was
probably the exterior of the unfinished pyramid before there was
another fundamental change in design, resulting in the building
of the Grand (or Ascending) Gallery, the most marvellous architectural achievement in the interior of any pyramid. It is 47 m long
and 8·5 m high and is corbelled in seven stages. On each side, near
the floor level of this gallery, are about twenty-five rectangular
holes, believed to be for receiving chocks or retaining beams,
which when removed enabled a series of granite plug blocks to be
slid one by one down the ascending gallery into the ascending ramp

to block it after the pharaoh had been buried. Three of these plugs (perhaps all that were eventually used) are still at the bottom of the ascending ramp. The workmen in charge of this blocking would have got away down the escape shaft leading from the bottom of the ascending gallery to a point near the bottom of the lower ramp. At the top of the ascending gallery is a short horizontal passage containing slots for three vertical granite portcullis slabs, beyond which is the sarcophagus chamber. The latter is rectangular and placed west–east, the granite sarcophagus being at its west end to associate the passing of the pharaoh with the setting of the sun. The sarcophagus lid is missing. The chamber is lined and flat-roofed with large granite slabs. Above the ceiling are five relieving chambers, all with flat granite roofs excepting the top chamber which has a pitched limestone roof. These relieving chambers contain inscriptions in red ochre stating that work had reached that stage in the seventeenth year of the reign of Kheops. From the walls of the sarcophagus chamber there extend to north and south narrow shafts; the north shaft at 31° to the Imperishable Circum-polar Stars, and the south shaft at 44° 5′ to Orion, both to facilitate the pharaoh's ascent to those parts of the sky (Badawy 1964; Trimble 1964).

A detail of interest is that the sarcophagus is *c.* 2 cm wider than the narrowest part of the ascending ramp; it must therefore have been put in position before the ascending ramp had been completed (Petrie 1883, 216).

Such, in bare outline, is the interior of the pyramid of Kheops. The evidence is usually interpreted as indicating three phases: (i) the unfinished lower chamber; (ii) the unfinished 'Queen's Chamber'; and (iii) the final 'King's Chamber'. A recent authoritative opinion, however, is that the internal arrangements 'belong to a sole project which was studied in every detail as a whole', excepting perhaps the escape shaft which could have been an afterthought (Maragioglio and Rinaldi 1965, 150–2). The architect may have been the vizier Hemon whose limestone statue is in the Pelizaeus Museum in Hildesheim.

Near the pyramid of Kheops are several boat-hollows (Chapter Nine). From the eastern boat-hollow on the south side a large boat, mainly of cedar of Lebanon, was removed in 1954; this has now been restored and will soon be exhibited in a specially built structure near where it was found. The hollow containing this boat was roofed by forty-one limestone slabs (one for each nome?), some inscribed in red ochre with the name of Djedefre who succeeded Kheops and was therefore responsible for his funeral arrangements.

Three small pyramids east and southeast of that of Kheops probably served for three of his wives. Each has its own temple on its east side. Each also has its entrance near ground level in the middle of the north face, from which a ramp descends by an ante-chamber and short passage through a right-angled turn to a sepulchral chamber placed west of centre.

The *Pyramid of Djedefre* is in a commanding position at Abu Rauwash on top of a plateau north of the Giza pyramid field. From the vestiges of the valley temple, indicated only by scattered blocks west of the village, extend the remains of a magnificent causeway for *c.* 1500 m along a natural ridge to a point near the northeast corner of the walled pyramid enclosure. On the east side of the pyramid are foundations of a funerary temple largely in mud-brick, suggesting a hurried completion after the pharaoh's early death. South of this temple is a deep hollow 37 m long for a funerary boat; in this hollow the heads of three statues of Djedefre were found (two in the Louvre, one in Cairo Museum). The pyramid is *c.* 98 m square and in its present unfinished state its maximum height is *c.* 12 m. The entrance is in the middle of the north face; from it an open ramp descends to a rectangular sepulchral chamber at the west end of which the sarcophagus was presumably intended to be placed. This chamber is at the base of a vertical shaft on whose walls Perring thought he detected the former presence of relieving chambers as in the pyramid of Kheops. Southwest of the pyramid is the remnant of a subsidiary pyramid. The funerary monument of Djedefre was never completed and has been used for centuries as a quarry. Many granite chippings show the extensive use of granite in its structure and the first three courses of the pyramid casing were probably in this material. It is believed that political reasons, the nature of which can only be conjectured, induced Djedefre to abandon the Giza plateau in favour of Abu Rauwash for his funerary monument.

The *Pyramid of Khephren*, Djedefre's successor, is on the Giza plateau southwest of that of Kheops. It should be approached from the granite valley temple just southeast of the Sphinx. This temple was originally reached from the Nile by a canal whose quayside was just east of the temple. North and south entrances to this temple lead to a narrow vestibule in a pit in whose floor the famous diorite statue of Khephren was found. A passage from this vestibule leads to a T-shaped hall of sixteen granite pillars, paved with alabaster. This contained twenty-three statues of Khephren, the places where they stood being indicated by depressions. These statues were lit by rays from oblique slits in the roof. South of the stem of the 'T' are two groups of three storerooms one above the other. North of the stem a corridor runs past a small chamber on the left and a stairway on the right to the roof into the causeway leading to the funerary temple. The causeway is 500 m long and mostly hewn from the natural rock. Its walls remain at its eastern end and may have been decorated with reliefs.

The funerary temple is rectangular and floored with alabaster. It includes a T-shaped hall with sockets for twenty-four pillars, a court whose walls were probably lined with twelve statues of Khephren, five long niches perhaps for similar statues, and behind them five storerooms. The occurrence of these elements in groups of five is probably connected with the pharaoh's five titles at this period. Behind these storerooms is a narrow corridor containing a recess for a large granite false door with an offering-table at its foot. Near this temple are five boat-hollows (Chapter Nine). Two long corridors leading from the ends of the T-shaped hall may have been to accommodate boats.

The pyramid is nearly as large as that of Kheops but much less complex internally. Its casing of Tura limestone is still in place for the top quarter of each face. The slope-angle, 53° 10′, is slightly steeper than that of Kheops, 51° 50'. The first two courses were of granite, of which traces remain. The interior is now electrically lit. There are two entrances, each just east of the middle of the north face. The lower entrance is on the ground level a few metres north of the base. From it a ramp descends through the bedrock to a vertical granite portcullis, south of which it becomes a horizontal passage; from there a short ramp descends westwards into a long rectangular chamber with pointed roof, apparently the sarco-phagus chamber as originally intended. After passing the short ramp leading to this, the horizontal passage continues as far as a ramp ascending to meet the passage from the upper entrance which is 11 m above the base. Its cover slab was inscribed by Belzoni in 1818. A ramp, lined and roofed with granite, descends into the bedrock to a vertical granite portcullis beyond which is a horizontal passage. After passing the top of the inner ramp from the lower entrance, this continues to a sarcophagus chamber with pointed roof, slightly north of the centre below the apex of the pyramid. Near the western end of this chamber is a polished granite sarco-phagus let into the floor, its lid being on the floor level. On the south wall of the chamber Belzoni left another inscription. In the middle of the south side of the pyramid is the site of a subsidiary pyramid.

The *Sphinx* originated as a natural knoll in the quarry from which the coarse limestone blocks were extracted for the body of the pyramids of Kheops and Khephren. This was converted into a recumbent lion with head as a stylized portrait of Khephren facing the rising sun, and with a statue of Khephren (now worn away) on its chest. The limestone casings are New Kingdom and later.

The *Pyramid of Mycerinus* is southwest of that of Khephren. The visit to this pyramid complex should begin at the valley temple about 400 m southwest of the Sphinx. This valley temple was begun in limestone but completed in mud-brick. The causeway extend-ing from it to the funerary temple is c. 630 m long and on a prepared limestone base, but was walled in mud-brick and probably roofed with palm logs. The funerary temple, which incorporates the main elements of others of Dynasty IV, was in parts completed in mud-brick, and elsewhere left unfinished. The pyramid is much smaller than those of Kheops and Khephren, being 105 m square and originally c. 66·5 m high, with a slope-angle of about 51°. The first sixteen courses are faced with granite. Around the entrance on the north side the face of these blocks is undressed and they retain the lugs which facilitated their being levered into position probably with the aid of palm logs. Around the entrance, the clear-ance of sand and rubble during the last few years has revealed on three of the granite casing blocks a hieroglyphic inscription which had been previously noted by Diodorus Siculus c. 50 BC: 'in the side towards the north, Mycerinus, the name of the founder, is ingraven' (Diodorus Siculus I, 63–4). This inscription, in about five lines, is badly weathered but it includes a cartouche which seems to enclose the name Menkaure (Mycerinus) and gives the date of his burial as the 23rd day of the fourth month of winter (about March), but the year has weathered away. It was probably carved during Dynasty XXVI when the replacement coffin was put into the pyramid.

72 The pyramid of Mycerinus: plan and section of the interior

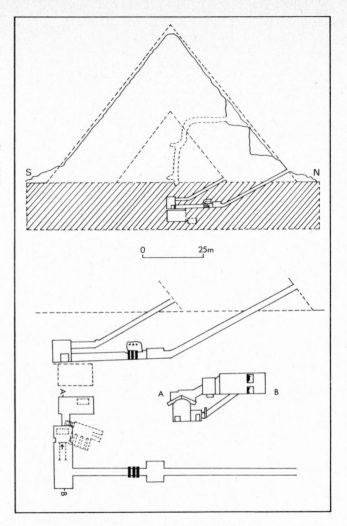

The entrance is in the fourth course of masonry. From it a ramp descends through the masonry (where it is lined with granite) into the bedrock for *c*. 31 m. From that point a horizontal passage begins with a panelled vestibule and leads past three granite portcullises into a rectangular chamber near the west end of which is an oblong hollow apparently intended to receive the sarcophagus. From the middle of this chamber, however, a ramp descends westwards to:

(i) six steps leading to a room with six rectangular cells, probably for the same purpose as six cells within the entrance to the funerary temple of Khephren;

(ii) just beyond this, a sarcophagus chamber walled and barrel-roofed in granite. On its west side was a basalt sarcophagus with palace façade decoration, lost off the coast of Spain on its way to England in 1838.

From the upper part of the original sarcophagus chamber there extend a horizontal passage and ramp to a dead end in the masonry of the superstructure. This may be at the entrance to the pyramid

73 The sarcophagus of
Mycerinus from his pyramid at
Giza

as originally planned, *c.* 40 m square. In the original sarcophagus
chamber Vyse found the lid of a wooden coffin inscribed with the
name of Mycerinus, a replacement dating from Dynasty XXVI
and now in the British Museum.

South and southwest of the pyramid are three small pyramids,
all unfinished, most likely of the wives and perhaps a daughter of
Mycerinus; east of each is a funerary temple of mud-brick.

Almost all the components of the funerary monument of
Mycerinus were either left unfinished or hurriedly completed in
mud-brick. His son and successor Shepseskaf evidently completed
his father's pyramid complex as rapidly as possible so that he could
start on his own funerary monument.

A reaction against the Heliopolitan solar cult which inspired
pyramid building caused Shepseskaf to build his funerary monument in the form of a large sarcophagus, on the east side of which
were the usual funerary temple and causeway doubtless leading
from a valley temple on the edge of the desert. The break with the
previous regime was emphasized by his abandoning Giza in favour
of a site at South Sakkara. His probable successor, Queen Khent-
kawes, had a tomb of similar type, but sited on the Giza plateau
between the causeways of the pyramids of Khephren and Mycerinus, thereby perhaps hinting at a partial return to the old regime.
The tombs of one or two late and obscure pharaohs of Dynasty IV
remain to be identified.

Dynasties V–VI (*c.* 2494–2181 BC)

The pharaohs of these dynasties reverted to the pyramid as their
tomb type. At least six pharaohs of Dynasty V built sun temples
as well, showing that the solar cult of Heliopolis had returned but
was being expressed in a new form. The labour available had therefore to be split between the building of pyramids and sun temples,

74 The pyramids of Abusir.
Reconstruction after Borchardt

but even so it barely equalled, for any one reign, that expended on the pyramid complex of Mycerinus.

The parentage of the early pharaohs of Dynasty V is uncertain; but as Khent-kawes is described in her tomb as 'Mother of two kings of Upper and Lower Egypt', she was with little doubt mother of two of the early pharaohs of this dynasty, Sahure probably being one.

The *Pyramid of Userkaf* is near the northeastern corner of the enclosure of the Step Pyramid of Zoser. It is by no means typical of the other pyramid complexes of this dynasty and was plundered by those who built the Saitic tombs near by.

The main pyramid field of Dynasty V is at Abusir, a short distance north of Sakkara. It comprises the pyramid complexes of Sahure, Neferirkare, Neferefre, and Neuserre, who succeeded Userkaf in that order. Of these the most typical is that of *Sahure*, the northernmost on the plateau. The valley temple near the desert edge has entrances at the east and south. From it a causeway extends for *c.* 200 m westwards to the funerary temple. The walls of this causeway were originally decorated with reliefs. The funerary temple comprised:

 (i) the entrance corridor
 (ii) an open court paved with basalt and surrounded by sixteen granite palm columns, and with limestone walls decorated with painted reliefs of the king vanquishing his enemies and in the presence of captured animals
(iii) five statue-niches just west of the open court
(iv) various storerooms including two double-storeyed groups of five

(v) the sanctuary at the western end of which was a granite false
    door with an alabaster altar at its foot

In the southeastern angle of the walled enclosure of the pyramid,
which includes the western part of the funerary temple, is a subsidiary pyramid 12 m square, entered from the middle of its north
side.

The pyramid of Sahure is 78 m square. Almost on ground level
just east of the centre of the north side is the entrance, walled and
roofed in black granite. A short ramp leads to an antechamber
ending with a vertical granite portcullis. Beyond this point the
horizontal passage to the sarcophagus chamber is blocked. The
sarcophagus chamber is beneath the apex of the pyramid, and
has a massive pointed roof of limestone blocks. The body of all
the pyramids of Dynasties V and VI normally comprised a series of
accretions walled with coarse or occasionally fine limestone, their
interspaces filled with sand and rubble. These accretions were held
together by the pyramid casing of Tura limestone but once this
was stripped these pyramids rapidly fell to ruin. From the top of

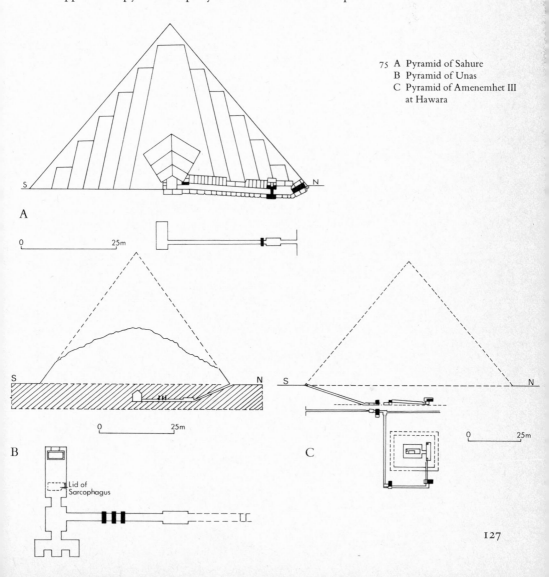

75 A Pyramid of Sahure
   B Pyramid of Unas
   C Pyramid of Amenemhet III
     at Hawara

this pyramid there is a fine view of the funerary temple, causeway, and valley temple.

The pyramid complexes of *Neferirkare*, *Neferefre*, and *Neuserre* follow a similar pattern. The lower temple and causeway of Neferirkare, unfinished at the time of his death, were incorporated into the pyramid complex of Neuserre. The funerary temple of Neferirkare is noted for the discovery within it, in 1893, of papyri relating to the administration of the pyramids of Dynasty V. From these we learn much about the temple furniture and how it was checked monthly and breakages reported on handing over to another official; records of the monthly rota and duties of the temple officials on ordinary and feast days; accounts of income and expenditure; and accounts of the distribution of food and clothing (Posener-Krieger and de Cenival 1968).

Neuserre was followed by *Djedkare-Isesi* who abandoned the royal necropolis at Abusir in favour of a site for his pyramid well south of the Step Pyramid of Zoser.

The *Pyramid of Unas*, southwest of the Step Pyramid of Zoser, opens a new phase in pyramid development – from now until the end of the Old Kingdom some of the walls of the pyramid interior are inscribed with Pyramid Texts.

According to the Egyptian king-lists, Unas was the last pharaoh of Dynasty V. This may and perhaps must be so, but several Egyptologists, including Baer (1960, 297–8), Lauer, and Fakhry (1969, 182), have suggested that Unas might have been the first pharaoh of Dynasty VI. Among the reasons for this suggestion are:

(i) Unas was the first pharaoh to have Pyramid Texts on the walls of his pyramid interior

(ii) during his reign there was a fundamental change in the ranking of the pyramid priesthood

(iii) late in Dynasty VI, when the ranking of the priesthoods of the pyramids of Dynasty V was reduced, the ranking of those of the pyramid of Unas was retained as though he were of the reigning dynasty

The site of the valley temple of Unas is by the road to the main group of monuments at Sakkara. Visible remains include a wall and parts of pink granite palm columns. It is connected with the funerary temple by a causeway *c*. 660 m long, originally roofed with slabs decorated with five-rayed stars. This causeway was walled with painted low reliefs, some being still in position. The subjects portrayed, in sequence as one moves towards the funerary temple, include gold-working and vase-making; boating; the transport by boat of granite columns and architraves from the Aswan quarries for the pyramid temples of Unas; animals in procession; a procession of divinities; and offering-bearers from various localities. South of the causeway's change in direction are two slab-lined boat-hollows side by side.

The funerary temple, now ruined, comprises the usual five elements: entrance corridor, rectangular open court, five statue-niches, groups of storerooms, and at the west end the sanctuary, including, on the east side of the pyramid, a false door, originally with an offering-table at its base.

Externally the pyramid is a ruin, but its interior is well preserved and of great interest. The entrance (originally closed by a plug) is near the centre of the north face, its ceiling being on the ground level. From it a ramp descends to a vestibule, beyond which a horizontal passage leads past three vertical granite portcullises to the antechamber, sarcophagus chamber and serdab. Both antechamber and sarcophagus chamber have a pointed roof decorated with five-rayed stars in relief. The serdab has three statue-niches.

The Pyramid Texts cover the walls of the horizontal passage south of the portcullises, the antechamber, the corridor between antechamber and sarcophagus chamber, and the sarcophagus chamber except for the walls around the sarcophagus which are lined with alabaster painted with a palace façade motif. The texts are concerned with the pharaoh's future. 'In the pyramid of Unas we find that the rebirth, the rising from the primeval waters, takes place in the corridor leading into the antechamber; in the antechamber he ascends to heaven, travels in the barge of the sun, and absorbs the substance of the gods; in the sarcophagus chamber his final exaltation takes place, and he is enfolded in the embrace of his father Atum, the All' (Piankoff 1968, 10–11).

Near the western end of the sarcophagus chamber is the sarcophagus, of polished black granite, with the lid on the floor near by. On the south face of the pyramid part of the casing remains, and bears a hieroglyphic inscription recording the restoration of the pyramid by Khaemwese, eldest son of Ramesses II. Southeast of the pyramid is the site of a subsidiary pyramid.

The pyramid complexes of *Teti*, *Pepy I*, and *Merenre*, at Sakkara, follow a similar general pattern but are less well preserved.

The *Pyramid of Pepy II*, the last pharaoh of Dynasty VI, is the main element in the southern group at Sakkara. Pepy II came to the throne at the age of six and held it until almost a hundred years old. The valley temple is approached by two ramps, one at each end of a long terrace. From this valley temple a causeway proceeds for *c.* 400 m southwest to the funerary temple. The walls of this causeway bear scenes similar to those in that of Unas but more fragmentary. The funerary temple follows the plan of that of Unas. One of the five statue-niches still contains the pedestal for a statue. The walls of the sanctuary were decorated with scenes of animals being sacrificed and of offerings being brought. The entrance to the pyramid is on ground level in the centre of the north side. It was originally within a small offering chapel whose walls were decorated with offering scenes in relief. From the entrance a ramp descends to a vestibule beyond which is a horizontal passage past three vertical granite portcullises to the antechamber, serdab, and sarcophagus chamber. From the vestibule onwards, all the walls bear Pyramid Texts excepting the walls of the serdab, and the walls surrounding the sarcophagus which have the usual palace façade decoration. The sarcophagus, of polished black granite, bears in hieroglyphs the name and titles of the king. The lid of the canopic chest is near. In the southeast angle of the temenos wall enclosing the pyramid is a subsidiary pyramid. Near by are the pyramids of three of the queens of Pepy II – Iput, Neit, and Wezebten – all with their interior inscribed with Pyramid Texts, and each with its subsidiary pyramid to the southeast.

76 Pyramid of Unas: the sarcophagus chamber from the east showing the star-decorated pointed ceiling; Pyramid Texts in vertical columns; and panelled decoration on walls surrounding the sarcophagus

The collapse and the First Intermediate Period (*c.* 2181–2060 B C)

Increasing strain on the economy, caused by the cost of maintaining a staff for each pyramid, contributed to the collapse following the death of Pepy II, and the end of the Old Kingdom. During the ensuing state of anarchy all the pyramids and their associated temples were doubtless plundered. Only one pyramid, that of Ibi, probably Dynasty VIII, east of the pyramid of Pepy II, can be attributed with certainty to this dark age. It is *c.* 31·5 m square and is crudely inscribed with Pyramid Texts.

The Middle Kingdom (*c.* 2060–1777 B C)

The Theban founder of the Middle Kingdom, Nebhepetre-Mentuhotep (Dynasty XI) built for himself a funerary monument of unique design between the Nile and the Theban Hills. Approached from a valley temple by a causeway *c.* 1200 m long, it comprised a central pyramid on a podium surrounded by a pillared hall beneath which was the funerary temple. A chamber beneath the pyramid, approached from the Bab el-Hosan to the east, seems to have been for a mock burial; the real tomb was in the cliff well west of the pyramid. This pharaoh's successor, Seankhkare-Mentuhotep, started building a similar funerary monument below the cliff to the south, but his reign ended when the work had barely begun.

From the beginning of Dynasty XII the Old Kingdom type of pyramid complex was resumed in principle but certain changes were made. The causeway between valley temple and funerary temple was shortened; the entrance to the pyramid was no longer always in the north side but often in one of the other sides; a highly complex substructure was designed to deceive the plunderer; there were no funerary texts on the interior walls; and a rather shoddily built superstructure was cased in Tura limestone, causing the pyramid to fall into ruin once the casing had been removed. The pyramids of Amenemhet I and Sesostris I at Lisht are accessible but their sarcophagus chamber is under water, the water table having risen since those pyramids were built. Apart from two pyramids of early Dynasty XIII at South Sakkara, none of the other Middle Kingdom pyramids can now be entered. The pyramids of this period are all between south Sakkara and the Faiyum.

The Second Intermediate Period (*c.* 1777–*c.* 1554/1551 B C)

Papyri relating to the royal tomb robberies of Dynasty XX mention several pyramids of Dynasty XVII near the entrance to the Valley of the Kings. The pyramids of Nubkheperre Antef and Sebekemsaf had been robbed, and the thieves described the quantity of gold, silver, and bronze objects found in the latter tomb. They apparently failed to reach the burial in the pyramid of Sekhemre Antef, and the inspectors reported as intact the pyramids of two Sekenenres and Kamose. These were all probably of mud-brick topped by a limestone pyramidion. There is little of them now to be seen, but the limestone pyramidion of Sekhemre Antef is in the British Museum.

The New Kingdom and after (*c.* 1554/1551 BC onwards)

The first pharaoh of Dynasty XVIII, Amosis I, built for himself a probably non-pyramidal tomb at Thebes and cenotaphs in the form of a pyramid at Abydos for himself and for his grandmother Tetisheri. From Tuthmosis I onwards the kings were interred in rock tombs in the Valley of the Kings until the end of Dynasty XX. After the pyramid had been abandoned by royalty, it was adopted by some of the Theban royal necropolis officials as the chief element in the superstructure of their own tombs at Deir el-Medina where several have been restored. Pyramid tombs were

77 Pyramid tomb, Deir el-Medina, Thebes. A restored example of the small pyramid-topped tomb adopted by some of the Theban aristocracy after the pyramid had been abandoned as a tomb form by the pharaohs

resumed by the Nubian kings of Dynasty XXV from Piankhi (*c.* 700 BC) onwards. They were occasionally built in Ptolemaic Egypt but none are known to have survived.

Conclusion

The factors which conditioned pyramid development were partly religious and partly those of security. The pyramid was the means by which the dead pharaoh ascended to the sky – hence its original stepped appearance. It was also a sun symbol, as suggested by several contemporary names of pyramids, for example 'Snefru appears'; 'Horizon of Kheops'; 'The Soul of Sahure shines'; 'Merenre shines and is beautiful'. The surviving pyramidia (of Amenemhet III and Khendjer) were inscribed on all four faces with the sun disc and with invocations to the sun-god. The sides of the pyramid may have been regarded as representing the sun's rays. As the Old Kingdom developed, changes in religious concepts resulted in modifications in the plan and arrangements of the valley and funerary temples, as well as the introduction of Pyramid Texts on the interior walls from the reign of Unas onwards. Security of the royal sarcophagus and the treasure in the tomb against the tomb robber was the chief factor conditioning the structural details of the interior of the pyramid.

It required less than 150 years for the pyramid to develop from its stepped origins to its climax in the pyramid of Kheops. The following thousand years (*c.* 2550–1550 BC) witnessed a decline halted only for a couple of centuries during the Middle Kingdom. The type of royal tomb which replaced the pyramid is the subject of the next chapter.

Note

Since this chapter was written, Kurt Mendelssohn (*The Riddle of the Pyramids*, London 1974, 79–132) has convincingly urged that the insecurity of the outermost section of masonry of the Maidum pyramid, in loosely packed horizontal courses, caused the pyramid to collapse before it was finished. This led, in his opinion, to the reduction of the slope angle of the upper part of the south pyramid of Snefru at Dahshur, and to the adoption of a low slope angle for the north pyramid of Snefru in the same locality.

Chapter Fourteen

The Valley of the Kings

The chief reason for the failure of the pyramid to provide security for the dead pharaoh and the treasure placed in his tomb was that the pyramid by its very nature proclaimed the location of the burial. Therefore the early pharaohs of Dynasty XVIII were obliged to consider other methods of tomb construction. The tombs of the first two kings, Amosis I and Amenophis I, have not yet been certainly located. As their mummies were found in the cache at Deir el-Bahri in 1881 their tombs cannot be far away from the Valley of the Kings. In that Valley are two tombs of very early type, VK 32 and VK 39 (inaccessible), which may be of these kings if they are not the tombs of sons of Tuthmosis I. From the reign of Tuthmosis I until the end of Dynasty XX, all the pharaohs (with the probable exception of Akhenaten) were buried in rock-cut tombs in the Valley of the Kings, and their funerary temples were separated from the Valley by the mountain known as the Gebel Asasif. It has been conjectured that the rather conical top of this mountain might have been regarded in antiquity as a natural pyramid, and that the New Kingdom pharaohs were interred near it for that reason.

Dynasty XVIII (c. 1554/1551–1305 BC)

In the absence of any certain information on the location of the tombs of Amosis I and Amenophis I, the founding of the royal necropolis in the Valley of the Kings is provisionally attributed to Tuthmosis I. The selection of the previously desolate Valley, the siting of the tomb of Tuthmosis I in a particularly remote and inaccessible part of it and the method of its construction, were directed by the royal architect Ineni who left on the walls of his own tomb (Thebes no. 81) his own account of the work:

'I inspected the excavation of the cliff-tomb of his majesty, alone, no one seeing, no one hearing . . . I was vigilant in seeking that which was excellent. I made fields of clay in order to plaster their tombs of the necropolis; it was a work such as the ancestors had not done which I was obliged to do there . . . I shall be praised because of my wisdom in after years, by those who shall imitate that which I have done.'

An effort was made to achieve maximum security by establishing at Deir el-Medina to the south a village for the necropolis workers, including quarrymen, draftsmen, sculptors and painters.

The tomb of *Tuthmosis I* (VK 38) is the smallest of all the royal tombs in the Valley. Being designed for concealment it has an inconspicuous entrance, 'more of a rabbit-hole than such a façade as suited the taste of the Ramesside pharaohs'. (Baikie 1932, 506). From this entrance a rough stairway descends to a corridor leading

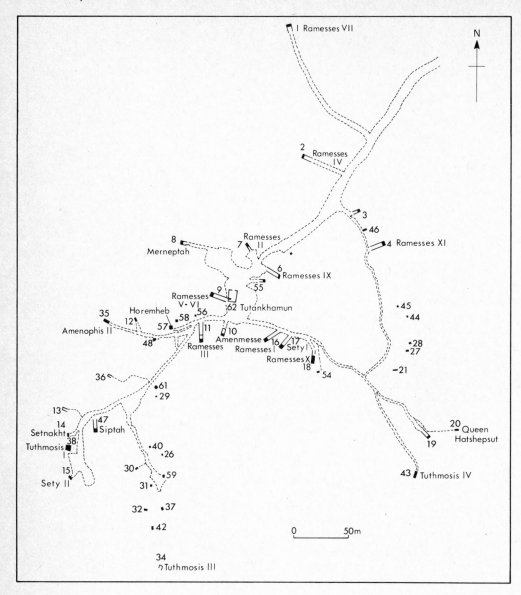

Tombs and labels on the plan:

I Ramesses VII

N

2 Ramesses IV

3

46

4 Ramesses XI

8
Merneptah

Ramesses II
7

6 Ramesses IX

55

9
Ramesses V·VI
62 Tutankhamun

35
Horemheb
12
57
58
56
48
Amenophis II

11
10
Amenmesse
Ramesses I
Ramesses III
16
17 Sety I
Ramesses X
18
54
45
44
28
27
21

36

61
29

13
14
Setnakht
47
Siptah
38
Tuthmosis
I

40
26

15
Sety II
30
59
31

20 Queen Hatshepsut
19

43 Tuthmosis IV

32
37

42

0   50m

34
Tuthmosis III

78 Plan of the Valley of the
Kings at Thebes

to an antechamber, from whose floor a flight of steps leads downwards to a burial hall in the shape of a royal cartouche ⬭,
with remains of a central pillar to support the roof. This hall
originally contained a cartouche-shaped quartzite sarcophagus
(Cairo Museum) and a canopic chest for the viscera of the deceased. The mummy of Tuthmosis I was transferred to the cache
at Deir el-Bahri at the time of the great tomb robberies (Chapter
Twelve) and was rediscovered there in 1881. Leading from the
burial hall is a niche for a statue. The curved axis of this tomb
heralds the L-shaped plan of the tombs attributed to the five suc-
ceeding pharaohs.

The tomb of *Tuthmosis II* has not been identified with certainty, but it could well be VK 42 which has a similar but L-shaped plan, with two pillars instead of one supporting the roof of the burial hall, in which is an uninscribed quartzite sarcophagus. The unfinished tomb of *Hatshepsut* (regent for her stepson Tuthmosis III when young) is VK 20 and comprises a long winding passage leading to an antechamber and burial hall with three pillars and three statue niches. The burial hall contained two red sandstone sarcophagi, both bearing her name, but one of them (in Boston Museum, USA) altered to that of her father Tuthmosis I.

The tomb of *Tuthmosis III* (VK 34) is the earliest tomb in the Valley to be lit electrically. A lengthy modern stairway up a rocky ravine leads to an inconspicuous entrance. From this an ancient stairway descends to a ramp, a room containing a second stairway, another ramp, and a shaft (crossed by a modern wooden bridge). From now until early Dynasty XIX this shaft is a normal feature of the royal tombs. Its main purpose was to protect the tomb against the robber; but another purpose may have been to receive rainwater from occasional heavy storms and prevent it from flooding the tomb beyond this point. Beyond this shaft a right-angled turn to the left is initiated by a two-pillared antechamber. From this a stairway descends to a two-pillared burial hall, cartouche-shaped, containing a red sandstone sarcophagus with its lid on the floor. The mummy of the king had been removed to the cache at Deir el-Bahri where it was found in 1881. The walls and pillars of the antechamber and burial hall are painted with texts and scenes from the Book of That which is in the Underworld, in some places unfinished, and barely started on the pillars in the antechamber. The ceilings of the shaft, antechamber, and burial hall are painted with yellow stars against a blue background. Offset from the burial hall are four niches for statues.

The tomb of *Amenophis II* (VK 35) follows closely in plan and section that of Tuthmosis III, except that it is more regular, the burial hall contains six instead of two pillars and is rectangular, and the quartzite sarcophagus is in a crypt beyond the last pair of

79 A Tomb of Tuthmosis III
  B Tomb of Amenophis II
    (After Lange and Hirmer)

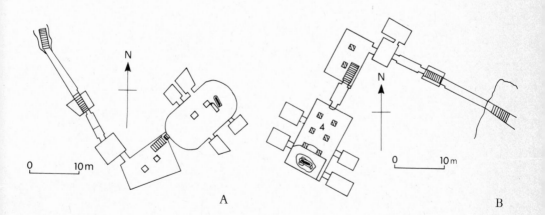

A

B

pillars. The walls of the burial hall are painted with texts and scenes of the finest quality from the Book of That which is in the Underworld. On the pillars of this hall are paintings of Amenophis II receiving Life from Osiris, Anubis and Hathor. The ceiling is painted with yellow stars against a blue background. Offset from the burial hall are four chambers. The king's mummy was found in his sarcophagus in 1898 but was disturbed by armed robbers in 1901.

The tomb of *Tuthmosis IV* (VK 43) is difficult of access. It is, however, of special interest in having two right-angled turns, the first just beyond the shaft and the second just beyond the antechamber. On the wall of the antechamber are two hieroglyphic inscriptions of Meya recording his restoration of the burial of Tuthmosis IV in the eighth year of Horemheb, showing that his tomb was robbed about seventy-three years (or less) after he was buried. The royal mummy was removed during Dynasty XXI to the tomb of Amenophis II but is now in Cairo Museum. This is the first royal tomb in which the figures of deities are coloured instead of being merely in outline. In it was found part of a royal chariot in gilded stuccoed wood (Cairo Museum).

The tomb of *Amenophis III* (VK 22), which also has two right-angled turns, is in the western part of the Valley of the Kings; it is not at present accessible.

Any tomb that may have been started for Amenophis IV (*Akhenaten*) at Thebes would probably have been in the western valley, and Miss E. Thomas has suggested that VK 23, in which Ay was buried, may have been started for Akhenaten when Amenophis IV. The tomb attributed to Akhenaten at Amarna cannot at present be visited, but both this and VK 23 introduce a straight axis, probably to enable the sun's rays to penetrate the whole length of the tomb in accordance with the Amarna religion.

The tomb of *Tutankhamun* (VK 62, formerly VK 58) is different in plan from any other New Kingdom royal tomb and it is certain that it was not originally designed as such. It was probably intended as a private tomb of a type which exists elsewhere in the Valley (Thomas 1966, 89). From the entrance a flight of sixteen steps descends to a doorway found in 1922 with its blocking still bearing the seal of the Theban necropolis (Anubis reclining above the figures of Egypt's nine traditional enemies). Beyond this doorway a corridor leads to an antechamber with annexe, to the right being the burial hall and the treasury. The four shrines of gilded wood (Cairo Museum) were originally placed one inside the other around the sandstone sarcophagus in which the mummy still reposes. This is not the place to describe the other funerary equipment about which much has been written by others. The walls of the burial hall are painted with funerary subjects including on the north wall a scene of Tutankhamun's successor Ay, wearing a leopard skin, performing the Opening of the Mouth ceremony before the dead king who is portrayed in the form of Osiris.

The tomb of *Ay* (VK 23), in the western valley, introduces into the Valley of the Kings the idea of a tomb on a straight axis, which was to continue (with the exception of the tomb of Ramesses II) until the abandonment of the Valley of the Kings for royal burial

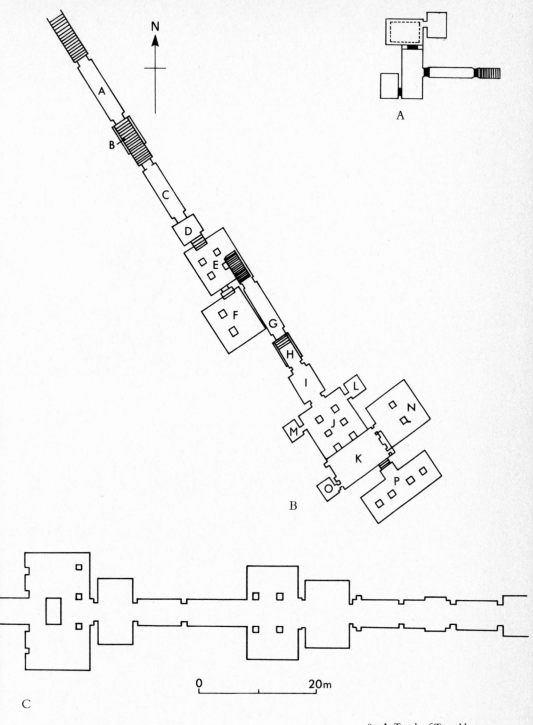

80 A Tomb of Tutankhamun
B Tomb of Sety I
C Tomb of Ramesses V–VI,
to the same scale. (After
Lange and Hirmer)

137

at the end of Dynasty XX. The idea was probably adopted from the plan of the tomb attributed to Akhenaten at Amarna, combining a straight general axis with two offset groups of chambers. From the entrance to the tomb of Ay, the straight axis is formed by a descending stairway, a corridor, a second descending stairway, another corridor, an antechamber, and a burial hall in the floor of which was a granite sarcophagus (Cairo Museum). Beyond the burial hall is another chamber, perhaps usurped from Akhenaten. It is thought by some that this tomb was originally intended for Tutankhamun and that as it was unfinished at the time of his death he was placed in the improvised tomb VK 62. Ay's motives for putting Tutankhamun into VK 62 may not therefore have been entirely disinterested. The decoration on the walls of the burial hall is remarkably similar to that in the tomb of Tutankhamun.

The tomb of *Horemheb* (VK 57), the last king of this dynasty, is among the most richly decorated in the Valley and is the earliest tomb in the Valley to have some of the wall decoration in relief. The burial hall still contains the sarcophagus of red granite.

Dynasty XIX (*c.* 1305–1196 BC)

The first king of this dynasty, *Ramesses I*, reigned probably for not more than two years, and therefore his tomb (VK 16) is small compared with those of most of his successors. Access to the burial hall is by a steep ramp between two stairways. The unfinished red granite sarcophagus is still in the burial hall whose ceiling is unfinished. There are three recesses in the walls of this hall. Some of the interior walls bear attractive scenes from the Book of the Dead.

The tomb of *Sety I* (VK 17) is among the longest and finest in the Valley. Its length, 100 m, is astonishing for a king who reigned for only about thirteen years. As the tomb has been open since it was explored by Belzoni in 1817, much of the decoration on the walls and ceiling near the entrance has faded or flaked off but the inner parts of the tomb still preserve their magnificent colouring. Space does not permit detailed descriptions of the scenes which cover almost every wall as far as the burial hall.

The plan and section follow closely those of the tomb of Horemheb. The finished wall-scenes are all in relief. A modern stairway descends to the original entrance which bears the royal titles. The ceiling of the first corridor (A) is decorated with a striking series of hovering vultures alternating with the royal titulary. Appropriately the walls of this corridor and the stairway corridor (B), which receive a good deal of daylight, bear the texts and scenes of the Sun Litany. Some of those on both sides of the stairway corridor are unfinished. Corridor (C) carries scenes of the journey of the sun during the fourth and fifth hours of night from the Book of That which is in the Underworld. A modern wooden bridge crosses the shaft (D) whose upper walls bear representations of the king with various deities. The walls of the hall with four pillars (E) carry scenes from the journey through parts of the underworld and the sides of the four pillars show the king with various gods and goddesses. The two-pillared room (F) is of special interest in that all the decoration (from the Book of That which is in the Underworld) has been sketched in outline only, first in red and afterwards in black. This may have been to lead robbers to conclude that the tomb had never been completed and did not proceed beyond this point. From the left part of the floor of room (E), a stairway (blocked by the architects after the burial) descends to the rest of the tomb, leading initially to corridors (G) and (H) which carry scenes of the Opening of the Mouth ceremony and related ritual. The walls of the antechamber (I) show the king with gods and goddesses of the dead including Osiris, Isis, Hathor, and Anubis. Next comes the outer part (J) of the great six-pillared burial hall whose walls carry reliefs from the Book of Gates. The pillars nearly all bear reliefs of the king with various deities; a missing relief is in Berlin. The Book of Gates is continued in side-chamber (L) where a stylized picture of a snake of twenty-four coils is among the most startling subjects in the whole tomb. Side-chamber (M) contains texts and scenes from the Book of the Cow. From (J) three steps lead down to the inner part (K) of the burial hall, with its famous astronomical ceiling (the earliest example of this motif on the ceiling of any royal tomb in the Valley), and walls carrying funerary scenes and inscriptions. The ornate inscribed alabaster sarcophagus, found here by Belzoni, is in the Sir John Soane Museum in London. Left of this hall is a chamber with two pillars (N) carved with a bench on its three long sides. Its walls are decorated from the Book of That which is in the Underworld. Right of this hall is a small undecorated room. Beyond the inner part of the burial hall is a four-pillared chamber (P) which has been closed for many years. From beneath the position of the sarcophagus a stairway descends to a tunnel which proceeds for a considerable distance and is believed to end in a cul-de-sac. The mummy of Sety I was recovered from the cache at Deir el-Bahri in 1881 (Cairo Museum).

The tomb of *Ramesses II* (VK 7) is not normally accessible as it is largely collapsed and therefore dangerous. The plan reverts to the L-shape of mid-Dynasty XVIII. For the first time the entrance doorway is decorated with the sun disc and deities on the lintel and with the royal titulary on the jambs. From now onwards all completed royal tombs in the Valley have an entrance decorated in this way. The interior wall reliefs follow the usual pattern, those near the entrance carrying the Sun Litany. The inner parts of the tomb are badly damaged. The royal mummy was recovered from the cache at Deir el-Bahri in 1881 and is now in Cairo Museum.

Ramesses II was followed by *Merneptah* whose tomb (VK 8), until recently accessible, is closed at the time of writing (1973). This tomb resumes the straight axis normal in this dynasty but is simpler in plan than those of Ramesses II and Sety I. For the first time the entrance doorway assumes monumental proportions which continue with all the royal tombs in the Valley until the end of Dynasty XX. It is decorated with the sun disc between Isis and Nephthys on the lintel, and the royal titulary on the jambs – the style initiated by Ramesses II though heralded by the royal titles on the door jambs of Sety I. It is curious that the two-pillared hall half-way to the burial hall, offset to the right of the main axis, resembles the corresponding hall (F) of Sety I in being unfinished: yet in the case of the tomb of Merneptah a glance at the plan shows that the reason cannot have been to deceive the tomb robber. The royal mummy is believed to have been placed in the innermost of four sarcophagi placed one inside the other. The rectangular outermost lid is in the antechamber; a fine pink granite lid in the form of a cartouche is in the burial hall.

The tomb of *Amenmesse* (VK 10), who probably followed Merneptah but reigned for only four or five years, is unfinished and contributes little or nothing to the history of the Valley of the Kings. The same applies to the tomb of *Sety II* (VK 15) who reigned for five or six years and whose tomb is of similar plan. For some years following 1922 it was used as a laboratory for treating numerous objects from the tomb of Tutankhamun. The tomb of *Siptah* (VK 47), the last king of the dynasty, has the usual straight axis. It has some fine decoration but the innermost portion is ruined. The name of Siptah has been erased throughout and then restored.

In addition to the various changes already noted, throughout this dynasty there is a tendency for the ramps and stairways to become less steep. From Ramesses II onwards the stairways usually have a ramp in the middle to facilitate the lowering of the sarcophagus.

Dynasty XX (*c.* 1196–1080 B C)

The tomb of *Setnakht* (VK 14), the first king of this dynasty, who reigned for only two years, was originally that of Queen Tausert (late Dynasty XIX) who may have reigned alone at the end of that dynasty. Her name and portraits have been plastered over throughout the tomb, which has a straight axis and a plan fairly normal for the period. Setnakht's sarcophagus remains in the burial hall.

Setnakht had previously started a tomb which was later to become that of *Ramesses III* (VK 11). It is among the most important in the Valley; but the antechamber, burial hall, and rooms beyond it are ruined and inaccessible. From an imposing entrance a stairway with central ramp descends, past two Hathor-headed pilasters on each wall, to a sloping corridor with one pair of side-chambers and a horizontal corridor with four pairs of side-chambers. These chambers, decorated chiefly with scenes of daily life, are a feature peculiar to this tomb. Beyond them the corridor continued but cut into the tomb of Amenmesse (VK 10), a circumstance which caused Setnakht to abandon this site. Ramesses III continued the tomb on a parallel axis a short distance to the right to avoid VK 10. His part therefore comprises a slightly ascending corridor leading past the usual shaft to a hall of four pillars with a chamber offset to the right; a ramp descends from the floor of this hall to a corridor, two antechambers, and a burial hall with eight pillars. The red granite sarcophagus found in the burial hall is now in the Louvre, its lid in the Fitzwilliam Museum in Cambridge. The royal mummy was among those found in the cache at Deir el-Bahri (Cairo Museum).

The tomb of *Ramesses IV* (VK 2) has the usual characteristics of the dynasty: an imposing entrance doorway, slightly inclined stairways with central sarcophagus-ramp, and corridors leading to the antechamber [waiting room], burial hall [House of Gold], and beyond it a small chamber with lateral offsets [the place of shabtis] and an end chamber [Treasury of the Interior]. The names in square brackets are translated from those given in hiero-glyphs on the contemporary plan of this tomb, on papyrus, in the Turin Museum: a most useful document describing the various parts of a royal tomb. The walls of this tomb bear about fifty Greek, Roman, and Coptic inscriptions – more than any other tomb in the Valley excepting that of Ramesses VI (VK 9), as it was used as a chapel and a place of pilgrimage in the early Chris-tian period.

The tomb of *Ramesses V* (VK 9) comprises the first five rooms of this tomb only; it was usurped, extended and completed by *Ramesses VI*. It was the rubble from the cutting of this tomb that concealed the tomb of Tutankhamun (immediately below) until it was discovered in 1922. It is among the most visited tombs in the Valley. Nearly a thousand graffiti on the walls, inscribed by visitors through the ages, show that it has been a show place ever since Classical times. The inscriptions are predominantly Greek, Roman, Coptic, and Arab, but of course there are the usual inscriptions of European visitors dating from the eighteenth century to the present day. It is 94·5 m long, only 5·5 m shorter than that of Sety I. The tomb has a straight axis and is unusual in having no stairways. The wall decorations are nearly all in sunk relief and well coloured, but their quality is inferior to those of the previous dynasty. The funerary texts from various parts of the Book of the Dead are here particularly comprehensive.

After an imposing entrance, three decorated corridors in succes-sion lead to a square shaft-chamber whose shaft was either never cut or has not yet been cleared. Beyond this is the usual four-pillared hall. As far as this point the tomb was constructed under Ramesses V whose cartouche appears everywhere altered to that of Ramesses VI, who did not choose to consider his predecessor a legitimate king. From this point onwards the tomb was hewn for Ramesses VI. From the floor of the four-pillared hall a ramp descends to two corridors, an antechamber and a burial hall with four pillars supporting a fine vaulted astronomical ceiling. In a recess in the floor is what is left of a gigantic red granite sarcopha-gus which probably contained at least one inner sarcophagus. During Dynasty XXI this tomb was broken into by five thieves, the confession of one of whom, transcribed on papyrus, has survived (Piankoff 1954, 6). It is uncertain whether Ramesses V was ever buried in this tomb but it seems unlikely. In any case the mummies of both Ramesses V and VI were transferred during Dynasty XXI, along with those of several other pharaohs, to the tomb of Amenophis II where they were found in 1898.

The tomb of *Ramesses VII* (VK 1), who reigned for only about a year, comprises merely a ramp and a corridor ending at a burial

81 Tomb of Ramesses VI, Valley of the Kings. Burial hall with remains of sarcophagus

hall with astronomical ceiling and containing a granite sarcophagus with unfinished lid. The tomb of *Ramesses VIII* has not yet been identified.

That of *Ramesses IX* (VK 6), who reigned for nearly twenty years, is the latest important royal tomb in the Valley. Its interest is increased by the survival of a contemporary plan on a limestone flake (Cairo Museum). From this we learn the original names (here in square brackets) of some of the parts of the tomb. From the entrance doorway a double stairway with inclined ramp in the middle leads to a horizontal corridor with two pairs of offset chambers. The stairway [corridor of the path of Shu], god of the air, is open to the sky. The horizontal corridor [corridor of the sun] is the farthest point in the tomb reached by the sun's rays. Two more corridors lead to the square room which was occupied by the shaft [Hall of Hindering], so-called from its original purpose of deterring the tomb robber (Thomas 1966, 278). Beyond this is the usual hall of four pillars [the Treasury?], from whose floor a ramp descends to a burial hall with vaulted astronomical ceiling. Let into the floor is a kind of rectangular double-recess to receive inner and outer sarcophagus but both are missing. The walls of the tomb are decorated throughout with funerary texts and scenes from the Book of the Dead.

The tomb of *Ramesses X* (VK 18), who reigned for about eight years, is unfinished and of little interest. It houses the electric power plant for lighting the other tombs in the Valley. The tomb of *Ramesses XI* (VK 4), the last king of the dynasty, who reigned for about twenty-eight years, follows the general plan of those of his forbears, except that the sarcophagus was apparently intended to be placed at the bottom of a pit at least 9 m deep in the centre of the burial hall. The tomb was never completed and has little decoration.

Conclusions

Most of the royal tombs of Dynasty XVIII were sited beneath fissures or ravines subject to occasional flooding, perhaps in the hope that the material brought down by these floods would assist in blocking and concealing the tomb. The tombs of the officials of each reign, which during the Old and Middle Kingdoms were usually placed in the vicinity of each pyramid, were grouped during the New Kingdom in the neighbourhood of the royal mortuary temples between the Theban Hills and the river Nile to avoid betraying the location of the royal tomb.

Towards the end of Dynasty XIX and throughout Dynasty XX, the pharaohs seem to have offset their declining power by building increasingly impressive tomb entrances, indulging in the wishful thought that while it was useless to try to conceal the tomb entrance from the robber, it would be possible to provide security against him by being buried in increasingly massive sarcophagi, often one inside the other.

The Valley of the Queens, in which princes as well as queens were buried, is omitted only by reason of the need to keep a sense of proportion between the Egyptian and the other regional sections of this study.

Note

Since this chapter was written, there has been published the late Professor J. Černy's unfinished manuscript, *The Valley of the Kings* (Cairo, 1973). From this it is learned that the death of a pharaoh and the accession of his successor were immediately announced at the same time to the Necropolis officials, who then arranged for completion of the pharaoh's tomb and commencement of that of his successor. Relationship between length of reign and length of tomb is not as close as might be expected. To the ancient Egyptian, the left and right sides of the tomb were considered from the innermost room looking towards the entrance – the reverse of the modern archaeologist's way of surveying the tomb, which is normally from the entrance looking inwards.

Chapter Fifteen

Mycenaean tholos tombs

The Mycenaean tholos tomb is always at least partly stone-built. It comprises the following elements:

(i) an entrance corridor (*dromos*) usually cut into a hillside; it was filled with rubble after each interment was made

(ii) a deep doorway (*stomion*) whose lintel is usually on the original ground level. The lintel slabs are normally of conglomerate, the only local stone that would span the width without the risk of breaking

(iii) a circular chamber (*tholos*) with a corbelled or beehive roof. Its base diameter is usually about the same as its height. In the floor there are usually pits, at least some of which were graves. In two instances (the Treasury of Atreus at Mycenae and the Treasury of Minyas at Orchomenos) there is a small side-chamber leading from the tholos

(iv) a circular mound or barrow probably always covered the upper portion of the tholos. The roof and walls of the latter were covered with layers of clay in the hope of preventing seepage of water into the tomb. Above this clay layer were placed the earth and rubble forming the mound or barrow. Sometimes the circular barrow was provided with a retaining wall (*krepis*) following the line of its circumference

Present opinion would place all the larger Mycenaean tholos tombs between *c.* 1600 and 1200 B C, but smaller and often degenerate examples continued to be built in Thessaly and Messenia until the tenth century B C. The larger tholos tombs are usually considered to be of royalty or of near-royal families. Royalty in this context should be understood to mean the ruling families of city-states which varied considerably in size and importance. The aristocracy were normally buried in chamber tombs (hewn entirely in the rock) which are much more numerous than tholos tombs.

Unfortunately nearly all the known tholos tombs, by reason of their ready accessibility, were robbed in antiquity and few have yielded interments. The Dendra/Midea tomb, which contained a substantial undisturbed area, revealed at least three extended burials with rich grave-goods, provisionally attributed to a king, a queen, and a princess. The tholos tombs in Messenia so far excavated have yielded rather more burials. The available evidence suggests that in the Argolid (Mycenae, Tiryns, and surroundings) tholos tombs contain the interments of royalty; but in Messenia the custom of building and using tholos tombs was not confined to royalty but spread to the aristocracy. In this province they are often smaller and more numerous and continue until the Proto-geometric period (tenth century BC). The principal burials in tholos tombs were always unburnt.

The origins of the Mycenaean tholos tomb have been discussed for many years. If they are not entirely a native product of the Greek mainland, they were probably derived from Minoan Crete. It is uncertain whether the circular stone-built tombs of the Cretan Mesara and elsewhere were originally vaulted; but the Cretan tholos tombs, of which about twenty are now known, seem to have developed from them. The recent discovery of numerous tholos tombs in Messenia, including some of early date, lends support to the idea of Minoan influence. It is certain that many more tholos tombs await discovery in Messenia, concealed under rank vegetation. The theory of their Minoan origin is strengthened by the presence of the site of a Minoan trading station (or colony) on the island of Kythera midway between Crete and Messenia.

Classification and chronology

The following chronological classification was developed by Wace (1923, 1949) for the nine known tholos tombs at Mycenae. His classification was based on the assumption that each tomb showed an architectural advance on its predecessors. To some extent, at least, it can be applied to other areas. His sequence seems to be supported by such finds as have been recorded from the tombs.

Type I (Wace's Group I). Rock-cut dromos, normally not lined with masonry. Doorway lintels have no relieving triangle. The innermost lintel has a straight inner edge (not curved to accord with the curve of the tholos). The tholos is of limestone rubble.
Type II (Wace's Group II). The dromos is still rock-cut but now lined with either limestone rubble or ashlar (coursed) masonry or a mixture of both. The jambs of the doorways are solidly built of coursed masonry. The doorway lintels, which are longer than in type I, have above them a relieving triangle. The innermost lintel has its inner side curved to the circle of the tholos. The tholos is of rubble masonry but sometimes on a bottom course of ashlar; and there is a tendency to shaping in much of the rubble coursing.
Type III (Wace's Group III). The dromos is lined with coursed ashlar, except at the Tomb of the Genii which has rubble walls on an ashlar base. The doorway is of finely dressed blocks. Two of the three tombs of this type at Mycenae had an engaged half-column on each side of the doorway. The lintels are surmounted by a relieving triangle, in at least two instances originally faced with richly decorated slabs. The doorway contained double doors of wood covered with bronze, or entirely of bronze. The tholos is built throughout of ashlar masonry.

THE THOLOS TOMBS OF MYCENAE form a compact group, all nine being within about 700 m from the Lion Gate. With the exception of no. 7 they are all near roads or paths. The tombs are topographically in three groups containing one of each of the types described above. West of the Lion Gate the Tomb of Aegisthus is type I, the Lion Tomb is type II, and the Tomb of Clytemnestra

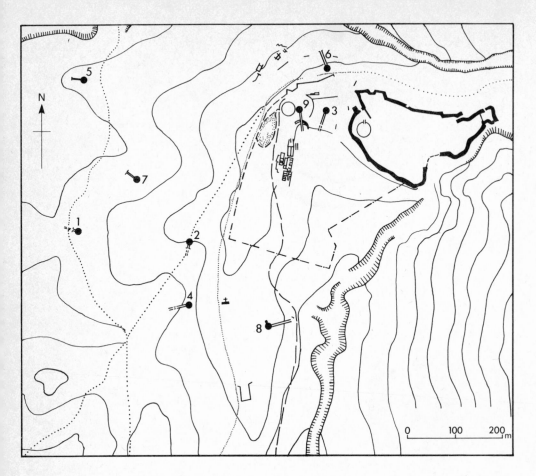

82 Plan showing location of the nine tholos tombs at Mycenae. (After H. Wace)

First chronological group: 1550–1450 BC
1 Cyclopean Tomb
2 Epano Phournos Tomb
3 Tomb of Aegisthus

Second chronological group: 1450–1400 BC
4 Panagia Tomb
5 Kato Phournos Tomb
6 Lion Tomb

Third chronological group: 1400–1200 BC

7 Tomb of the Genii (Tomb of Orestes)
8 Treasury of Atreus (Tomb of Agamemnon)
9 Tomb of Clytemnestra

is type III, all three being within 150 m of each other. The Epano Phournos Tomb (type I), and the Panagia Tomb (type II) are quite near to the Treasury of Atreus (type III). The third group, comprising the Cyclopean Tomb of type I, the Kato Phournos Tomb of type II, and the Tomb of the Genii of type III, is a little more scattered but all three tombs are fairly near the same path. For convenience the tombs are here described in Wace's order.

Type I (Wace's Group I); *c.* 1550–1450 BC
Tomb 1 (the *Cyclopean Tomb*), about 650 m southwest of the Lion Gate, is somewhat ruined. It is the smallest of all the tholos tombs at Mycenae. The dromos is devoid of any slab lining. The doorway is of rough masonry and the lintels, of which only one is in place (1969), are of rough slabs. The tholos proper, the upper part of which is missing, is of largely uncoursed 'Cyclopean' rough blocks. Its diameter is only 8 m and its height was probably about the same. The lowest course of blocking across the doorway is still in position.
Tomb 2 (*Epano Phournos*) is just outside the southwest corner of the Hellenistic lower town wall. This tomb also is ruined. The dromos has no slab lining. The doorway narrows slightly towards the top and is of coarse rough blocks; the lintel slabs are likewise rough. The tholos is of slabs which are rather better dressed than those of

the Cyclopean Tomb. Above the lintels the tholos is missing. From the doorway and dromos came Late Helladic II potsherds of *c.* 1500–1450 BC.

Tomb 3 (the *Tomb of Aegisthus*) is just west of the Lion Gate. The dromos is lined with rough small blocks except for the lower part of the walls near the doorway where the original rock-cut sides were unlined. In this structural feature this tomb therefore forms a link between type I and type II. The walls of the doorway are of more finely dressed masonry than tombs 1 and 2. The tholos is of courses of small slabs. Its top is missing and open to the sky. The innermost lintel slab has been cut to a concave curve to fit the circumference of the tholos – another feature which links this tomb with those of type II.

Type II (Wace's Group II); *c.* 1450–1400 BC

Tomb 4 (the *Panagia Tomb*) is about 180 m down the hill slope west of the Treasury of Atreus. It is named from the Panagia Chapel near by. The dromos, facing west, is lined with rubble walls. The doorway has walls of well-dressed blocks, and its inner lintel is concave to fit the curve of the tholos. Over the lintel was a relieving triangle of which only a small corner of the lower portion remains. At the ends of each lintel is a triangular nick to facilitate its transport and positioning. The tholos, which is 8 m in diameter, is of small coursed masonry, with larger and more finely cut blocks around the entrance.

Tomb 5 (*Kato Phournos*) is just west of the N–S track about 550 m west of the Lion Gate. The dromos, facing west, is lined with courses of finely cut masonry, and its entrance retains the lowest course of its closing wall. It is apparently the earliest tholos tomb to have this feature. The innermost of the lintel slabs has been dressed concave to fit the curve of the circumference of the tholos. The latter is 10 m in diameter but above the level of the lintel it is open to the sky. In the southern part of the floor is a rectangular pit which was found empty in 1892. Pottery found 'in or by the tomb' (Wace) is Late Helladic II, which if contemporary with the tomb would confirm the date attributed on typological grounds.

Tomb 6 (the *Lion Tomb*) is so-called because it is just over 100 m northwest of the Lion Gate. The dromos, facing north, is lined with finely dressed coursed masonry. Its entrance was probably closed by a wall of which only one slab is shown on Wace's plan. The masonry of the doorway and its surroundings is extremely fine. The innermost lintel slab is cut to fit the curve of the inner circumference of the tholos. The outer lintel (fallen) has on its underside the pivot holes for a double door. Above the lintel there was probably a relieving triangle which has now gone. The tholos is 14 m in diameter and would probably have been 15 m high but the whole of its upper part above the lintel is missing. Remains of the circular stone retaining wall of the barrow covering the tholos were found. In the eastern part of the floor of the tholos are three rectangular pits, in which 'nothing of importance' was discovered.

Type III (Wace's Group III). *c.* 1400–1200 BC

Tomb 7 (the *Tomb of the Genii*, known locally as the Tomb of

I

2

3

83 The three main types of tholos tomb at Mycenae
1 Type I: Epano Phournos Tomb
2 Type II: Kato Phournos Tomb
3 Type III: Tomb of Clytemnestra

84 The Lion Tomb at Mycenae
from above, showing finely
coursed masonry around the
doorway

Orestes) is situated about 500 m west of the Lion Gate. It is among
the best at Mycenae and is in exceptionally fine condition. The
dromos, facing northwest, is lined with small rough blocks mostly
of limestone but some of conglomerate. The entrance to the dromos
still retains much of its blocking wall. As this is not bonded with its
extensions on either side of the dromos, it would seem that there
had been at least one opening and re-closing. The doorway has its
innermost lintel curved to fit the curvature of the tholos. Above
the lintel is a relieving triangle, missing masonry from which
indicates that the tomb was plundered through that opening, the
roof of the tholos being still intact. On the underside of the inner
lintel are pivot holes showing that there were double doors. The
tholos is architecturally almost up to the standard of the Treasury
of Atreus, each block of coursed masonry being carefully dressed
both horizontally and vertically on its inner face to contribute to
the overall effect. Its internal diameter is 8·40 m and its height about
8 m. In the floor are three grave pits, which when found in 1896 still
had their roof slabs in place, but they were empty. Scattered over
the floor were, however, various beads and other ornaments
probably from necklaces. Among them were plaques showing
libations being poured over a column or pillar by Genii (from
which the tomb derives its present name).

Tomb 8 (the *Treasury of Atreus*, known locally also as the Tomb of
Agamemnon), is just west of the modern road. This tholos tomb
is unquestionably the finest at Mycenae. The dromos, facing east,
is on an exceptionally large scale, being 36 m long, 6 m wide, and
10 m high where it reaches the doorway. The entrance to the
dromos preserves the first course of part of its closing wall.

The doorway has several features of interest. As usual its walls
converge slightly towards the top. It is framed on all sides by
recessed panelling. Above the enormous lintel is a relieving triangle originally masked by masonry carved with horizontal rows
of scroll designs alternating with blank horizontal strips. On each

85 The Treasury of Atreus,
Mycenae. Note the lowest
courses of a temenos wall
continuing across the entrance
to the dromos

86 Façade of the Treasury of
Atreus, Mycenae. Reconstruction
by Higgins and others

149

side of the doorway is a low rectangular plinth on which stood a green marble half-column. The slots by which this was attached to the wall are still visible. These half-columns are carved with a zig-zag motif filled with running scrolls; specimens of this decoration are in the Athens and British Museums. The presence of pivot holes in the sill and lintel shows that the doorway contained double doors probably either of wood covered with bronze, or entirely of bronze. Holes carrying nails by which the door frame was fixed to the wall are still visible (Higgins *et al.*, 1968).

The tholos is 14·5 in diameter and 13·2 m high. It is built in thirty-three courses of beautifully cut conglomerate, gradually getting smaller as the height increases. Each block is carefully dressed both horizontally and vertically on its inner face to accord with the horizontal and vertical lines of the tholos as a whole. From the fifth course upwards there are nail-holes arranged in horizontal rows at various levels; these are believed to have been the means by which ornaments, possibly rosettes, of bronze or gilt bronze were fixed to the wall. On the north side of the tholos a door with relieving triangle leads to a side-chamber with rock-cut flattish roof. In the floor of this side-chamber are two pits. The doorway into this side-chamber contained double doors within a

87 The Treasury of Atreus, Mycenae. View of the interior by E. Dodwell (died 1832)

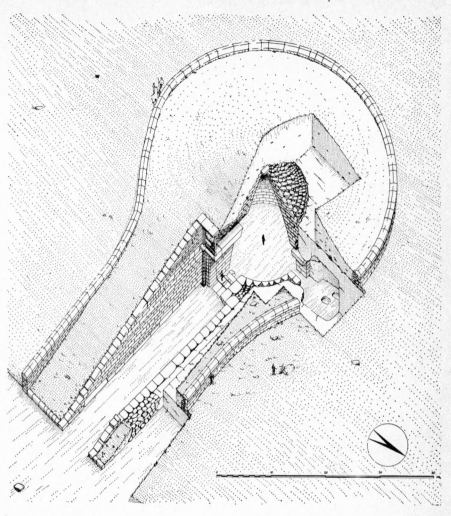

frame; the nail-holes for fixing them to the wall are still visible. Two fragments of gypsum bull-reliefs in the British Museum probably came from this side-chamber. The tholos is still covered by its barrow which retains traces of its retaining wall (*krepis*). The original contents of this tomb are unknown. Gold fragments and beads from the dromos and doorway may or may not date from the tomb's construction.

Tomb 9 (the *Tomb of Clytemnestra*) is between the tomb of Aegisthus and Grave Circle B. It was while restoring the roof of this tomb about 1951 that Grave Circle B was discovered. The dromos faces south, and is 37 m long – slightly longer than that of the Treasury of Atreus, and is 6 m wide. On its left side near the doorway is a rectangular pit-grave which contained a burial with two bronze mirrors having carved ivory handles (Athens Museum). Many centuries after the dromos was filled and the existence of the tomb had been forgotten, its site was covered by a Hellenistic theatre, the front row of whose seats, stone-built, is still to be seen on both

89 Menidi: entrance to tholos tomb with relieving slabs above the lintel

sides of the walls of the dromos. The doorway is similar to that of the Treasury of Atreus, being enclosed by double recessed panelling and flanked on each side by a half-column of gypsum supported on a low plinth, in this case semicircular. Above the lintel is a relieving triangle which was doubtless originally faced with decorated slabs perhaps likewise of gypsum. Just above the lintel, at the lower right corner of the relieving triangle, is a slab carved with a horizontal row of raised circular discs, believed to simulate the ends of wooden beams. The presence of pivot holes in the central lintel and other holes in the walls of the doorway shows that it contained double doors within a door frame perhaps of wood. The tholos is 13·4 m in diameter and was probably about the same height. It is built of beautifully cut and jointed ashlar masonry similar to that in the Treasury of Atreus, but has the added refinement of a course of slabs on the level of the lintel and the same thickness as the lintel, thereby forming a more solid basis for the upper part of the corbelling. The latter has been restored since 1950. An arc of retaining wall found 1952–4 showed the barrow to have been *c.* ·50 m in diameter. This tomb has suffered from water seepage ever since it was built, and even the original builders provided a catchment pit in the floor of the tholos, from which a drainage duct extends along the dromos to carry away the water.

It will have been noticed that many of these tombs are now named after figures in Homeric legend (Aegisthus, Agamemnon, Atreus, Clytemnestra, and Orestes), but this does not necessarily mean that those people were buried there. It is doubtful whether the task of marrying tradition to the results of archaeological research at Mycenae will ever be satisfactorily accomplished.

Some other tholos tombs

TIRYNS. The tholos tomb is near a path on the east side of the road between Nauplia and Tiryns, about 1 km from the Tiryns citadel. The dromos faces west and is lined with coursed masonry. The walls of the doorway converge towards the top as with the tholos tombs at Mycenae. There is no relieving triangle above the lintel which is much smaller than those at Mycenae and would probably not have needed any relieving element. The tholos proper is well preserved and built of small blocks of coursed masonry resting on a bottom course of larger blocks. The barrow remains above the tholos. This site was attributed by Wace to his third period – most likely sometime during the thirteenth century BC following Mylonas' revision of Wace's chronology.

MENIDI (Acharnai). This tomb, about 8 km north of Athens, was excavated by the German Institute in 1879. The dromos, which faces southeast, is 26·5 m long and 3 m wide and its walls are lined with rather roughly coursed masonry. Remains of the sealing wall are still visible at its entrance. The doorway is of much larger but still rather rough blocks, and the stomion which it faces is 3·35 m deep. The outer lintel is unusual in being surmounted by four horizontal relieving slabs with spaces between them, rather

90 Orchomenos: tholos tomb
from above showing the main
entrance and doorway to
side-chamber. The so-called
'Treasury of Minyas'

in the manner of the relieving chambers above the roof of the
'King's Chamber' in the pyramid of Kheops at Giza. The innermost lintel, which is surmounted by a relieving triangle filled with
small masonry, is curved both vertically and horizontally to
conform to the lines of the interior of the tholos. The latter is 8·35
m in diameter and 8·76 m high. Its roof has been restored, and
presumably also the covering barrow may be partly a restoration.
The finds included pottery of Late Helladic IIIB (c. 1300–1230 BC)
and the tomb is therefore both typologically and chronologically
in Wace's Group III. Other finds included an ivory pyxis decorated
with rams, an ivory lyre, and some green-glazed imitation boars'
tusks from a helmet probably of leather (Lolling 1880). These finds
are in Athens Museum.

THE TREASURY OF MINYAS AT ORCHOMENOS is about midway
between Athens and Delphi. In several ways it resembles the
Treasury of Atreus and indeed it may have been built by the same
architect. The dromos is 5·1 m wide but its original length is
unknown as it was largely destroyed about a century ago. The
doorway is over 5 m high and its sides converge towards the top in
the usual manner. The inner side of the lintel is curved to accord
with the curvature of the tholos. The tholos, of which only the
first eight courses remain, is 14 m in diameter. From its fifth course
there are at intervals nail-holes implying the former attachment of
ornaments, perhaps bronze rosettes, to the wall. A doorway leads
from the south side of the tholos to a rectangular side-chamber,
the ceiling of which was decorated with a most beautiful pattern
of spirals, rosettes and other motifs carved in green stone. On the

floor of the tholos is the pedestal of a Macedonian tomb (Mylonas 1966, 125).

MARATHON, 1 km west of the Soros, near Vraná. The dromos, which faces east, is 25 m long and without masonry lining. It narrows as it slopes downwards towards the doorway. Within the outer (top) end of the dromos was a remarkable burial of two horses placed symmetrically. They may have been attached to a funerary hearse but of this no trace was found. Above the doorway lintel is a relieving triangle. The tholos, of roughly coursed masonry, is nearly 7 m in diameter and about the same height. In its floor are two rectangular stone-lined pits each of which contained a burial. One had already been plundered; the other yielded (1957) a gold cup now in Athens Museum. Late Helladic II pottery apparently associated should give a date in the fifteenth century BC. The tholos is now crowned with a tumulus and retaining wall (both restored).

Pylos and Messenia

In general the tholos tombs of this region are smaller and more numerous than those of Mycenae and the Argolid.

PYLOS, 80 m northeast of the Palace of Nestor. The dromos of this tomb faces southwest and is 10 m long and 4 m wide at its outer end. Its walls have no masonry lining. The doorway seems to have had no relieving element. The tholos is 9·35 m in diameter and was originally about 7·5 m high. Its domed roof was restored in 1957 and the original covering barrow was removed by the farmer some years previously. Excavation by Blegen in 1953 brought to light many small objects left behind by the early plunderers, including gold leaf; beads of amethyst, amber, gold and paste; arrowheads of flint, chert and obsidian; and a gold pendant in the shape of a figure-of-eight shield, similar to one from the tholos tomb at Menidi (Acharnai). The doorway had contained no door but had been blocked after the burial (Blegen 1954).

MALTHI, between Tripolis and Pylos. Here three tholos tombs have been excavated, of which only one (Malthi I) is now accessible. The dromos, which faces west and is lined with coursed masonry, is 13·5 m long. Its outer end was closed by a sealing wall. The doorway has its lintel surmounted by a relieving triangle. It faces a stomion 3 m deep which has the exceptional feature of being wider in front than at the back. The doorway had been blocked by masonry of which five courses remained. The upper courses had been removed by plunderers who had entered through the tholos roof. The single lintel covering the whole depth of the stomion has its inner edge curved to the circular line of the tholos. The latter is 6·85 m in diameter and 5·8 m high, and its lowest course is set in a rock-cut bedding groove. The covering barrow has gone, exposing the cover-slab of the tholos (Valmin 1938, 208–15).

PERISTERIA/MOIRA, in the same general area. Here Marinatos has excavated some tholos tombs one of which is of special interest. The dromos, which is lined with masonry, leads to a doorway of finely dressed blocks some being incised with Minoan Linear A script, including a branch symbol and a double-axe symbol on the left jamb. The tholos is 12 m in diameter and work on restoring it began in 1971. From another tholos tomb near Peristeria came three magnificent gold cups and a quantity of gold jewellery now in the Chora Museum (Mylonas 1966, 125).

In conclusion, it seems advisable to make it clear that Wace's arrangement of the tholos tombs at Mycenae, on the basis of progressive architectural development, does not provide for the possibility of degeneration such as is known to have occurred with the Egyptian pyramids. Neither does it take account of possible differences in standards of workmanship. Indeed it has been stated that 'the whole problem of chronology of the tholos tomb groups should be re-examined' (Mylonas 1966, 118 note 35).

92 Peristeria/Moira: Linear A signs (behind glass frame) on the left jamb of entrance to tholos tomb

Chapter Sixteen

The necropolis at Salamis in Cyprus

If any link were needed between the last chapter and this, it is provided by the fairly recent discovery and excavation, by J.-C. Courtois of the French Archaeological Mission at Enkomi-Alasia, of two Mycenaean tholos tombs within the Bronze Age city of Enkomi, just north of the Sanctuary of the Ingot God, between 4th and 5th Street. One, of rough masonry, had been plundered long ago but was probably built in the fifteenth century BC. The other includes an oval tholos of coursed and well-cut masonry alternating with courses of bricks, entered by a somewhat awkwardly placed doorway of trilithon type (an upright slab for each side and a third for the lintel). It yielded fragments of typical Mycenaean and other vases dated *c.* 1320–1280 BC (Courtois 1969). Near by are some fine built tombs of other types.

As Cyprus was not affected by the Dorian invasion of the Greek mainland, Mycenaean tradition survived in the island for several centuries. In our description of the royal and other tombs at Salamis, mention will be made of Royal Tomb 3, with its curious brick-built tholos placed not directly above the chamber, and covered by a large tumulus in the manner of the Mycenaean tholos tombs – and yet some centuries later in date. Other Mycenaean survivals in Cyprus have been studied and published by Karageorghis (1962).

The Bronze Age city and port of Enkomi was abandoned and succeeded by Salamis about the eleventh century BC, partly because its inner harbour had silted up. The tombs about to be considered are therefore those of the royalty and aristocracy of Salamis and not those of the last centuries of Enkomi. They belong to the eighth and seventh centuries BC. Two of them (3 and 77) are still covered by large tumuli. There is strong reason to believe that at least some of the others were originally covered by tumuli which have been removed for agricultural purposes. Even today traces of mounds can be detected over some of these tombs by the practised eye.

It will be noted that it was the custom during this period for the burial ceremony to include the deposit of the remains of a horse-drawn hearse or other vehicle for royalty, and the remains of one drawn by asses for the less opulent burials of their non-royal contemporaries. In most instances, after the first horse or ass was killed, its companion or companions took fright and in one or two instances twisted and broke their neck around the yoke.

Tomb 1, just southeast of the Great Tumulus (3), is the earliest accessible tomb in the group. The dromos faces east and slopes downwards towards a façade of limestone blocks with a corniced

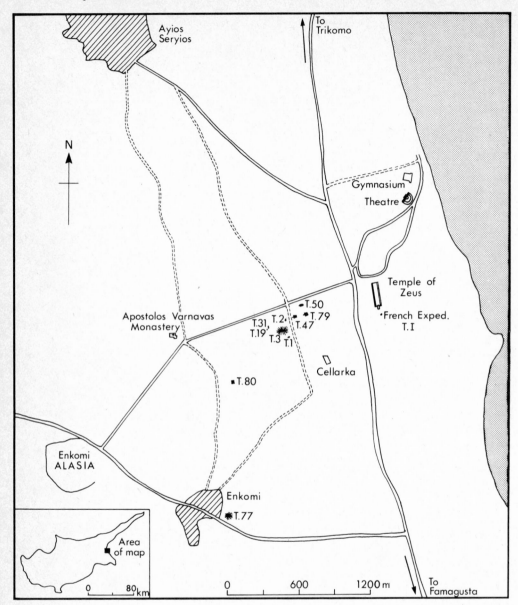

93 The necropolis of Salamis, Cyprus. (After Karageorghis)

roof. In the centre of this façade is a recessed doorway with a free-standing pillar on each side. The door leads to a rectangular chamber, 4·7 m × 5 m, which contained two interments. The earlier, placed in a pit in the floor, comprised a deposit of burnt bones wrapped in cloth and placed in a bronze cauldron. This cauldron also contained a necklace of gold and rock-crystal beads and some fragments of sheet gold identical with others found among the ashes of the funeral pyre in the dromos. The cremation ceremony therefore took place in the dromos after which as many bones as possible were picked out, wrapped in cloth and placed with the necklace in the cauldron in the pit in the floor of the burial-chamber. Pottery from the chamber and dromos date this inter-

94 Tomb 2 at Salamis showing
cornice and doorway with
closing slab

ment to the mid-eighth century BC. The later interment was a
disturbed inhumation probably of the early seventh century
BC. After the burials had been made the doorway was sealed by a
massive limestone slab. In the dromos were remains of a chariot
with two horses sacrificed with the earlier interment and a chariot
with four horses sacrificed with the later burial.

Tomb 2 is just northeast of the Great Tumulus (3). Its dromos,
which faces slightly west of north, is 9 m long and slopes downwards towards the doorway. The entrance is in the centre of a
façade of limestone blocks having a cornice roof of white limestone
slabs. It had been closed by a massive slab now propped up at right
angles to it. The doorway leads to a rectangular burial chamber
3·1 m × 2·2 m. This chamber contained the greatly disturbed
remains of two interments, one by inhumation and the other
uncertain. In a shallow pit in the floor was a silver bowl having two
periods of decoration; the earlier is an 'Egyptianizing' composition
of human figures, and the later includes Egyptian hieroglyphs
arranged apparently without meaning and therefore probably not
done in Egypt but perhaps Phoenician. Pottery from the chamber
and dromos indicate that the first interment was made *c.* 700 BC
and the second *c.* 600 BC. In the dromos in front of the doorway
were the remains of a hearse drawn by two asses; after the first
had been killed the second took refuge in a corner where he was
stoned and buried alive in earth. This hearse had belonged to the
second burial, but it had probably disturbed a chariot burial of the
period of the first interment. Near the top of the filling of the
dromos was the extended skeleton of an individual whose hands
had been bound in front.

Tomb 31, just west of the Great Tumulus (3), has its dromos (about
9·7 m long) facing slightly west of north. On its floor Karageorghis
found the skeletons of two asses in a symmetrical position as though
they should have accompanied a hearse but no trace of it remains.
This and the last tomb (2) have dromoi which are much shorter
than those about to be described and seem to have been non-royal

tombs with ass-drawn instead of horse-drawn vehicles. This tomb
had contained two interments, both probably made between 700
and 650 BC. *Tomb 19* near by is of similar type.

Tomb 79, just south of the Prison (or Tomb) of St Catherine, has
an eastward facing dromos 16·8 m long. This slopes downwards
to a façade of monumental proportions with central recessed
doorway, behind which is a rectangular burial chamber composed
of two enormous stone blocks, one above and one below. Its
internal dimensions are 3·2 m × 2·4 m, and it has a gabled ceiling
1·8 m high.

The sequence of interments which the chamber had probably
contained was indicated by the stratification of the filling in the
dromos. The first burial had been made *c.* 710–700 BC, when a
light chariot drawn by four horses and a richly decorated hearse
drawn by two horses were placed in the dromos. These were
moved to the south to make way for the second burial and its
accompaniments a few years later. The second burial included a
war chariot drawn by two horses, and a horse-drawn hearse. The
chariot had four standards, one on each side of each horse. The
horse trappings from these interments included richly decorated
items, some of them bearing strong orientalized Egyptian and
probably also north Syrian motifs. Other finds included two
bronze cauldrons (one on an iron tripod), a pair of fire-dogs, and
(most exciting of all) furniture including a richly decorated ivory
chair or throne with orientalized Egyptian openwork plaques, two
other richly decorated chairs, and the remains of a wooden bed
with applied ivory bands both carved and plain. The furnishings
in this tomb are the richest so far published from any Cypriote
prehistoric tomb. During the Roman period it was again used for
burials for which graves were made in various places.

Tomb 47 is midway between the Great Tumulus (3) and the Prison
of St Catherine, and is among the largest in the necropolis. Its
dromos, which faces east, is 20 m long and 13·65 m maximum
width. It had an ashlar lining which has been nearly all pillaged by
searchers after building stone. The dromos slopes downwards to
reach a flight of four steps up to a paved platform fronting a façade,
the roof of which was originally corniced. Placed centrally in
this façade is a doorway leading to a burial chamber 4 m by
2·2 m. It had been totally robbed and is now roofless. Removal of
the filling from the dromos (1964–7) revealed the remains of a
hearse drawn by two horses, which had accompanied the earlier
burial. An Egyptian scarab with the prenomen of Osorkon I
(926–881 BC), most likely associated with this burial, must have
been an heirloom as the pottery shows the first burial to have been
made *c.* 700 BC. On the platform before the entrance were the
remains of a hearse and six horses, believed to have accompanied
the later burial, made between 700 and 650 BC. This deposit is
preserved on the site beneath a glass frame.

Tomb 50 (the Prison, or Tomb, of St Catherine) is the well-known
building about 1100 m east of the Monastery of St Barnabas. It is
in fact a normal tomb of the period of this cemetery, with a vaulted
chamber added much later and now used as a chapel dedicated to
St Catherine. Its identity was masked by the later structures until

95 Tomb 50 ('Prison of St Catherine') at Salamis. The 'greenhouse' covers the horse sacrifice

1965 when it was noticed that the cornice around the interior of the vaulted chamber was similar to the cornices roofing the façades of several of the other tombs. Excavation then revealed an ashlar-lined dromos facing east, sloping downwards for 28 m westwards to a wide flight of four steps up to a platform before a cornice-roofed entrance façade, in all these respects similar to the features in tomb 47 just described. (The four steps leading up to the platform before the façade are no longer visible as they were covered by the vaulted chamber some centuries later.) The original entrance in the centre of this façade leads to a rectangular chamber 4·1 m × 2·4 m, with a gabled roof 2·4 m high. It had been emptied probably by the Roman period. On the floor of the dromos there was a burial of two horses originally yoked to a chariot, impressions of the yoke and pole of which were still in the soil. The rest of the chariot had gone and may have been detached to accompany the interment (c. 700–650 BC) in the burial chamber. The remains of this chariot burial are now covered with a glass frame on the site. The later history of this tomb is noted in Chapter Ten.

Tomb 3 (the Great Tumulus) is the enormous mound southwest of the Prison of St Catherine. It is still about 60 m in diameter and 10 m high. The preservation of the tumulus is due to the fact that it is too high and steep to be ploughed over. The dromos, facing north-east, slopes downwards for 24·6 m to a recessed door. The walls of the dromos are lined with mud-bricks as they approach the door-way. The site was dug last century in an unscientific manner by a team from the British Museum, a record of whose activity sur-vives to this day in the date 1896 painted on the gabled ceiling of the burial chamber. The latter is rectangular, 2·93 m × 2·38 m, with a well-built gabled roof 2·83 m high. It is worth noting that the doorway comes into the burial-chamber at its east corner and not (as normally) in the middle of one side. The siting of the bulk of the chamber west of the door has parallels in Egypt (Chapter Thirteen). No burial has been recorded from this chamber but excavation in the filling of the dromos (1964) revealed that there had been only one burial. On the floor of the dromos in front of the doorway were substantial vestiges of a war chariot drawn by

96 Tomb 3 at Salamis with
covering tumulus in form of
tholos and closing slab beside
the entrance

two horses and fragments of a hearse to which two horses had been
yoked. With the war chariot were bundles of iron arrowheads,
traces of a quiver of wood and leather (?), parts of a circular bronze
shield, and an iron sword. The heads of three bronze standards
(there had originally been four) were found, one on each side of
each horse's head. On the floor of the dromos were several
amphorae, one bearing a Greek inscription indicating that it
contained olive oil. There were also traces of a large pyre on which
the body had been cremated. After the defunct had been interred
in the burial chamber, its doorway was closed by a slab the back of
which is deeply flanged to fit the aperture.

The most remarkable feature of this tomb, however, is that a
sort of tholos of mud-bricks, 9·4 m in diameter at its base, was built
not above the burial chamber, but directly above the deposit
found in the dromos. This tholos certainly seems to be a survival
of a Mycenaean tradition.

Tomb 80 is just east of the path between Enkomi and the Monastery of St Barnabas. It is among those most recently explored (and has not yet been visited by the author). It is really a burial chamber built into an earlier tomb which had a short dromos. The special interest of the later tomb is that it has a vaulted ceiling decorated with painted blue and purple stars and rosettes, and its walls are painted with long-stemmed blue and purple lotus plants some-what in an Egyptian style. Water seepage has unfortunately caused these paintings to deteriorate. The tomb is believed to have been built between 560 and 525 BC during the period when Cyprus was under strong Egyptian influence in the reign of the pharaoh Amosis II (*c.* 569–525 BC).

Cellarka. About 600 m south of the Prison of St Catherine, between the footpath to Enkomi and the road from Famagusta to Salamis, is a large rectangular area uncovered by Karageorghis between 1964 and 1967, where a hundred tombs have so far been examined, and doubtless many more remain to be explored. They are almost all rock-hewn chamber tombs, most of them having a dromos descending by a series of steps to the burial chamber. The earlier tombs normally have their dromos facing east towards their settlement area (as also do the 'royal' tombs); the later tombs are often smaller and usually have their dromos facing south. Only in one or two instances have horse burials been found in the dromoi of these tombs. Of special interest is *Tomb 105* the chamber of which is lined with ashlar masonry, and this is in fact the only built chamber so far found at Cellarka. On a wall in this tomb is a well-executed sketch of a ship with oars and mast (Egyptian ?). The funeral pyres among these tombs contained many miniature earthenware copies of jewellery and other offerings to the dead. All the evidence suggests that we are here dealing with the more modest tombs of families well below the rank of royalty – prob-ably the upper or middle classes of Salamis.

'*Tomb 77*' (cenotaph of King Nicocreon ?) is immediately east of Enkomi village, and is easy to find as it is mostly covered by a tumulus about 50 m in diameter and 10 m high. It was excavated in 1965–6 by Karageorghis. His removal of about three-quarters of the tumulus by a vertical cutting revealed its stratification and showed that it was built on a specially prepared surface. The mound had been constructed in layers with various walls of rubble and mud-brick incorporated in its structure to bind it together. The south side of the mound covered a rectangular platform of mud-brick, 17 m × 11·5 m, ascended by a ramp in the middle of the west side and by a flight of four steps on all four sides (recalling the broad stairways between the dromos and the chamber of many of the Salaminian tombs). On the centre of this platform there was a conical pile of stones beneath which was a pyre containing, in addition to charcoal and ashes, funerary offerings including about a hundred gilded vessels of clay or gypsum, gilded bronze wreaths, rosettes and leaves of gold, and several (probably originally sixteen) painted clay statues moulded around wooden poles which had been placed in holes encircling the pyre. As these statues are late fourth century BC, it was concluded that this is a cenotaph of the last king of Salamis, Nicocreon, who committed suicide with his family in 311 BC.

Chapter Seventeen

Etruscan cemeteries and tombs

Following the pioneer work of Bradford (1957, chapter 3), the C.M. Lerici Foundation of Milan has developed the under-mentioned processes for exploring Etruscan cemeteries:

Aerial photography and plotting;

Geophysical survey;

Periscope inspection and periscope photography;

Excavation of the more important sites revealed by periscope photography.

Following up the evidence of aerial photographs by geophysical survey, it is possible to ascertain more or less precisely the point where the ground should be pierced by the periscope and its camera. This camera is sent down a vertical tube 10–12 cm in diameter which penetrates the ceiling of the tomb. With the aid of a rotating cylinder, the camera then takes twelve photographs through 360°, thereby obtaining a complete record of the wall decoration (if any) in each tomb, as well as a preliminary record of its furnishings. An excavation programme is then arranged to achieve the most rewarding results (Lerici 1960, 1962). At Tarquinia alone more than six thousand new tombs, including thirty-seven with wall paintings, have been found by these methods.

Etruscan tombs and cemeteries were always placed outside the cities; and so incidentally were those of the Roman period.

97 Plan of the Monterozzi cemetery at Tarquinia. (After Moretti)

1 Tomb of the Lionesses
2 Tomb of Hunting and Fishing
3 Tomb of the Charuns
4 Tomb of the Triclinium
5 Tomb of the Funerary Bed
6 Tomb of the Leopards
7 Tomb of the Typhon
8 Tomb of the Shields

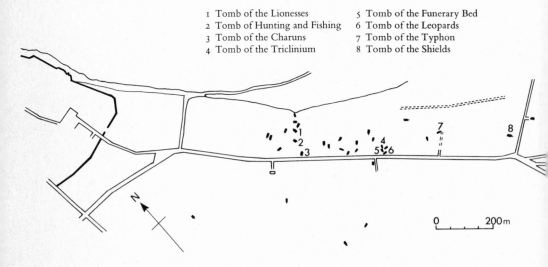

The main group of chamber tombs near Tarquinia is on a long hill called Monterozzi (the red hillocks) from numerous tumuli of reddish soil, many more of which were seen by English and other tourists during the eighteenth century, but which have subsequently been eroded by the plough.

The idea of the chamber tomb may have been introduced at Tarquinia by immigrants from Asia Minor. The important tumulus cemetery at Bin Tepe in Anatolia includes the 'Tomb of Alyattes', still 69 m high and 355 m in diameter and therefore much higher than the 40 m of Silbury Hill in Wiltshire. These tumuli are enclosed by a retaining wall, entered from a dromos, and have other features similar to those of Etruscan tombs, including interior furnishings reproduced in stone; they date probably from the seventh century B C.

The cemetery at Monterozzi extends over a length of about 5 km and a width of about 1 km. The chamber tombs in this area have nearly all been robbed in antiquity and it is therefore impossible to date them from their contents. It is, however, possible to arrange them in approximate chronological order from the style and content of their wall paintings. The following account is concerned mainly with the painted tombs which are either normally accessible (by arrangement with the custodians at Tarquinia Museum), or which have had their paintings transferred to canvas and reconstructed in tomb form on the second floor of Tarquinia Museum.

A detail that applies to most of the painted tombs is that a 'closed-in' feeling is largely overcome by the use made of stylized trees, plants, flowers, animals, and birds to provide a pastoral environment for the scenes portrayed.

9 Tomb of the Orco	13 Tomb of the Chariot
10 Tomb of the Black Sow	14 Tomb of the Ship
11 Tomb of the Baron	15 Tomb of the Olympiad
12 Tomb of the Bulls	16 Tomb of the Augurs

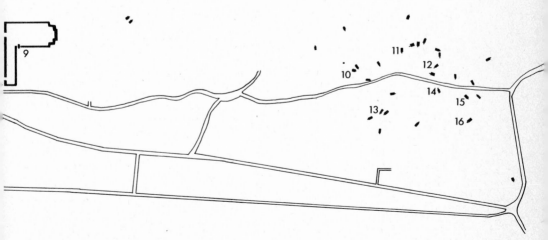

The orientalizing and primitive period (*c.* 550–480 B C)

The *Tomb of the Bulls*, dated *c.* 550–540 B C, is probably the earliest known accessible painted tomb at Tarquinia. A steep stairway from the west descends to an entrance chamber and two small chambers behind it, each having a bench on three sides. It still retains most of its covering tumulus. It is the only Etruscan tomb to have one of its walls (in the entrance chamber) decorated with a Homeric scene: Achilles ambushing Troilus who is shown on a horse; between Achilles and Troilus is an ashlar-built well on top of which are two crouching feline animals. Above this scene is an inscription in Etruscan. The presence of this scene reflects contacts with Greece and Asia Minor. The tomb is named from the paintings of bulls (one with human head) and other figures including a winged sphinx, above the doorways into the two small chambers. There are erotic human scenes beside each bull. The remaining scenes are concerned mainly with the joys of life, including banqueting, music, dancing, and athletic sports.

The *Tomb of the Augurs* is believed to have been decorated between 530 and 520 B C. It is entered by a descending stairway from the west. The burial chamber has a gabled ceiling with central beam painted red. On each side of this beam are painted little red and black flowers on a neutral background. In the centre of the end wall there is a painting of a heavily studded doorway either to the tomb or to Hades; on each side is a dignified human figure standing in an attitude of sorrow and respect. In the pediment above is

98 Tomb of the Bulls, Tarquinia, *c.* 550–540 B C. This scene of Achilles ambushing Troilus illustrates the strength of Greek influence in the early painted tombs at this site

depicted a wild goat seized by two feline animals. To the right are two wrestlers holding each others' wrists. A pile of three bowls between them is interpreted, somewhat doubtfully, as the prize for the winner. To the right of this is a revolting scene of a blind-folded man armed with a club being savaged by a dog: an un-pleasant act depicted in several Etruscan tombs, and known as the *Phersu* from the name of a bearded man who took part in it. The name of this tomb is derived from the fluttering birds portrayed above these scenes. Left of the main wall is a bearded man dancing with a bird above and below. In the rear end of the floor are two pairs of small rectangular hollows, probably where sarcophagi were originally fitted.

The *Tomb of the Lionesses* is usually dated between 525 and 515 BC. The entrance is by a descending stairway from the north. The deceased was cremated and the urn containing the burnt bones was placed in the niche at the bottom of the wall at the end. The tomb is named from two facing feline animals (panthers?) formerly thought to be lionesses, painted on the pediment. Below this is a tripartite scene, the central element of which is a festooned krater with a figure on the left playing a cithara and one on the right playing a double flute. To the left is an animated but somewhat overdressed female dancer, and to the right are a male and a female dancer. Below this tripartite scene, on each side of the door, is a frieze of birds and dolphins above a band of sea waves. On the side walls are the reclining figures of four men (two on each side) at the (funerary?) banquet.

The *Tomb of Hunting and Fishing* is usually dated *c.* 520–500 BC. A wide flight of rock-hewn steps descends to two chambers of which the inner is just over 3 m square. There is a scene of the re-turn from a hunt on the pediment above the door leading from the outer to the inner chamber. On each side of this door are frag-mentary scenes including dancers and trees with festoons hanging from them. The scenes on the walls of the inner chamber are among the most beautiful in any known Etruscan tomb. Facing the door is a delightful seascape with dolphins, and a boat with an eye painted on its prow, from which a youth is fishing. The sky is almost filled with birds, one of which is being aimed at by a youth with a catapult. On the wall to the left the seascape continues with more dolphins, another boat, more birds, a youth climbing a rock and another diving from the top of this rock into the sea. On the right wall the seascape continues in similar style. Wreaths or fes-toons hang from a ceiling of coloured horizontal bands. In the floor near the rear of the inner chamber are two pairs of cut rect-angles, probably for fitting sarcophagi.

The *Tomb of the Olympiad* is dated between *c.* 540 and 500 BC. It is among the most important painted tombs discovered since 1956 by the Lerici Foundation. Its wall paintings have now been removed to the Villa Giulia Museum in Rome. The tomb was discovered on 26 March 1958, and the pictures on its walls were televised within a few hours from the periscope camera to the USA and elsewhere before the tomb had even been opened. It was named from the athletic scenes on the walls, and because the Olympic Games were due to be held in Italy in 1960. The left-hand wall

shows boxers and a race between four chariots each drawn by two horses; one of the chariots has come to grief. On the end wall are portrayed a male and a female dancer. The right-hand wall has three runners, a jumper, and a disc-thrower, as well as the remnant of a *Phersu* scene of the type already noted in the *Tomb of the Augurs*. The decoration in this tomb was inspired by the Attic vases of the period (Åkerstrom 1970).

99 (*Opposite*) Tomb of Hunting and Fishing. Tarquinia, *c.* 520–500 B C, noted for the scene of bird-catching and fishing on the end wall which is continued on the side walls

The *Tomb of the Baron*, dated *c.* 500 B C, is so-called because it was discovered by Baron Kestner in 1827. It is also known, more appropriately, as the *Tomb of the Horses* from the most conspicuous features in the decoration. It still retains much of its original tumulus. The entrance is from the S S E, and is by a rock-cut stairway descending to the burial chamber (4·5 m × 3·9 m) which has a sloping ceiling with central beam painted red. The wall paintings are exceptionally well preserved. The scene on the rear wall includes a man holding a dish (*kylix*) with his arm on the back of a boy who is playing the double flute. They stand before a lady with upstretched arms. Above this scene are representations of sea-horses. On each side of the main group is a youth on horseback, and on the side walls are youths dismounted from their horses and possibly (on the right) appealing to a referee to decide who was the winner. The style of these paintings is very restrained, and they provide a natural transition from this group to the group shortly to be described.

The *Tomb of the Chariot* is named from the chariots and horses shown (along with wrestlers and jumpers and other athletes, originally about a hundred figures in all) in the narrow frieze on the wall of the chamber. The paintings, dated between 500 and 490 B C, have been removed to Tarquinia Museum. The main scene on the rear wall is an all-male banquet; and male and female dancers are shown on the side walls. What remains of these paintings suggests that this was originally among the most lavishly decorated tombs at Tarquinia.

The period of Attic and Classical art (*c.* 470 B C onwards)

The *Tomb of the Leopards* is immediately north of the road from Tarquinia and is believed to date from between 470 and 450 B C. It is named from the leopards or panthers facing each other on the pediment of the rear wall of the chamber. A stairway from the west descends to the burial chamber which is *c.* 4 m square. The ceiling is of red, blue, and white squares, and the central beam is decorated with large and small circles. From now onwards the decoration on the rear wall is almost invariably a group of three couches on each of which are pairs of banqueters. On the left wall there are musicians followed by offering-bearers. On the right wall is an exceptionally well-executed scene of a man carrying a dish (*kylix*), a youth playing a double flute and a youth playing a cithara.

The paintings in the *Tomb of the Triclinium*, which are of exceptionally fine quality, have been removed to Tarquinia Museum. They comprise delicate and graceful portrayals of

100 Tomb of the Leopards,
Tarquinia, c. 470–450 BC. This
tomb is named from the
leopards (or panthers) facing
each other on the end wall
above a banqueting scene

subjects similar to those in the Tomb of the Leopards just
described. The tomb is dated c. 470 BC.

The paintings in the *Tomb of the Funerary Bed* have also been
moved to Tarquinia Museum. They are believed to be mid-fifth
century BC. The tomb is named from the large funerary bier, or
catafalque, with two pairs of pillows on top, in the middle of the
rear wall.

The *Tomb of the Ship* is among the most important discoveries
by the Lerici Foundation and the paintings have been removed to
Tarquinia Museum. They are believed to date from c. 450 BC. The
tomb is named from the rather damaged painting of a large
cargo ship with high prow and stern and masts, and a pair of oars
serving as a rudder, on the left wall of the chamber. To the left are
traces of other ships. On the right of the large ship are portrayed
two amphorae on a low table and two dishes of *kylix* type hanging
from the wall. To the left of these vases is a standing figure, and to
the right is a figure of a man playing a cithara. The rear wall is
decorated with a fine scene of three couches each with two occu-
pants. This scene continues on the right wall where there are traces
of another couch. The top register of the rear wall contains remains of a banqueting scene on each side of the bracket supporting
the central beam.

The *Tomb of the Black Sow* was found by George Dennis in the
nineteenth century and afterwards lost. It was recently rediscovered by the Lerici Foundation and the paintings have now been
removed to Tarquinia Museum. They are dated by Moretti
between 400 and 350 BC. The tomb is named from the chief

animal painted beneath the central beam on the rear wall, interpreted by Dennis as a black sow but by Moretti as a dark brown male boar with a red female boar. Each is shown being speared by a hunter and near by are the remains of hounds. The central register comprises the usual banqueting scene which continues into the rear parts of the side walls. The lower register of all three walls includes a miniature menagerie comprising two pigeons and four other birds, a marten, a dog and the back part of another, and a buck.

The *Tomb of the Orco* is at present closed to the public, but is too important not to be mentioned. The wall paintings are Hellenistic (*c.* 340–280 BC) and the figures all have their names written in Etruscan. They include the head of a young lady of the Velchia family and a winged figure of the Etruscan god of the dead, Charun, bearded. Behind this chamber is a later chamber, the walls of which are decorated with Hellenistic and Etruscan mythological figures including one of Tuchulca holding a snake, between Theseus and Pirithous (the last almost faded away). These paintings are dated between 280 and 180 BC.

Access to the *Tomb of the Shields* is also at present denied to visitors. This tomb gets its name from the row of circular shields painted on the walls of one of its three side-chambers. It comprises a large central chamber 6 m square with three small side-chambers, each with a door and two windows cut through the rock, simulating a house, in the manner of many of the tombs at Cerveteri but unusual for Tarquinia. The paintings are late Hellenistic and probably within a few years of 250 BC. The rear wall includes a banqueting scene with an inscription in Etruscan, and the right wall is decorated with a banqueting scene and musicians playing a cythara and a wind instrument.

The *Tomb of the Typhon* is also at present closed, but is among the best examples of its late period (between 150 and 30 BC). The ceiling is supported in the centre by an unusual rock-cut object, apparently a very thick pillar with a seat or altar at the side. The two sides of this pillar are painted with a winged giant or Typhon with arms supporting the roof and legs ending below the knee as serpents. At the back of this altar is a winged figure of Victory. The lower parts of the walls are occupied by three tiers of rock-cut benches for sarcophagi and cremation chests, parts of some of which remain in position. On the right wall are figures including Charun whose skin is coloured green (the colour used in Egypt for Osiris, god of the dead). The late date of the human figures is shown by their shading, and by the inscriptions being in Latin, which show that it was the tomb of the Pumpu family. It may here be added that the recently discovered *Tomb of the Charuns* in the Monterozzi necropolis contains no less than four finely preserved figures of Charun.

Among the painted tombs discovered by the Lerici Foundation is one known as the *Tomb of the Warrior, or of the Armour,* one of the walls of which is decorated with paintings of shields, helmets, and other armour, much of it closely resembling the objects carved in the Tomb of Painted Reliefs at Cerveteri (pp. 177–8). This tomb is dated to the second century BC.

The Pietrera tomb near Vetulonia

This is among the finest of the large tumulus tombs of the orientalizing period (eighth to seventh centuries BC). It is about 2 km northeast of Vetulonia as the crow flies, and south of the Via dei Sepolcri. It is approached from the north by a long walled dromos in the manner of the Cypriote 'royal' tombs of Salamis. This leads by a stomion (deep doorway) to a corridor with side-chambers beyond which is the original (lower) chamber, about 5 m square.

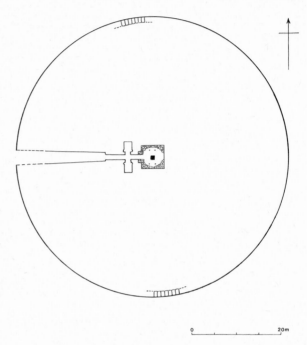

101 Plan of the Pietrera tomb, Vetulonia. (After Pincelli)

0   20m

This collapsed soon after it was built, probably because it was of poor-quality masonry. This lower chamber has a central pillar tapering towards the top, where it was probably intended to be clear of the roof, and this pillar is thought to have been some kind of cult symbol. Similar pillars occur in the domed chambers of other large tumuli of this period, such as La Montagnola north of Florence, and Casale Marittima north of Populonia (now reconstructed in the garden of the National Archaeological Museum in Florence).

Over the wreckage of this lower chamber the upper chamber was built, and this also is 5 m square. It has a corbelled roof, now completed in modern brick. This chamber has squinches in the angles to convert the square into a circular shape to receive the dome. This upper chamber was decorated with perhaps the earliest known Etruscan reliefs depicting human figures who appear to be personifications of the dead; they are in an orientalizing Greek style. Any burials there may have been in either chamber had been robbed. Placed superficially in the covering circular tumulus (63 m in diameter and 13·7 m high) were seven trench graves, three of which were rich in goldsmiths' work. As the sculptured figures in the upper chamber are shown wearing jewellery identical with that found in the trench graves, it is clear that they are contemporary, and they are dated between 700 and 650 BC (Pincelli 1943). One wonders whether the two chambers were a 'blind' to deflect tomb-robbers from the burials in the covering tumulus.

Cerveteri

In many ways the most important tomb in this area is the *Regolini-Galassi Tomb*, named from its early explorers, General Alessandro Regolini and Archpriest Vincenzo Galassi, who cleared the tomb of its vast contents in about twenty-four hours early in 1836 (Pareti 1947).

There is good reason to believe that the entrance to the main burial-chamber was from the circumference of an original tumulus *c.* 28·5 m in diameter, and that this was enlarged to a tumulus *c.* 48 m in diameter, from various parts of the circumference of which five other burial-chambers were entered; these five secondary chambers had all been destroyed before 1906 when the tomb was re-examined by G. Pinza. The whole tomb was probably completed by adding masonry including a stone perimeter wall to form a total diameter of 57 m.

The main chamber is approached by a stairway which descends from the west through an antechamber with a pair of rock-cut oval side-niches. Both antechamber and chamber have a steeply gabled upper portion and ceiling of fine-quality masonry, resting on rock-cut walls. The burial in the main chamber was of a

102 Cerveteri: the Regolini-Galassi tomb, *c.* 700–650 BC, so-called from its explorers, General Regolini and Archpriest Galassi, whose twenty-four hours of hectic activity in 1836 brought to light the richest assemblage of funerary furniture yet found in any Etruscan tomb. The finds fill a room in the Gregorian Etruscan Museum in the Vatican

woman with very rich accompaniments including a gold pectoral, gold and silver jewellery and utensils, including richly decorated silver bowls and dishes, and two (probably originally three) great bronze cauldrons. Although the early explorers mentioned no burial there was probably an inhumation. The antechamber contained a male inhumation lying on a bronze bed; two (?) tripods, one at the head and the other at the foot of the bed; a four-wheeled chariot; iron javelins and other objects. To the walls were fixed bronze shields, and to the ceiling were nailed fluted bronze bowls. In one of the side-niches was a bucchero vase (*olla*) containing burnt bones. The three interments may have been roughly contemporary. Many of the richly decorated metal objects show marked Egyptian and other 'orientalizing' features. The date of the tomb is probably between 700 and 650 BC. As neither Regolini nor Galassi were properly equipped to cope with a find of such magnitude and their notes were hopelessly inadequate by modern standards, there is a good deal of doubt as to the precise arrangement of the finds in the tomb. They are now displayed in the second gallery of the Gregorian Etruscan Museum in the Vatican.

Cerveteri: the Banditaccia cemetery

103 Cerveteri: the Sepulchral Way in the Banditaccia cemetery, lined with tumuli on each side

Cerveteri was an Etruscan neighbour city to Tarquinia, and there was sometimes antagonism between them. Indeed an early Roman inscription at Tarquinia records a Tarquinian who conquered a king of Caere (Cerveteri). The following account is concerned mainly with the tombs in the Monumental Enclosure as this is

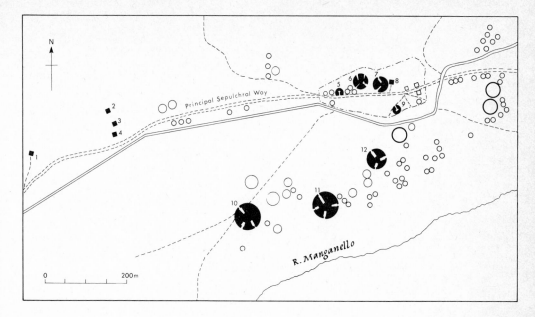

104 Cerveteri: the Banditaccia cemetery. (After Pallottino and Bradford) Almost the whole of the area north of the River Manganello is covered with tombs of which only the main groups are shown here. Those described in the text are indicated in black.

1 Tomb of the Five Chairs
2 Tomb of the Tarquinii
3 Tomb of the Sarcophagi
4 Tomb of the Triclinium
5 Tomb of the Capitals
6 'Tumulus II'
7 'Tumulus I'
8 Tomb of Painted Reliefs
9 Tomb of the Cornice
10 Tomb of the Ship
11 Tomb of the Painted Animals
12 Tomb of the Shields and Chairs

the only section suitable for a general visit. The tombs in this section have been extensively excavated and are a fair cross-section of the necropolis as a whole. The Monumental Enclosure includes a long stretch of the Principal Sepulchral Way, still retaining its original vehicle ruts and lined on both sides with tumuli, mostly large and small circular examples with stone retaining walls, but with some rectangular tombs. Others are hewn in the rock and are without any covering tumulus. From this road there are subsidiary roads also lined with tombs, several of which are covered with tumuli. Here and there are earlier Villanovan tombs of much more modest proportions. Many of the tumuli were restored by Raniero Mengarelli who devoted much of his time to the investigation and restoration of this area between 1911 and 1935. As nearly all the tombs were robbed long ago, their dating has been worked out mainly from details of their structure and decoration.

Tumulus II is the largest tumulus in the Monumental Enclosure, being *c.* 40 m in diameter. It stands on a circular rock-hewn drum near the top of which is a cornice of five raised cordons. It is among the earliest tumuli in the Banditaccia cemetery and among the first to have cornice moulding. The two parallel walls at right angles to the circumference, on the southeast side, are believed to have enclosed an altar. This tumulus contains four tombs:

(i) The *Tomb of the Hut with the Thatched Roof* is believed to be the earliest, and is dated *c.* 620–600 B C. The rock-cut entrance, facing north, leads to a chamber in the form of a rock-hewn imitation of the interior of a rectangular hut with stone ledge around the walls. A rounded doorway at the far end leads to a small chamber. The main chamber has a gabled roof with a raised strip along the top.

105 Cerveteri: Tumulus II in the Banditaccia cemetery. This is the largest tumulus in the public part of the Monumental Enclosure, and covers the Tomb of the Hut with the Thatched Roof, the Tomb of the Dolii (storage jars), the Tomb of the Funerary Beds, and the Tomb of the Greek Vases. Their date ranges between *c.* 620 and 450 BC

(ii) The *Tomb of the Dolii*. An entrance leads from the north past a pair of side-chambers to two main chambers. The interior contained several storage jars (*dolii*) and other vases which are now in the Villa Giulia Museum in Rome; they include a complete group from the Alari chamber.

(iii) The *Tomb of the Funerary Beds*. The entrance leads from the southwest past two side-chambers to two main chambers. There are raised rock-hewn funerary beds with pillows on each side of the main chamber which has a doorway with a solid arch between two narrow windows.

(iv) The *Tomb of the Greek Vases* has an entrance from the southeast which leads past the usual pair of side-chambers to a four-bedded chamber whose rear portion is tripartite, each part containing two funerary beds. Within this tomb were found a fine series of Greek vases, now in the Villa Giulia Museum in Rome. Their dates suggest that the tomb was used between *c.* 550 and 450 BC.

Tumulus I is separated from Tumulus II by groups of later and much smaller tombs. It is not as large as Tumulus II, being 32 m in diameter. It stands on a circular drum decorated with a cornice of two cordons separated by a plain course. It is about the same date as the last. It contains two tombs with interior doorways moulded in a Doric style similar to those of the false door façades of the rock tombs at Castel d'Asso northeast of Tarquinia. Each entrance leads past a pair of side-chambers to a main chamber but the southwestern entrance leads to two main chambers.

The *Tomb of the Capitals* is between the ticket office and Tumulus II, and its entrance is on the north side of the Principal Sepulchral Way. It is dated to the early sixth century BC. The entrance leads past a pair of side-chambers to a main chamber whose ceiling is supported by two columns with so-called 'Aeolian' capitals. The ceiling is carved with imitation parallel wooden beams supporting what appears to be a simulated thatched roof. Against the walls are eight round-headed funerary couches – four on each side of the entrance. The rear end of the main chamber is tripartite and contains more funerary couches, some with squared and others with rounded ends, possibly to differentiate between male and female usages.

The *Tomb of Painted Reliefs* is the most spectacular in this cemetery. It is dated to about the third century BC by the *kylix* dishes carved on the walls and by the other carvings. Its entrance faces south, and was guarded on each side by a life-size statue of a lion, of which only the head of that on the right remains, mounted not very suitably on a cube-shaped plinth. A stairway descends to a rectangular chamber 7·6 m × 6·7 m. The ceiling, which has a slight slant, is supported by two pillars with richly decorated capitals. The two outer sides of each pillar are carved with various objects. Arranged at right angles to the walls are thirty-two funerary beds divided by raised ridges, and in addition there are, in wall-niches, another thirteen beds each with two pillows painted red.

The decoration includes a circular shield below the capital of each pilaster excepting those at the far end. Above the entrance to the chamber are carvings of two bulls' heads in a rope harness. On each inner side of the door is a carving of a two-handled metal dish, beneath which is a large circular hoop with central bar (similar objects occur on the walls of the *Tomb of the Warrior* recently discovered at Tarquinia). On the floor is a marble cippus bearing an inscription in Etruscan, which indicates that the tomb belonged to the Matuna family.

The principal interment was probably in the middle of the rear end of the chamber where excavations directed in 1850 revealed the skeleton of a warrior and portions of a suit of armour. Precise identification of all the objects carved on the walls is

106 Cerveteri: Tomb of the Painted Reliefs, *c.* third century BC, with walls carved in relief with representations of warrior equipment, various household objects, furnishings and animals

still sometimes uncertain; but the general picture is clear. On top of the walls immediately below the ceiling are swords placed horizontally with red or yellow caps between them. On the architraves just beneath are circular shields painted yellow to represent bronze; bronze helmets with greaves on each side; a double string of large stones or pebbles for use in sling warfare or hunting; and leggings. The reliefs on the pilasters flanking the principal burial place include a bust, a handled jug, a bronze two-handled dish, a fan, and a wand or stick. Beneath this burial place is a figure of Charun with serpentiform legs, carrying a rudder in his right hand and a snake in his left. He faces an animal resembling a dog with three heads, before which is a snake. Behind Charun is a relief of a rectangular stand with a cushion on top and shelves beneath.

The front of the left pillar is decorated with reliefs of a truncheon, a handled jug, an axe, a knife, a coil of rope, two rods, and at the bottom a cat with a mouse in its mouth. The right side of this pillar is carved with objects including a two-handled bronze dish, an object resembling a stool or table on wheels, a handbag covered with netting, and a goose feeding.

The front of the right pillar has reliefs of two long rods, a circular gong (?), an axe, two small knives in a stand, and a circular object on another stand. The left side of this pillar bears reliefs which include a rectangular frame, a gong (?), a pair of pincers, a ladle, a goose, a dog with a lizard, and a tortoise. There is probably no more accurate representation of the furnishings of an upper-class Etruscan house of this period.

The *Tomb of the Cornice*, usually dated to the fifth century BC, is on the south side of the Via IX (delle Cornici) which turns off sharply on the South of the Principal Sepulchral Way, a short distance east of the tomb just described. It retains its own beautifully formed circular tumulus in almost perfect condition. The entrance is from the northwest and leads to an interior the plan of which is almost identical with those of the Tomb of Capitals and the Tomb of the Greek Vase. On each side of the entrance is an antechamber containing two funerary beds. The main chamber has a chair and two couches to the left and right of its entrance. At the rear are three chambers with windows, entered by panelled doorways; there are two funerary beds in each of these chambers. The tomb is named from the cornice on three sides of the main chamber.

It remains to describe some of the more important and accessible tombs outside the Monumental Enclosure. The *Tomb of the Five Chairs*, west of this Enclosure, is often water-logged, as are the next two tombs to be described which the writer has not been able to see for this reason. Our account of these tombs is therefore brief. The present tomb is named from the five rock-cut chairs in the left side-chamber. The *Tomb of the Triclinium* contains, within its doorway, reliefs of a wild boar on one side and a panther tearing its prey on the other. On the left wall are traces of a painted banquet scene, and the other walls also have traces of paintings. Other tombs at Cerveteri may originally have been painted but the rock-cut surfaces in this area are not such as to preserve tomb paintings.

The *Tomb of the Tarquinii or of Inscriptions* contains a large chamber
c. 10·7 m square with sloping ceiling supported by two pillars,
one painted with a circular shield. Set into the walls are thirteen
sepulchral recesses, mostly double, and nearer the floor are two
tiers of rock-cut benches for further bodies. This tomb could
therefore have accommodated well over a hundred burials.
Numerous wall inscriptions, some in Etruscan and others in
Latin, show that it was occupied for eight generations by a group
of presumably related families some of whom were named
Tarchna. It is clear, however, that they were probably not connected with the traditional Kings of Rome called Tarquinii. The
inscriptions of the last three generations are in Latin. The tomb
seems to have been used for burial from the third to the first
century BC. The *Tomb of the Sarcophagi* is known for the richly
decorated sarcophagi which it contained, one being in the Gregorian Etruscan Museum in the Vatican. All the tombs just
described are close together and about midway between Cerveteri
and the Monumental Enclosure.

Between the road leading to the Monumental Enclosure and
the river Manganello are three exceptionally large circular
tumuli. The western example, the *Tomb of the Ship*, is named from
the painting of a ship (now almost gone) in the second chamber.
The central example, the *Tomb of the Painted Animals*, contains
four groups of tombs, one with walls decorated with animal paintings only the slightest traces of which remain; it is, however, of
great interest because the antechamber has its ceiling decorated
with ribbed spokes radiating from a circle in the manner of a
gigantic sun symbol which it may well be. The entrance stairway
of this tomb is exceptionally massive and imposing. The eastern
tumulus, the *Tumulus of the Shields and Chairs*, dates probably
before 500 BC. It is approached from the east by a descending
stairway which passes two side-chambers to reach a main chamber
at the rear end of which are three inner chambers. On each side
of the central inner chamber is a beautifully carved chair with
footstool at its base and circular shield above, from which the
tomb derives its name. Fourteen more circular shields are carved
on the walls of the main chamber which contains six funerary
couches. The wall paintings in the *Tomb of the Painted Lions* in the
same tumulus have almost vanished; but this tomb contains
another example of ceiling of ribbed spokes formed by cut-out
rectangles, the part near the entrance assuming the form of a
gigantic sun symbol. Its date is probably sixth century BC.

In 1967 the Museo Nazionale di Cerveteri was opened in the
sixteenth-century castle adjoining the main square in the town.
Arranged on modern lines, it presents a fully illustrated picture of
the development of the Etruscan cemeteries at Cerveteri. Among
the exhibits are some of the painted tiles which have come from
both the ancient city and the tombs in the Banditaccia cemetery.

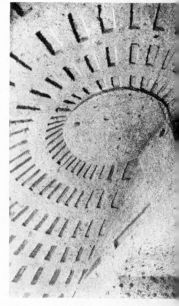

107 Cerveteri: 'sun-ray' ceiling
in the Tomb of the Painted
Lions, *c.* sixth century BC

Chapter Eighteen

Sardinia and Corsica

Sardinia

The earliest tombs so far identified in Sardinia are several circular cairns with retaining walls, each containing a central stone cist, in the area of Li Muri near Arzachena in northern Sardinia. The rite used was in at least one instance inhumation, and the grave-goods included a steatite bowl of Aegean origin, stone axes, mace-heads, a necklace of stone beads, and flakes of obsidian and flint.

Between 2400 and 1600 BC a Copper Age culture, known as the Ozieri culture after a town in northern Sardinia, flourished and had contacts with other parts of the Mediterranean, especially Malta. It is represented by two important cemeteries and various other tombs mostly in the north of the island.

The necropolis of *Anghelu Ruju* includes about thirty-five accessible tombs. They are not numbered and no accurate plan has yet been published, but ill. 108 is accurate enough for the present purpose. The tombs, of varying orientation, are all rock-cut and below ground level, and are approached either by a ramp or by a rock-cut stairway, or a combination of both. The doorways are sometimes carved to simulate the wooden door frame of a house and some are rebated to receive a closing slab. Each tomb comprises between one and six or eight chambers arranged often along a central axis, sometimes paired, but frequently haphazardly.

The finds from these tombs include bell-beakers from tombs I, III, V and XIII; V-perforated 'tortoise-buttons' from tombs XIII, XVII and XXX; tanged copper daggers from tombs I and XXX; three figurines of Cycladic type but made locally, and several tanged flint arrowheads from tomb XX *bis*; a perforated wrist-guard and beads including a cowrie from tomb XXX; and a whetstone or wristguard in a bone case from tomb XIII. Analysis of the metal objects from these tombs suggests that three awls and a dagger probably came from Spain; a ring was from eastern Europe; and a flat axe and an awl were most likely from Ireland. These objects illustrate the cosmopolitan character of the Ozieri culture. The rite of interment in this cemetery was collective inhumation.

The carved tombs at Anghelu Ruju have now to be described. Tomb XIX is entered from the north by a long passage leading into an antechamber with bull's horn carvings on each side of its entrance; beyond this is the main chamber in the centre of which is a pillar bearing on its outer side two bull's head carvings. Tomb XX *bis* is approached from the east by a short stairway continuing as a ramp into a chamber with two pillars, one being carved with two bull's heads one above the other. Tomb XXX is noted for both its architecture and the finds already mentioned. It is entered

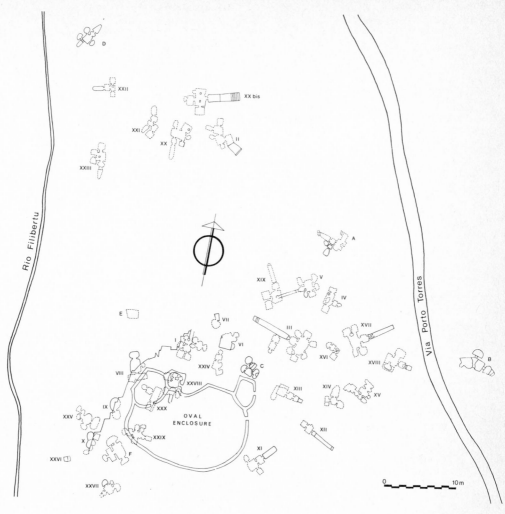

108 The necropolis of Anghelu Ruju, Sardinia. (After Levi and Contu)

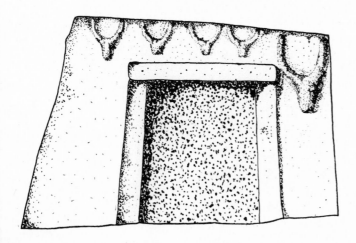

109 Tomb A at Anghelu Ruju. (After Contu)

110 Tombs at Sant Andria Priu, Sardinia, general view. The best tombs are beneath the horizontal groove but are difficult of access. They are remarkable for their rock-cut architectural details simulating the interior of houses built of wood

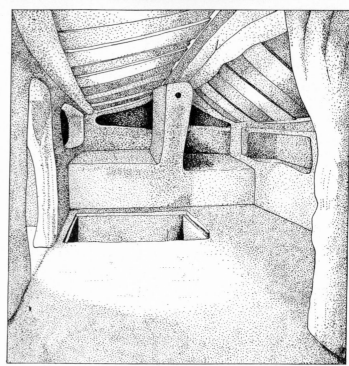

111 Interior of tomb at Sant Andria Priu. (After Guido)

from the small enclosure within the northwest corner of the Oval Enclosure. The tomb has an antechamber with bull's horns carved on its opposing walls, and beyond this is a large rectangular chamber with a smaller chamber to the right. Tomb A, near the road, has the greatest number of bull's head carvings: four large and two small ones in a row above a doorway; another on the wall to its right; and two more in cell 2. Some of the bull's-horn carvings in these tombs were originally painted with red ochre.

The tombs at *Sant Andria Priu*, about 6 km east of Bonorva, are cut into the face of a trachite cliff. There were originally at least

twenty tombs here but only a few are now accessible, parts of the rock face having collapsed. At least one was approached by an impressive stairway which has fallen. Others have rounded interior doorways. Access to the three most important tombs, marked by a deep horizontal groove above them, has to be by a tall ladder. All three are cut with architectural details simulating those of the roof and walls of a house built mainly of wood. They have been compared with the carved tombs at Cerveteri but seem to be Copper Age, on the evidence of a beaker sherd and a tanged triangular arrowhead from other tombs in the group.

Of other tombs attributed to this period those cut in the Elephant Rock, about 3 km east of Castelsardo, are among the best known and easiest to find. This rock contains several chambers presumed to be for burial, and that cut into its eastern side has a fine but stylized bull's head carved on each inside wall of its entrance.

The Giants' Tombs

These tombs may have developed from the dolmens of which about forty are known, nearly all in the north of the island. Among the most accessible is that near the railway station at

112 (*Upper*) Elephant Rock at Castelsardo, Sardinia, showing entrances to tombs

113 (*Lower*) Elephant Rock at Castelsardo. Tomb with bull reliefs

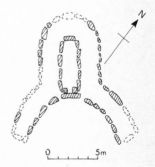

114 Plan of Giant's Tomb at Fontana Morta, Sorgono, Sardinia. (After Guido)

183

115 Giant's Tomb at Borore/
Imbertighe, Sardinia. The
entrance slab is between the
horns of a forecourt behind
which is an elongated mound

116 Giant's Tomb at Molafá,
Sardinia, general view

Birori, east of Macomer. The dolmens vary in plan from circular through oval to rectangular, the last being in plan closest to the Giants' Tombs.

The distribution of the Giants' Tombs is similar to that of the nuraghi (habitations comprising round towers and accessory structures) and they are accordingly considered to be of this culture (*c.* 1500–300 BC). Around three hundred of these tombs are known. In plan they resemble the head and horns of a bull, and in view of the bulls' heads carved in many of the tombs of the Ozieri culture, this could well have been intended to symbolize the power of procreation of the bull as a means of rebirth into an after-life. A few Nuraghic sherds have bulls' heads in relief, and there are stone and bronze bulls' heads of Nuraghic age. Other indications of a fertility cult are the occasional presence in the burial chamber of carved female breasts, carved phallic emblems and the presence in the forecourt of baetylic stones carved with female breasts. Incised slabs from two Giants' Tombs at Rio di Palmas near Sulcis bear carvings of large spoked wheels, perhaps sun symbols.

The horned entrance usually faces between south and east, and the forecourt (sometimes with an offering-table) bounded by the horns was used for burial ritual. Behind the entrance is a rectangular chamber 2–18 m long and 1 or 2 m wide, in which the interments were placed. The walls of the chamber and forecourt are of coursed masonry or upright slabs. The chamber was roofed by either transverse slabs or corbelling. In the wall of the chamber there is occasionally a niche for a lamp or for offerings. Some of the more impressive Giants' Tombs have a tall entrance slab cut in the form of a false door with rounded top, the real door into the tomb being in the lower part of this slab. This door is, however, usually too small to have admitted a burial and may have been to receive offerings. The burials were unburnt and of both sexes and all ages. Up to fifty or sixty burials have been found in a single tomb used probably for several centuries. Recent excavation of four Giants' Tombs (Li Lolghi, Coddu Vecchiu, Li Mizzani, and Oridda) has shown that they had been rebuilt many times (Castaldi 1969, 155–6).

Two of the best Giants' Tombs are near Borore south of Macomer. Borore/Imbertighe is the better example and has a perfectly preserved monumental entrance slab. Borore/S. Gavino has an entrance slab that is similar but less well preserved. Its mound is *c.* 9 m long and 60 cm high. In each case the entrance slab is *c.* 3 m high. A Giant's Tomb with an exceptionally typical forecourt and mound is at Is Concas near Quartucciu east of Cagliari.

The *Tombe des Géants,* 200 m north of Molafà railway station, between Alghero and Sassari, is a rock-cut tomb of similar type. In the centre of a rock-cut crescentic forecourt is the monumental entrance with the upper part solid and rounded in the manner of a false-door, beneath which is the entrance to the burial chamber. The latter is rectangular, *c.* 2·7 m × 1·8 m, and has on three sides a raised bench similar to those in many of the sepulchral caves of Majorca. With its arched ceiling, it has been called 'an adaptation

117 Giant's Tomb at Molafà. Detail of entrance in the centre of a rock-cut crescentic forecourt. It leads to a rectangular chamber with arched ceiling and raised bench on three sides

118 The dolmen at Fontanaccia near Sartène, Corsica. This is the finest of the Corsican dolmens

to limestone country of a type of tomb which is most at home in regions of Sardinia where nature provides ready to the hand of the builders the great slabs which are so characteristic a feature in the construction of the Tombs of the Giants' (Mackenzie 1910, 124).

All who are interested in the Sardinian tombs should visit the Cagliari and Sassari Museums. The latter has recently been re-arranged, a feature being a splendid series of casts of the various reliefs and some paintings in the tombs of the Ozieri culture.

Corsica

Although Filitosa is the best-known and most spectacular pre-historic site in Corsica, it is in some ways surpassed in academic interest by the sites south and southwest of Sartène where most of the stones in the alignments are more or less in their original posi-tions. Before discussing the sites it should be mentioned that Corsica comprises a granite plateau excepting around Cap Corse in the extreme north where schist and limestone occur, and around Bonifacio in the south where there is also limestone. During the Early Neolithic period the dead were interred in natural caves.

Grosjean divides Corsican prehistory from Late Neolithic on-wards into Megalithic (I, II, and III) when relations with Sardinia are attested by the presence of obsidian, and the burial rite was inhumation; and Torrian, when he believes the funerary rite to have been cremation. Megalithic I–III are almost entirely coastal and riverine in their distribution, but the Torrians sometimes penetrated into higher ground for siting their defended villages.

To the final phase of *Megalithic I* (c. 3500–2300 BC) has been attributed some dozens of *coffres mégalithiques* (stone cists, but often enclosing a larger area than usually indicated by that term), mostly in groups but some in isolation. They can be up to 3 m long and 2 m wide, and are sometimes at or near the centre of a circular peristalith which presumably originally enclosed a covering tumulus. An example at Tivolaggiu (southwest of Porto Vecchio) has a double peristalith (13 m in diameter), possibly indicating two structural periods. Objects found in or near these cists, which have almost always been pillaged, include V-perforated and other stone beads, worked flakes of obsidian and (more rarely) flint, and diorite axes; but these can be no more than circumstantial evidence for dating the cists. The rite was almost certainly inhumation as no bones have been found and only cremated bones would survive in this acid soil. There are usually one or more menhirs near each stone cist. These sites are mostly in the south of the island, especially between the Taravo and Ortolo rivers, and are probably contemporary with the similar sites near Li Muri in northern Sardinia.

Megalithic II and III (*c.* 2300–1600 BC) are distinguished from one another only by the latter having more developed statue-menhirs. Stone cists with peristaliths continued to be built. Near the alignment at Palaggiu is one of special interest which includes a cist-slab decorated with a rectangle enclosing three rows of small cup-depressions, apparently derived from an earlier structure as the decorated part is broken off at one end. Excavation in this cist revealed five pots, a triangular copper knife or dagger, a whetstone or archer's wristguard, a gold annulet (earring?) and parts of a silver ring (dress fastener?). There were no bones and an inhumation can be inferred. It appears to be the only grave-group so far published from any Corsican site of this type. Near by is the stump of the usual menhir (Peretti 1966).

Dolmens are believed to have been introduced during Megalithic II. The best-known example, at Fontanaccia near the alignments of Cauria, is *c.* 3·15 m × 2·05 m and 1·65 m high, and has its entrance facing ESE. It may have been originally in a mound, and there is the stump of a menhir near by. The dolmen at Settiva (commune of Petreto-Bicchisano) is within a stone setting, roughly circular excepting for the part flanking the entrance at SE, which has the appearance of a façade resembling those of the Giants' Tombs of Sardinia. The Corsican dolmens have their entrance at SE, or at S if in line with a stone alignment, all the Corsican alignments being orientated N–S. All the Corsican dolmens have one or more menhirs near, most likely symbolic of the person(s) interred in the dolmen.

Whenever statue-menhirs occur in alignments they always face eastward. This might be interpreted as indicating that they are memorials of the dead and face the rising sun for religious reasons. If, however, the swords and daggers carried by some of them are of north Italian type (Lilliu and Schubart 1968, 29), these figures could be facing the land of their origin and still be memorials of the dead. Some of them at least were originally painted with red ochre which has been detected on them by infra-red photography.

It is uncertain whether Megalithic III survived the invasion of the Torrians (*c.* 1600 BC), and in the author's opinion it is doubtful whether any of the torri were intended for burial.

Chapter Nineteen

The Balearic Islands

The prehistoric cultures of Majorca and Minorca are in the following sequence:

Pre-Talayotic I: Late Neolithic/Copper Age, *c*. 2000–1800 BC.

Pre-Talayotic II: Copper Age/Early Bronze Age, *c*. 1800–1500 BC.

Talayotic, named from its chief surviving monuments, the talayots (round towers), fortified elements of the homesteads and villages. This period is subdivided into Talayotic I, *c*. 1500–1000 BC; Talayotic II, *c*. 1000–500 BC; and Talayotic III, *c*. 500 BC until the Roman conquest of 123 BC which it may have survived for a few decades.

Pre-Talayotic I is represented in Majorca by inhumations in natural caves, including Vernissa near Santa Margarita and Sa Canova near Petra, dated by pottery of Chassey and other types. A few artificial caves with one chamber only, distributed near the south coast of Majorca, may also be of this period.

Pre-Talayotic II is closely related to other Copper and Early Bronze Age cultures of the western Mediterranean. It is strongly represented in Majorca by most of the hundred artificial sepulchral caves described by Veny (1968). Those in Minorca have not yet been studied in detail. The cemeteries of Son Sunyer, Son Toni Amer, and Cala San Vicente now to be described include most of the finest examples in Majorca.

Artificial sepulchral caves of pre-Talayotic II

There seems little evidence that human remains have ever been found in the artificial caves here described as sepulchral. Their funerary purpose is assumed partly from the character of the objects found in them: pottery which might have contained food for the dead; bronze daggers with two, three, or four rivets; bronze arrowheads; bronze awls; buttons (often V-perforated) and beads; and occasional whetstones or wristguards. This assemblage is consistent with what is known of grave-goods of the period in the western Mediterranean, but the finds from the caves classed by Veny as for habitation are, however, only slightly more varied, if they show any difference at all.

The *Son Sunyer Cemetery* comprises caves IV to XII of Veny. It is situated on a low scrub-covered hill near the Son Sunyer Barbecue, just southeast of Palma Airport. The tombs are here described from west to east, Veny's numbering being followed:

Cave IV. A short ramp descends from the N through a small vestibule to a rectangular chamber with rounded corners, 5 m × 3·7 m. Along the length of each of the parallel long sides there is a ridged shelf. The chamber has an arched rock-cut ceiling *c*. 1·7 m high.

Cave V is entered by a passage from the NW, which proceeds through a vestibule and down a short ramp to a rectangular chamber 6·1 m × 2·5 m and 1·9 m high. A few potsherds of pre-Talayotic type were found in this chamber by Rossello-Bordoy.

Cave VI is entered from the NNW through a small vestibule leading to a rectangular main chamber 6·2 m × 3 m, at the rear of which is an end chamber. Both chambers have an arched rock-cut ceiling.

Cave VII is among the more developed in this group, but its roof is nearly destroyed. It has a slightly curved axis. Before the entrance is a three-sided trench which must have contained some kind of screen. The entrance leads through the remains of two vestibules to the main chamber which has two side-chambers on the right and one on the left. In the floor of this chamber is a rectangular hollow. Part of a globular round-based vase with opposed horizontally perforated lugs was found by Rossello-Bordoy while clearing this tomb.

Cave VIII also has a slightly curved axis. An entrance from the NW proceeds through two vestibules to a sub-rectangular chamber 8·5 m × 3 m, at the rear end of which is a small end chamber. The interior of the main chamber has been hollowed to form a ledge around the walls. Within this tomb have been found nine fragments of bronze awls, several V-perforated bone buttons, and sherds of five round-based vessels, three with horizontally pierced lugs. A sherd from a sixth vessel may have had a flat base.

Cave IX comprises a short ramp leading to a roughly circular chamber. Excavations by Rossello-Bordoy yielded a few worked flints and some pottery including parts of two round-based and two probably flat-based vessels.

Cave X has in front of the entrance a three-sided trench (for a screen ?) similar to that in Cave VII. A ramp leads from the entrance to a rectangular chamber with three side-chambers on the right. On the left is a chamber from the rear end of which there extends a passage.

Cave XI comprises a ramp descending to a rather shapeless chamber with arched ceiling. *Cave XII* is known only from an early reference.

The *Son Toni Amer Cemetery* comprises Caves XXV–XXIX of Veny. It is on top of the hill east of the road between Campos and Puerto de Campos (or Colonia de Sant Jordi). The tombs, which are cut in fine-quality sandstone, are described from west to east, Veny's numbering being used:

Cave XXV is entered from the NW by a short stairway leading straight into a long rectangular chamber, 8·5 m × 2·1 m and 1·2 m high, with an arched rock-cut ceiling. The central axis of the floor is hollowed to form a continuous ledge around the walls. This is the only cave in this group from which finds are known. They include a three-riveted dagger and parts of the blades of two other bronze daggers; three bronze awls; and parts of at least five round-based pots, some with everted rim.

Cave XXVI, the outer part of which is destroyed, was of similar type and size, but in the left corner of the rear end there is a small rounded niche.

Cave XXVII is the most interesting in the group. From the NW an entrance descends through the remains of a vestibule to an elongated oval main chamber 5·5 m × 2·45 m from the long sides of which there are three pairs of side-chambers (one chamber is destroyed), and one pair of narrow ledges on a higher level. At the rear end of this chamber is an end chamber with rebated doorway. The long axis of the main chamber is hollowed for the length of the three pairs of side-chambers, to form a shelf which is divided by ridges into compartments, in the manner of tombs 7–9 at Cala San Vicente described below.

Cave XXVIII, partly destroyed, is approached by a modern doorway. The main chamber is rectangular and there is a side-chamber at the rear end on the left.

Cave XXIX is entered from the SW by a flight of steps, leading to a rectangular main chamber 6 m × 3·5 m at the rear end of which are two small square chambers. The main chamber has been altered for modern purposes.

In the *Cala San Vicente Cemetery*, Caves LXXIX–LXXXII are easy of access. Veny dates this cemetery to his latest phase of the pre-Talayotic period, perhaps *c.* 1300–1200 BC, and a little later than those just considered. Each cave has a roughly quadrangular forecourt. Beginning with the westernmost, these are the main features:

Cave LXXIX (Hemp 6). The doorway still retains traces of a rebate probably to receive a closing slab. The entrance leads from the SW straight into a rather roughly-hewn elongated main chamber 10·7 m × 2·4 m at the rear end of which is a small end chamber. There is a hollow cut into the central portion of the long axis of the main chamber to form a ledge around the walls. This cave is poorly preserved and perhaps unfinished.

Cave LXXX (Hemp 7), the best in the group, and indeed among the finest in Majorca. The forecourt is 5·5 m square. The entrance doorway, which faces slightly W of S, is *c.* 67 cm high and 55 cm wide, and has rather weathered traces of a rebate. It leads through a small vestibule to a pair of side-chambers and then to a beautifully formed main chamber, rather cigar-shaped, with the rear end rounded. This chamber is 9·15 m × 1·8 m. There is the usual central hollow to form a shelf around all four sides; this shelf is divided into compartments by four ridges on each long side. The average height of the ceiling, which is beautifully rounded, is 1·8 m above the floor of the central hollow. There is a well-cut cornice between the ceiling and the shelves. The doorways to main and side-chambers have slots for the timbers of wooden doors. The irregular hollow at the rear end of the main chamber looks fairly recent. Finds include a V-perforated conical bone button from a groove in the floor at the inner entrance doorway, and a few potsherds.

Cave LXXXI (Hemp 8). From the centre of the quadrangular forecourt, in which three square hollows have been cut probably for timber posts, the entrance leads through two vestibules to a main chamber 8 m × 2 m. For most of this length there is a central hollow whose floor is 1·9 m below the ceiling which is rounded in the manner of cave LXXX. There are remains of ridges dividing

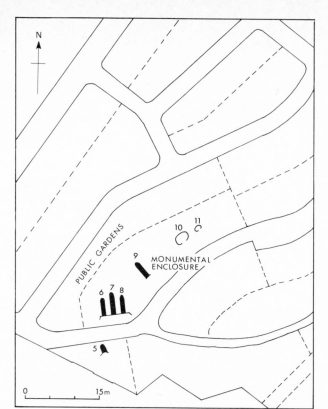

119 Plan of Cala San Vicente cemetery, Majorca (Hemp's numbering). (After Falcon)

120 Sepulchral cave LXXX (Hemp 7) at Cala San Vicente. View looking towards entrance showing the central hollow with shelf or bench on each side, divided into compartments by ridges. The cornice beneath the arched ceiling is unusual

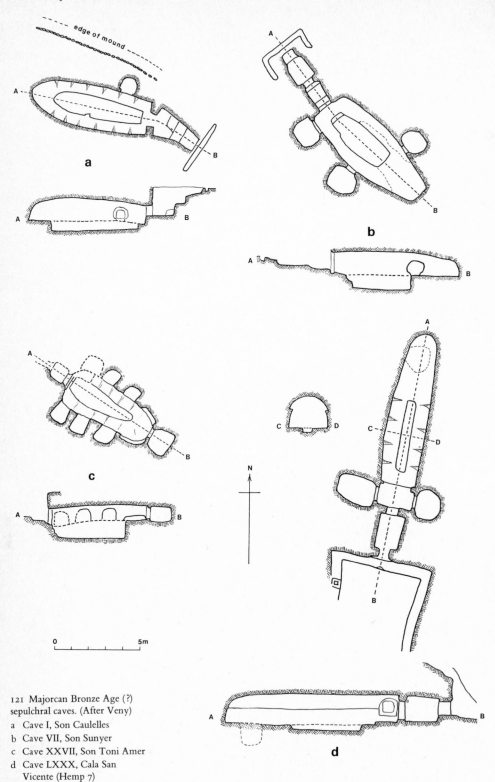

edge of mound

A

B

a

A

B

b

A

B

A

B

c

A

B

C

D

C

D

N

A

B

A

B

d

0   5m

121 Majorcan Bronze Age (?)
sepulchral caves. (After Veny)

a Cave I, Son Caulelles

b Cave VII, Son Sunyer

c Cave XXVII, Son Toni Amer

d Cave LXXX, Cala San
   Vicente (Hemp 7)

the shelf on the long sides into compartments. To the right of the main chamber is a small round side-chamber.

Cave LXXXII (Hemp 9) is about 30 m northeast of cave LXXXI. In the floor of the forecourt are two square holes presumably for wooden posts. In the centre of the façade of this forecourt is the entrance which faces south. A few steps descend through a vestibule to the main chamber (7·75 m × 2·2 m), at the rear end of which is a small chamber; there are two side-chambers on the right and one on the left, all roughly circular. In the wall of the doorway into the main chamber are two sockets for horizontal timbers of some kind of door. In the floor of the main chamber is the usual long hollow forming a shelf around the walls, divided on the long sides into compartments by ridges. The ceiling is rounded and about 2 m above the floor of the central hollow. *Cave LXXXIII* (Hemp 12), about 300 m to the east, is now nearly destroyed.

Of individual sepulchral caves that at *Son Caulelles* (Veny I) is of special interest because of the resemblance of its plan to that of the navetas next to be described. In front of its entrance is a trench which must have received a screen. A short stairway descends into the main chamber in the floor of which is the usual long hollow, forming around the walls a shelf which is subdivided in the usual way. On the north is a side-chamber, and on the south of the hollow is a pilaster of unknown purpose. There may be traces of a covering mound to this tomb.

The Talayotic period is the period to which most of the visible prehistoric monuments in Majorca and Minorca belong. They include more than a thousand talayots in Majorca and over five hundred in Minorca. Many of these are the fortified elements of villages, of which the most notable examples in Majorca are Ses Paisses near Arta, and Capicorb Vey southeast of Palma. Although talayots sometimes contain burials, they are omitted from this discussion as the most authoritative opinion is that they were never constructed for funerary purposes only (Pericot 1972, 59).

Navetas of Talayotic I

These are stone-built collective tombs in which the rite was inhumation. They were first given their name by the rather imaginative Dr Juan Ramis (1818) from their resemblance to upturned boats, one end being squared and the other apsidal. There is reason to believe that the naveta is a tomb in the form of the house of the period, and numerous navetiform structures occur among other house types in the talayotic villages of Majorca and they are also known in Minorca (Pericot 1972, 59–61). On the other hand the resemblance of the naveta to the most developed of the Majorcan sepulchral caves (such as Son Caulelles) has already been noted. The naveta also resembles, in both plan and elevation, the Giants' Tombs of Sardinia without their 'horns', believed to be contemporary with the Sardinian nuraghi which are themselves of the same period as the Balearic talayots.

The true naveta is almost confined to Minorca, where their estimated number has varied between forty and sixty-five accord-

122 Naveta of Els Tudons, near Ciudadela, Minorca. The classic example of Minorcan naveta with both upper and lower chamber

ing to where one draws the line between the naveta and the naveti-form structure. Navetas are all built of ashlar (Cyclopean) masonry without the use of any mortar, but clay or mud was probably used to seal the closing slabs over the entrance doorways.

The *Naveta of Els Tudons* (the woodpigeons) is surrounded at a distance by a modern stone wall for protection. It is orientated WSW/ENE, the entrance being at WSW, between two flat slabs in the centre of a slightly concave façade. The entrance doorway is rebated to receive a closing slab. The monument is *c.* 14·3 m × 6·5 m and *c.* 4·55 m high but it would originally have been *c.* 6 m high. The slope of the façade is steeper than that of the tail end. The site was excavated and restored in 1959–60 under the supervision of Pericot. The entrance leads by a short passage to an antechamber and then another short passage to the main chamber (6·3 m × 2 m), essentially rectangular but with a central bulge. The ceiling of this chamber has an average span of 1·5 m and is flat and *c.* 2·1 m above the floor. Above this is an upper chamber which is slightly longer. Finds made during the excavation included remains of at least a hundred human skeletons (one with trepanned skull), V-perforated buttons and bronze bracelets.

Rafal Rubi 1 (SE) naveta. The outer door is not rebated. The entrance faces SW, and is slightly s of the centre of the façade. The structure is 13·75 m × 8·5 m, the façade being 8 m wide. The doorway in the inner end of the antechamber is cut from a single slab and is rebated for a closing slab. Traces of clay mortar in the entrance passage may be the remains of the original sealing. The main chamber is 6·4 m × 2·4 m and the ceiling is 2·3 m above the floor. Above this is an upper chamber which was excavated in 1968; the finds included remains of at least twenty-four human skeletons and Talayotic pottery, suggesting that the tomb was used from the beginning of the Talayotic until an advanced stage of that period (Serra Belabre and Rossello-Bordoy 1971). The monument had been pillaged and rebuilt on several occasions and doubtless put to many uses.

Rafal Rubi 2 (N W) naveta. This is orientated s s w / N N E and is 14 m × 9 m. The entrance is in the centre of the s s w end and has no rebate. From it a corridor leads to an inner door cut from a single slab and rebated for a closing slab. This door leads to the main chamber (5·3 m × 1·7 m and 2 m high). There may be an upper chamber which has not yet been explored.

Of the remaining navetas, *Biniac East* (L'Argentina) has been altered in later times by the addition of a stone stairway and an upper entrance. *Cudia Cremada*, just southwest of Mahon, is of interest by reason of its present use as a shrine of St Mary Magdalene dating from the last century. *Son Mercer de Baix*, southwest of Ferrerias but difficult to find, has the roof of the main chamber supported by columns of Cyclopean masonry, and it is therefore uncertain whether it is a naveta or a hypostyle court (Pericot 1972, 80). *Sa Torreta*, between Mahon and Fornells, yielded remains of fifty-eight skeletons to Dr Margaret Murray in 1931.

Micro-navetas and sepulchral caves of Talayotic II and III

It is thought that full-sized navetas were not built after Talayotic I although those already in existence may have continued to be used and sometimes rebuilt. At Son Real on the northeast coast of Majorca, about 40 km southwest of Minorca, is a remarkable cemetery of which seventy-two tombs, placed very close together, have so far been investigated. About one-third of them are *micro-navetas*, similar in plan to navetas but averaging only 3 m × 2 m, and 1 m high, and of no fixed orientation. They nearly always have two trenches dug into the floor at right angles to their axis. Some have one, two, or three rectangular holes in the upper part of the end wall for a purpose not yet determined. Each tomb contained between one and six crouched inhumations, with the head towards the straight end and usually facing east. The finds date them around the seventh to sixth centuries B C, and are in the Alcudia Museum. Other tombs in this cemetery are circular and rectangular, and some yielded cremations with glass paste beads of Punic origin dating from the fifth century B C. The cemetery was probably re-used in Roman times (Pericot 1972, 61–7).

The sepulchral caves are abundant in groups along the south coast of Minorca. The most notable is at Cales Coves, a site of great beauty. On both sides of the ravine are rock-tombs of which ninety-five have so far been located. Plans and sections of twenty-five tombs and illustrations of finds have recently been published by Veny (1970) whose numbering is here followed. Some of the entrance doorways are rebated for a closing slab. Most of the caves comprise one chamber only, either circular, oval, or rectangular.

Sometimes there are two or more chambers, occasionally with niches in their walls. Cave XXV has one large chamber and three smaller chambers or niches and is the most elaborate of those so far published. Finds include socketed spearheads, spirally twisted wire perhaps of necklaces or bracelets, rings, and circular spoked discs – all of bronze, and a triangular bronze tanged blade of a type found also in navetas. Iron objects were found in three caves only. Bone objects include circular discs with dot-in-circle decoration and pins. The pottery is usually flat-based and flowerpot-shaped, with one solid handle of circular section, and often decorated with incised parallel lines, straight on the body but curved to fit the handle. Cave XXV contained three black glass beads decorated with white circles. Human skeletons have been reported from many of these caves. The cemetery 'began to be used in the middle of the ninth century BC and continued until the Roman period' (Veny 1970).

Among the best of the other ravine cemeteries is that at Cala Morell or Son Morell Nou (Ciudadela), where seventeen caves include some with rebated doorway and one (no. 12) with a carved doorway surround rather resembling those from some of the Etruscan tombs.

Ibiza was never colonized by the bearers of the Talayotic culture. It has an important Punic cemetery on the hill called Puig des Molins, and the contents of its tombs make a fine display in the Ibiza Museum adjoining the cemetery.

123 (*Opposite, upper*) Son Real cemetery, Majorca, including micro-navetas, by the coast between Alcudia and Arta. The standing figure is the distinguished Balearic archaeologist, Sr José Mascaró Pasarius

124 (*Opposite, lower*) Cales Coves, Minorca. A group of sepulchral caves in an idyllic setting

Chapter Twenty

The Channel Islands

The prehistoric tombs of the Channel Islands are largely an insular extension of those of Brittany and Normandy, which have been discussed by several writers including Daniel (1960) and Giot (1960), and more recently by L'Helgouach (1965).

Guernsey

Local names in this island indicate that the number of surviving megalithic monuments is probably less than half of that which at one time existed. The best-known tombs are the *passage-graves* of which the chief are La Varde on the western part of Lancresse Common; Le Déhus on the northeast coast; and Le Creux des Faies near Fort-Saumarez opposite Lihou Island.

The passage-grave of *La Varde* is within a roughly circular mound *c.* 19 m in diameter, edged by a retaining circle. The entrance from the S E, leads to a single chamber 10 m long, which expands as one proceeds inwards. At the north side of its western end is a recess. The chamber is now roofed by six slabs of which the innermost and largest has since 1890 been supported by a modern granite pillar. There were originally seven or more roof slabs to this chamber. Excavation by F. C. Lukis in 1837 yielded human remains of several individuals, some unburnt, others burnt (uncertain whether by fumigation or cremation but probably the former); a V-bored conical jet button; and nearly forty pots and sherds of more than a hundred others. These finds suggest the use of the tomb for burial extending over centuries. The pots include well-decorated bell-beakers (Lukis Museum at St Peter Port).

The passage-grave of *Le Déhus* is the best-known prehistoric tomb in Guernsey. It is within a roughly circular mound bordered by a retaining circle *c.* 19 m in diameter. The entrance, from the east side, leads into a main chamber *c.* 6 m long, which expands as one proceeds inwards. On each side of the passage are at least two (doubtfully originally three) side-chambers. A feature of special interest in the main chamber is that the second roof slab from the far end is incised on its underside with a representation of a human figure, the face and two hands being well defined; beneath the hands is a crescent-shaped object resembling a small bow. As part of the design extends behind a wall-slab, it is most likely that this roof slab was incised before being put in position. The monument was excavated by F. C. Lukis in 1837, and in 1932, at the expense of Sit Robert Mond, by Miss V. C. C. Collum, whose interpretations were somewhat individual (Collum 1935). The finds indicated that at least five inhumations had been interred. The artifacts included a tanged copper dagger, a green polished

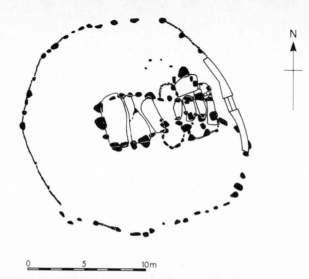

N

126 Passage-grave of Le Déhus, Guernsey. The face of the carved figure

0   5   10m

serpentine axe-head, six round-based pots from the side-chambers, two well-formed bell-beakers, and parts of several other beakers (Lukis Museum). The monument was restored late in 1932 and reopened to the public by the States of Guernsey in 1933.

Le Creux des Faies passage-grave was originally in a circular mound bordered by a retaining circle which was removed long ago. The entrance faces east, and leads via a passage which blends into the chamber, giving an overall length of 8·5 m and a height of nearly 2 m. Finds made by F. C. Lukis in 1840 included human remains, two fine bell-beakers and other beakers, and two barbed-and-tanged flint arrowheads, the latter near the surface.

Of the two statue-menhirs on the island, *La Gran'mère du Chimquière* was probably re-modelled in Gallo-Roman times. *Le Câtel*, with its 'necklace' and pair of breasts, strongly resembles examples from megalithic tombs in France, and may indeed have formerly been part of a gallery-grave (Kendrick 1928, 27; Daniel 1960, 68 note 2).

Jersey

This island has not only *passage-graves* but also *gallery-graves* such as occur over most of western France including Normandy and Brittany. The passage-graves include La Sergenté, Les Monts Grantez, La Hougue Bie, La Pouquelaye de Faldouet, Mont Ubé, and Mont de la Ville (now in the grounds of Temple Combe near Park Place, Henley-on-Thames). The gallery-graves are Le Couperon and Ville-ès-Nouaux.

PASSAGE-GRAVES

La Sergenté, on the southwest coast near Petit Port, includes the lower portion of a circular chamber *c.* 3·4 m in diameter, with a tendency to corbelling; the walls are now less than 1 m high; it is approached from the s s e by a short passage. On the southwest side of the chamber is a crescent-shaped area partitioned off by slabs and sometimes interpreted as a bed. It has for long been discussed whether this is a house or a tomb, but present opinion is that it is a tomb (J. Hawkes 1937, 90, 248; Daniel 1960, 67). It has yielded four round-based plain pots ('Jersey bowls').

Les Monts Grantez, overlooking St Ouen's Bay, comprises an entrance from the s e, leading by a passage to a somewhat V-shaped main chamber, with a side-chamber to the northeast, most of the cover-slabs being still in position. The structure is in a low mound *c.* 18·4 m × *c.* 6 m, but this may not have been its original shape which was most likely circular. Excavation in 1912 revealed seven crouched human skeletons in the main chamber, and one 'sitting' in the passage; artifacts included two 'vase-supports' and fragments of others, a round-based bowl, and two fragments of a bell-beaker.

La Hougue Bie, between St Helier and Gorey, is among the most impressive passage-graves in western Europe. The passage and chambers are covered by a vast mound *c.* 57 m in diameter and *c.* 12·3 m high, surmounted by two medieval chapels (Chapter Ten).

A splayed entrance from the east leads to a passage *c.* 10 m long, varying in height from *c.* 1·4 m to 2 m, and then to the main chamber nearly 10 m long and *c.* 2 m high. There are side-cells at the north, south, and west of the main chamber. The northern side-cell is of special interest in that its eastern wall-slab bears about eighteen large and three small cup-marks, most of which were, however, hidden behind dry-walling when the tomb was completed. In the far end of the main chamber are three short 'menhirs' and there is a fourth at the rear end of the western cell, each of the four being *c.* 30 cm high. The tomb was thoroughly robbed in antiquity, but excavation in 1924 revealed the remains of eight inhumations and nineteen 'vase-supports'.

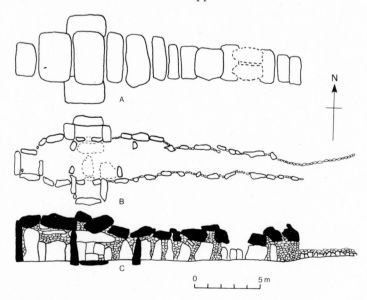

128 Plan and section of La Hougue Bie passage-grave, Jersey. (After Rybot)
A Plan of capstones
B General plan
C Longitudinal section

La Pouquelaye de Faldouet is on the hill between Gorey and Mont Orgueil Castle. It comprises a passage leading from the east to an outer chamber with four cists, and a horseshoe-shaped inner chamber still retaining its cover-slab. The distance from the entrance to the far end of the inner chamber is 14 m. The site was originally covered by a mound, probably circular, and apparently with inner and outer retaining circles, nearly all traces of which have now gone excepting on the east side. As the monument was 're-stored' by a former excavator, Rev. F. Porter, about 1868, there is some doubt whether the cists in the outer chamber are all original or later. Finds included two or three human skeletons, two 'Jersey bowls', two 'vase-supports' on which the bowls may have been resting when found, a tiny cup, two polished axes (one of greenstone, the other of flint), and two segmental perforated pendants (one of greenstone, the other of dolerite).

Mont Ubé, southeast of St Helier, is similar in plan to those of Guernsey, a rather narrow passage leading from the entrance at SSE to an oval or bottle-shaped chamber. This seems to have been divided into about four compartments but only two of the dividing slabs now remain in position. The cover-slabs have gone and the passage and chamber are open to the sky. They were most likely within a circular mound limited by a retaining circle of stones, a few of which were still present when the tomb was discovered in 1848. Finds included a 'Jersey bowl', a grape-cup of the type which occurs in the Wessex culture, and beaker sherds.

Mont de la Ville passage-grave was discovered when ground was being levelled for defence works on the site of Fort Regent, St Helier, in 1785. Two years later it was presented to General Conway, Governor of Jersey, on his retirement, and in 1788 he had the stones transported and re-erected in the grounds of his residence

129 Mont de la Ville passage-grave, Jersey, removed in 1788 to the grounds of Park Place, Henley-on-Thames

at Park Place, Henley-on-Thames. This estate was broken up in
1946 and the part containing the monument is now known as
Temple Combe (private). The passage-grave seems to be an essentially accurate reconstruction of the original tomb. It comprises an
entrance facing S E, with a passage leading to a roughly circular
chamber *c.* 8 m in diameter, within the circumference of which are
five chambers or cists. This unusual arrangement somewhat resembles the Meayll circle in the Isle of Man where the circumference
is, however, formed by six T-shaped triple cists.

GALLERY-GRAVES AND CIST

Le Couperon is sited on a spur overlooking Rozel Bay on the northeast coast. Its essential feature is a long stone cist, 8·2 m long and
1 m wide, with transverse cover slabs orientated W N W / E S E. It
was surrounded on all sides by a rectangular stone setting which
remains except on the northwestern side. The slab at the southeastern end has a semicircular concavity which might have been
paired with another to form a port-hole. It was placed in this
position in 1919, having been pulled from the site and used as a
cover slab in a 'restoration' done by Rev. F. Porter in 1868. It is
suspected that it is one half of a port-hole in an internal partition
or septal slab (J. Hawkes 1937, 257–8). Finds of the period of the
monument comprised only potsherds and flint flakes.

Ville-ès-Nouaux is easy of access, being in a small public garden at
the village of that name, on the coast west of St Helier. The long
cist is *c.* 10·2 m long and *c.* 1·2 m wide, and seven of its cover slabs
remain. The cist is placed W N W / E S E. It is flanked on its north
side by a stone setting; although there is no record of similar
settings on the other sides, such may formerly have existed.

Excavators in 1883 thought they saw signs of two side-cists at the

130 Gallery-grave at Ville-ès-
Nouaux near St Helier, Jersey

east-southeastern end, but this seems unlikely. Finds from the long cist in 1869 and 1883 include several bell-beakers and other pottery, and a stone wristguard holed at each end. Those found in 1869 are nearly all in the Lukis Museum (Guernsey), and those found in 1883 are in the Museum of the Société Jersiaise at St Helier; a few finds are also in the British Museum.

Just north of the gallery-grave is a perfectly preserved stone cist still with its cover slab, in the centre of a retaining circle *c*. 6 m in diameter, which formerly enclosed a round barrow. No significant finds are known from this cist.

A final point is that shells from shellfish, especially limpets, have been frequently found in megalithic tombs in the Channel Islands, and must have been either offerings to the dead or the remains of funeral feasts, or both.

Chapter Twenty-One

The British Isles I: Wessex and the Southwest

The Severn-Cotswold chamber tombs

The scope of this work permits only the briefest selection from material already published by various writers including Daniel (1950) and Corcoran (1969). No contribution is here offered to the already extensive literature on the origins of these tombs, but the writer would accept the view of Daniel (1963) that the gallery-grave with transepts is likely to have been introduced into the regions bordering the Severn estuary from Brittany. The following sites are among those most accessible and worth visiting.

Parc le Breos Cwm (Glamorgan): SS 537899
This site, in eastern Gower, was excavated by Atkinson in 1960 and shown to be a trapezoid cairn 20·2 m long, 12·3 m maximum width, and at present 1·3 m maximum height. From the sse an entrance leads to a gallery with two pairs of side-chambers but, curiously enough, no end chamber, although the gallery continues very slightly beyond the inner pair of side-chambers. At least thirty-one individuals, including young children, had been interred in the chambers and gallery. After the final burial had been made the forecourt was blocked with slabs laid horizontally. The mound has a roughly built inner and well-built outer retaining wall (Daniel 1937 and information from Prof. R. J. C. Atkinson).

Stony Littleton (Somerset): ST 735572
This fine trapezoid long barrow is c. 30 m long, 15 m broad, and 2·7 m high, and has its entrance at se, where there is a fine ammonite cast on the western door jamb, illustrating Neolithic man's interest in fossils. Between the horns is the entrance leading to a gallery 14·6 m long and 1·2 m high, with three pairs of side-chambers and an end chamber, of upright slabs with dry-stone walling filling in gaps here and there. It is the only known British long barrow with three pairs of side-chambers, but the destroyed site of Fairy's Toot, Butcombe (north Somerset) may have had more. Two human crania found in 1816 at Stony Littleton long barrow are in the City Museum, Bristol (Grinsell 1957c).

Wayland's Smithy (Berkshire): SU 281854
This well-known monument is just north of the Ridgeway above the Vale of White Horse. It has been so-called since the tenth century when it may have received its name from an Abingdon monk versed in Norse literature. Excavation in 1962–3 showed two structural phases (Atkinson 1965). Phase I comprised fourteen burials within a wooden mortuary enclosure floored with sarsens (the local sandstone slabs of the area), the whole then covered with a mound less than 20 m long. On this was superimposed Phase II, the structure as we now see it, comprising a trapezoidal long barrow with sarsen kerb c. 54 m long and c. 14 m maximum width, placed sse/nnw with entrance at sse. This entrance leads to a

131 Chambered long barrow at
Stony Littleton, Somerset

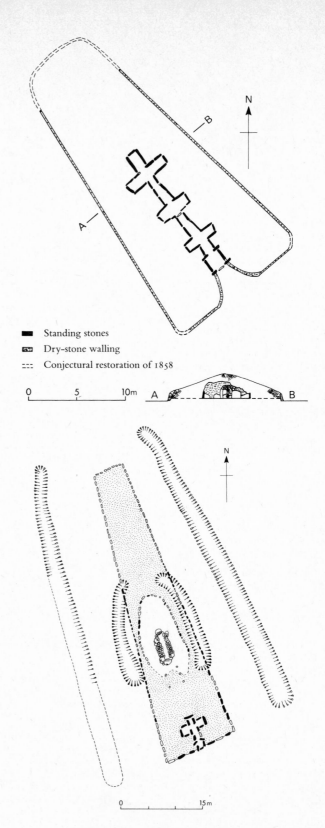

■ Standing stones

▨ Dry-stone walling

╌╌ Conjectural restoration of 1858

0   5   10m   A   B

132 Wayland's Smithy
chambered long barrow,
Berkshire. (After Atkinson)

0   15m

gallery with one pair of side-chambers and an end chamber, the whole presenting a cruciform plan. The sarsen kerb enclosed a mound of chalk rubble derived from side-ditches which are separated from the mound by a fairly wide berm. The entrance is placed centrally at the SSE end between the slabs of a monumental façade *c.* 3 m high. At least eight individuals had been buried in Phase II of this site.

WEST KENNET (Wiltshire): SU 104677

This is on a vastly larger scale than any other accessible British chambered long barrow, the mound being 100 m long, 24 m wide, and *c.* 3 m high, placed E–W, with the entrance originally placed centrally in an imposing forecourt at the east end. This entrance leads to a gallery with two pairs of side-chambers and an end chamber, all five chambers varying in height between 1·8 m and 2·9 m, enabling an adult of average height to stand erect in them. The inner pair of side-chambers had blocking slabs. The internal walling is of sarsens with the interstices filled with dry-stone walling of Corallian and Great Oolite slabs from the Colerne and Frome regions (from which binding material for Neolithic pottery was also obtained). The finds include the remains of at least forty-six individuals of both sexes and all ages; flint leaf-arrowheads and scrapers; a polished-edge flint knife; beads of bone, shell, and stone; bone pins and scoops; and pottery ranging from Windmill Hill Neolithic and Late Neolithic wares through bell-beakers to long-necked beakers, implying a use of the tomb for sepulchral purposes for a period of the order of a thousand years. An unusual feature is that the slab at the entrance to the southwestern chamber was extensively used for polishing axe-heads of flint and stone; axe-sharpening or polishing marks occur also on other sarsens here, including the lower part of the southern blocking slab in front of the original forecourt. After the monument had ceased to be used for burial, the gallery and chambers were filled to the ceiling with chalk rubble, the forecourt was filled with sarsen boulders and sealed by three large slabs arranged from north to south across the entrance, with two at right angles to them in line with the gallery. The site was restored by the (then) Ministry of Public Building and Works about 1962, who had little or no option but to make the present entrance in the southern corner of the final blocking. The core of the mound is of sarsens, covered with chalk rubble derived from the side-ditches. Between these ditches and the mound is a berm *c.* 12 m wide (Piggott 1962*a*). The East Kennet long barrow, 1·4 km to the southeast, is of even more massive proportions but has not yet been excavated.

HETTY PEGLER'S TUMP, Uley (Gloucestershire): SO 790000

This is the only accessible Cotswold example of a transepted gallery-grave with its cover slabs still in position. Finely sited above the escarpment between Dursley and Stroud, the monument was 36·6 m × 25·9 m and 3 m high, but it has overspread to cover a larger area. At the eastern end is the entrance, leading to a gallery with two pairs of side-chambers and an end chamber. The two northern chambers have been blocked since the site was found in 1821 while being pillaged for road material. Remains of fifteen human skeletons were found in the chambers in 1821, and eight

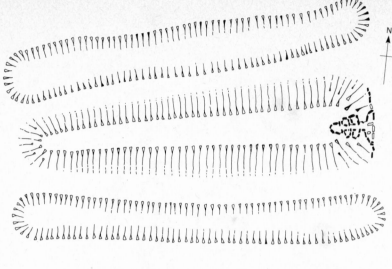

0 _____ 25m

133 Chambered long barrow at West Kennet, Wiltshire. (After Piggott)

135 (*Opposite, lower left*) long barrow Belas Knap, Gloucestershire

134 (*Opposite, upper*) Belas Knap long barrow, Gloucestershire, showing the false entrance between the horns of the forecourt and the entrances to the chambers in the long sides. The monument was reconstructed *c.* 1930–31

136 (*Opposite, lower right*) Burial chamber with a port-hole entrance, from a long barrow near Avening, Gloucestershire

human skeletons found by Thurnam in 1854 may or may not have been in addition. Parts of the interior walling have been restored within the last 150 years, but it is fairly easy to distinguish between the prehistoric and the modern work (Grinsell 1970).

BELAS KNAP (Gloucestershire): SP 021254

This is the finest known false-entrance long barrow on the Cotswolds, and is situated near the western edge of the Cotswolds between Cheltenham and Winchcombe. Its dimensions are 54·7 m long, 18·4 m wide, and 4 m high. Most unusually its axis is N–S, the (false) entrance being at the north end, in the forecourt between two convex horns. An excavation in 1863–5 revealed the skull of a round-headed young adult male (probably of Beaker stock) in the blocking of the false door, hinting that there was sometimes conflict between the Neolithic and the Beaker peoples in this area. Two opposed polygonal chambers are entered by short passages on the west and east sides of the mound, and there is another chamber, of much smaller stones, in the south part of the east side. The roofs of all three chambers are modern reconstructions of 1930–31, it being uncertain whether the original roofs were flat, corbelled, or a mixture of the two. A supposed south chamber in the tail end, represented by a single slab, may have been a cist. From the chambers came thirty inhumations – fourteen from the northwest chamber, twelve from the northeast chamber, and four from the southeast chamber. The entrance portal and chambers are of upright oolitic slabs combined with dry-stone walling. The revetment wall limiting the mound is of a most carefully laid dry-stone walling (Grinsell 1966).

THE AVENING PORT-HOLE CHAMBER (Gloucestershire): ST 879984

In a field by the river west of Avening are three burial chambers removed from a local long barrow in 1806. The most interesting has a port-hole entrance, formed by cutting a semicircle from two slabs and then placing them side by side. It is, with the possible exception of the Men-an-tol in Cornwall, the only example now

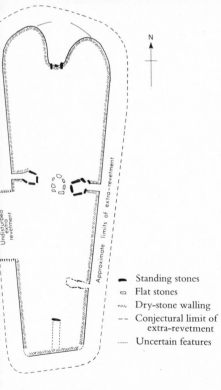

- ▬ Standing stones
- ⬭ Flat stones
- ⋗⋗⋗ Dry-stone walling
- -- Conjectural limit of extra-revetment
- ⋯⋯ Uncertain features

0 5 10m

Undisturbed extra revetment

Approximate limits of extra-revetment

N

visible in England, the two port-holed chambers in the Rodmarton long barrow having been re-buried for protection
(Clifford and Daniel 1940).

'Wessex Culture' round barrows

Until now, these regional chapters have been limited to sites which
can be entered. We are departing from this policy to have a glance
at a unique feature in the round barrows of western Europe: the
Early Bronze Age round barrows of bell, disc, and other 'fancy'
types of the 'Wessex culture' spread over Wessex with outliers elsewhere. They have been discussed in detail on several occasions
(Grinsell 1958, 1959, 1972; Piggott 1973), and only the briefest
description can here be given.

The two main types of 'fancy' round barrow in Wessex are the
bell-barrow and the disc-barrow. The bell-barrow has a berm,
usually 3–5 m wide, between a fairly large mound 2–5 m high and
the surrounding ditch, the overall diameter being 33–50 m;
occasionally there is a bank outside the ditch, making the overall
diameter *c.* 10 m more. The disc-barrow comprises a circular
ditch with outer bank, the overall diameter being 30–73 m, with
an average of 50 m; within the circular ditch is a small tump placed
centrally; sometimes there are one or two additional tumps between the central tump and the ditch. Both bell-barrows and disc-
barrows occasionally occur as oval twins, and triple bell-barrows
are known. Analysis of the grave-goods from bell-barrows
(unfortunately largely from the nineteenth-century records)
shows a rarity of beads and a fair frequency of masculine equipment including grooved bronze daggers, axe-hammers and archery
equipment, leading to the conclusion that they are essentially the
graves of men – presumably Wessex chieftains. By contrast,
analysis of the contents of the disc-barrows (again unfortunately
largely from the nineteenth-century records) shows a predomi-
nance of objects of female adornment, beads occurring frequently,
and an absence of masculine 'warrior' objects, leading to the conclusion that these are the graves of women, presumably the female
element in the Wessex aristocracy. In Dorset there is a rather
smaller variant of the disc-barrow, in which the bank may be
either on the inside or the outside of the ditch. Over Wessex as a
whole there is also the saucer-barrow, resembling the disc-barrow
but with the mound spread over the whole of the area bounded
by the ditch, the mound in this instance being less than 1 m high
and lower than that of the bowl-barrow (the normal type of
round barrow on the chalk downland of southern England and the
Wolds of Yorkshire and Lincolnshire, comprising a circular mound
with a surrounding ditch which provided most of the mound
material). Of nearly six thousand round barrows now known in
Wessex, *c.* 250 are bell-barrows and *c.* 150 are disc-barrows, but as
it is easy for disc-barrows to be eliminated by cultivation, there
were probably originally as many disc-barrows as bell-barrows in
Wessex. There are *c.* sixty-three recognizable saucer-barrows. The
last type of 'fancy' barrow is the pond-barrow, of which more than
fifty are known in Wessex. The pond-barrow comprises a saucer-

137 Winterbourne Stoke Cross-roads group of barrows, Wiltshire

shaped depression limited by a circular bank – similar to an 'inverted round barrow'. These 'fancy' barrows often occur among groups of barrows the rest of which are bowl-shaped. Among the most typical and accessible groups are the Winterbourne Stoke cross-roads and Normanton groups near Stonehenge, the Poor Lot group in south Dorset, the Oakley Down group on Cranborne Chase, and the Lambourn Seven Barrows in Berkshire.

THE WINTERBOURNE STOKE CROSS-ROADS GROUP (Wiltshire): SU 101417

Several of the barrows in this group are aligned on a long barrow, most likely of the founder of the cemetery. The group includes two bell-barrows, two disc-barrows, and two pond-barrows. One of the pond-barrows appears to overlap the southwestern bell-barrow, yet the ditch of the latter is modified to take account of the pond-barrow and their relative chronology can perhaps be decided only by excavation. If the early records are reliable, the long barrow contained one primary and six secondary crouched skeletons, and most of the round barrows of all types contained primary cremations. One of the bell-barrows (Winterbourne Stoke 4 or 5) yielded a presumably primary inhumation in an elm tree-trunk coffin, two bronze six-riveted daggers, and a bronze awl with bone handle. Parts of a handled urn of red ware, formerly considered of Armorican type which indeed it much resembles, is now claimed to be from an Iron Age haematite-coated bowl, despite the fact that it seems to have been with the primary interment (Thomas and ApSimon 1966; Piggott 1973, 371).

THE NORMANTON GROUP (Wiltshire): SU 115413

This fine group resembles the last in being essentially a linear cemetery but with scattered barrows off the line. It includes three bell-barrows, a twin bell-barrow, seven disc-barrows, one or two saucer-barrows and more than a dozen bowl-barrows. Among the latter is *Bush Barrow*, opened in 1808 by Hoare and Cunnington,

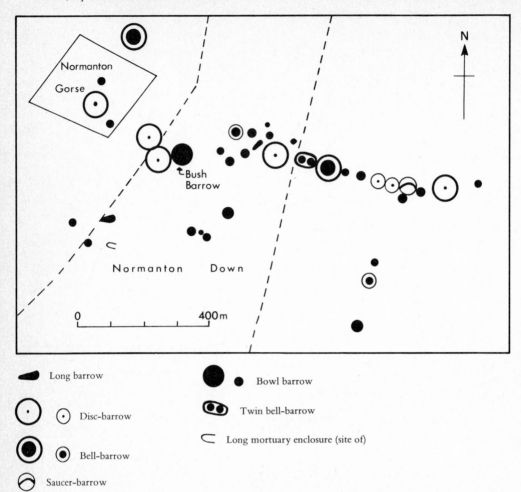

Long barrow

Disc-barrow

Bell-barrow

Saucer-barrow

Bowl barrow

Twin bell-barrow

Long mortuary enclosure (site of)

138 Plan of the Normanton group of barrows, Wiltshire

who found in it the (extended ?) skeleton of 'a tall and stout man', placed with the head to the south. Near the head was an object interpreted as a wooden shield with bronze fittings, but which might as well have been a helmet; by his shoulder was a flanged bronze axe wrapped in cloth the impression of which was preserved in the bronze corrosion; at his (right ?) side were two six-riveted bronze daggers, one with the hilt decorated in zig-zag pattern with thousands of minute gold pins; by his right hand was a smaller dagger; on his breast was a diamond-shaped gold plate encasing a thin piece of wood; and near his legs was a mace-head of fossil *tubularia* from the Teignmouth area in south Devon, and zig-zag shaped cylindrical bone mountings of a shaft, similar to those from shaft-grave Iota in Grave Circle B at Mycenae, and a small gold lozenge which may have been fixed to the shaft. There was also a gold scabbard hook. This is so far the richest known grave-group from Bronze Age Wessex. The bell-barrow north of Normanton Gorse contained an adult male skeleton on a plank of wood, a bronze dagger in a wooden case, a 'drinking cup' (lost) and antlers, the deposit being surrounded by wooden poles possibly of a hut. The two fine disc-barrows near Bush Barrow contained cremations, one with beads of amber, faience, and shale. Several of the other barrows in this group yielded notable grave-groups (Grinsell 1957a, 196–7).

THE POOR LOT GROUP (Dorset): SY 589907

This includes, to the north of the road, a twin bell-barrow and a fine disc-barrow; the main group, south of the road, includes three 'Dorset' type disc-barrows. Unfortunately there are no known excavation records.

THE OAKLEY DOWN GROUP (Dorset): SU 018173

This group is noteworthy for its fine disc-barrows, of which two (one an oval twin) are cut by the Ackling Dyke Roman road, which enabled Stukeley about 1723 to infer that disc-barrows are pre-Roman. Three of the other disc-barrows have one or more tumps in addition to the central tump. Southwest of a bell-barrow is a disc-barrow with ditch and outer bank reduced by later cultivation; this yielded to Hoare and Cunnington a cremation wrapped in (linen ?) cloth, beneath an inverted collared urn around the rim of which are eleven holes for tying on a cover of cloth or leather; in this respect this urn is apparently unique. The finds from these barrows are in Devizes Museum.

139 Oakley Down group of barrows, Dorset, remarkable for the fine disc-barrows

THE LAMBOURN SEVEN BARROWS (Berkshire): SU 328828

This group with its outliers comprises more than thirty sites, but the main group is arranged in two parallel rows north of the road between Kingston Lisle and Lambourn. It includes two pairs of twin-barrows, bell-barrows, a disc-barrow, and saucer-barrows, and there are the remains of a long barrow to the northwest. Finds from mid-nineteenth-century excavations are in the British Museum, and those from recent excavations in the long barrow are in Reading Museum (Case 1957; Wymer 1966).

Dartmoor: stone cists, cairns, and alignments

This granite upland contains a unique assemblage of sepulchral monuments of the Copper and Early Bronze Age. Well over a hundred stone cists are still visible, nearly all being orientated SE/NW. Most of them are in or near the centre of the stone retaining circle of a circular cairn 4–12 m in diameter; occasionally (as on the north edge of Fernworthy Reservoir) there were two stone cists in one cairn (one is now in Torquay Museum). Occasionally also a cairn has two, three, or even four retaining circles (as on Shuggle-down and Yellowmead Down), most likely indicating periodical enlargements for later interments. Many of these cist-cairns have a stone row, either single or double, proceeding from the cairn downhill and ending in a terminal stone at right angles to the axis of the row. It is therefore clear that we are dealing with composite funerary monuments comprising a stone row as well as stone cist and enclosing cairn.

The larger stone cists are big enough to have contained a crouched burial, but unburnt bones do not survive in the acid soil of Dartmoor. The vast majority of Dartmoor stone cists are, however, smaller and some certainly contained cremations. Nearly all of them have been robbed in antiquity. Finds from them have included beakers and other pottery and burnt bones.

Perhaps the most impressive group of sepulchral sites on Dartmoor is at Drizzlecombe (Ditsworthy Warren) where stone rows proceed downhill from three out of four small cairns, and there are two cists exposed in small cairns in the immediate vicinity. (It is only when a cairn has been pillaged that the stone cist is visible in it.) This site involves a long walk; a more accessible site, though not with such a strong sepulchral element, is at Merivale, south of the road between Tavistock and Princetown.

The importance of the association of stone rows with cairns on Dartmoor is underlined by excavations during the last decade or so in barrows on the heaths behind Bournemouth, where two round barrows have been shown to have had rows of wooden posts extending from them (Case 1952; Ashbee 1956). A double row of post-holes was found extending from barrow 75 on the Noordse Veld at Zeijen in the Netherlands (De Laet 1958, 119–20). Doubtless dozens of such instances will be found as soon as excavators dig outside as well as inside their barrows.

In quite a different category, and probably of slightly later date, are the large cairns usually on the hill tops. These large cairns are

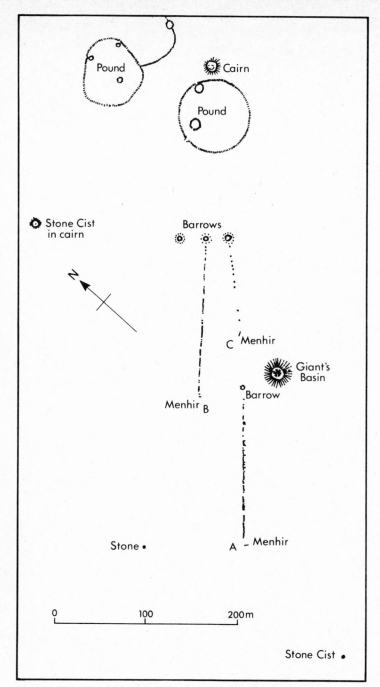

140 Bronze Age monuments at Drizzlecombe, Dartmoor. (After Worth)

scarcely ever associated with stone rows, and any apparent exceptions could have resulted from the enlargement of small cairns. A notable large cairn, on Hamel Down, opened in 1877, contained a cremation with a grooved bronze dagger, the amber pommel of which was decorated with minute gold pins in a manner similar to that of the dagger in Bush Barrow (Kendrick 1937).

Chapter Twenty-Two

The British Isles II: Ireland, Wales, and Scotland

Some passage-graves

THE BEND OF THE BOYNE (Co. Meath)

The elevated ground north of the Boyne at its large bend between Slane and Drogheda contains the greatest assemblage of passage-graves in the British Isles. Attention will here be given only to the three chief tombs – New Grange, Dowth, and Knowth.

New Grange is the most imposing of the cemetery. Its mound is a pebble cairn with an outside layer of white quartz pebbles around the entrance. It is *c.* 85 m in diameter and still 11 m high (excluding the addition of modern material now under consideration). When Edward Lhuyd saw it in 1699 there was a standing stone on top of the mound, but it was removed shortly afterwards. The cairn was surrounded at a distance by a circle 103·6 m in diameter of about thirty-eight standing stones, twelve of which remain. The circumference of the cairn is limited by a kerb of ninety-seven vertical slabs, of which slabs 1 (the entrance slab), 52 and 67 are richly decorated. The entrance slab has a superb decoration of double-spirals, lozenges, and arcs; slab 52 has an elongated oval overlapping concentric arcs with triangles in their centre; and slab 67 has an S-shaped spiral between lozenges, with a network of triangles to its left. Decoration is being revealed as other kerb-stones are uncovered.

On the right of the entrance is the blocking-stone which originally closed the tomb. Above the entrance is a 'roof box' with lintel decorated with a horizontal row of triangles within rectangles; the sun shines through this box at dawn on midwinter day, and therefore it would seem to be a fanlight. From the entrance (at the SE) a passage proceeds northwest for 18·9 m to the main chamber from which extend two side-chambers and an end chamber (hereafter to be called recesses), the complete plan being therefore cruciform. All the wall-slabs of the passage are dressed and many are decorated, as are also most of the wall-slabs of the recesses. The height of the passage varies from 1·5 m near the entrance to 3·6 m where it enters the chamber, so that it is easy to examine most of the carvings while erect. The height of the main chamber, to the top of the magnificent corbelled ceiling, is 6·1 m, that of the recesses being 2·4–2·7 m. One wonders whether the main chamber had any function other than as the entrance to the three recesses, each of which bears wall-decorations and has on its floor one or more large stone basins (the northeast recess has two basins one above the other, the upper one with two circular depressions near its edge). These basins were presumably for burials or offerings or both. The decorations in the passage and recesses are mostly spirals, lozenges, chevrons, triangles, and meanders. Slab C4 (in the left-hand recess) contains a fern pattern and a design con-

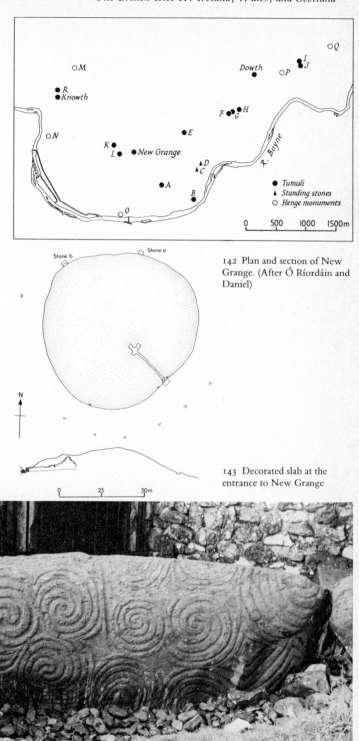

141 The great barrow cemetery at the Bend of the Boyne, Co. Meath. (After Ó Ríordáin and Daniel)

142 Plan and section of New Grange. (After Ó Ríordáin and Daniel)

143 Decorated slab at the entrance to New Grange

jectured to represent a ship with sun symbol, but the representation is too crude to inspire much confidence. The wall-slab on the right side of the end recess bears a superb carving of a three-spiral motif, and the roof slab of the right recess is richly decorated with a combination of the chief elements in the megalithic art of New Grange (O'Kelly 1967).

Dowth is 1·8 km northeast of New Grange. The great cairn is *c.* 85 m in diameter and 14 m high. It is limited by a stone kerb, one of the slabs on the east side of which is incised with several rayed circles (sun symbols ?). There are two known entrances, both on the west side. The principal entrance ('Dowth North') leads to a passage 8·2 m long ending in a cruciform arrangement of main chamber with two side-chambers and an end chamber, but additional chambers extend from the southern side-chamber. The main chamber contains a roughly rectangular large stone basin. The other entrance ('Dowth South') comprises a short passage, a circular chamber, and one side-chamber, on the lintel to which Coffey thought he saw other possible ship-carvings similar to that on slab C4 at New Grange. The roofing of all the passages and chambers at Dowth is believed to have been lintelled, but that in 'Dowth South' is now in modern concrete. A feature of this tomb is the number of sill-stones: three in the passage of 'Dowth North' and others at the entrance to nearly all the chambers beyond both entrances (Ó Ríordáin and Daniel 1964, 65–72). In the west part of the cairn there is also a souterrain of much later date.

Knowth is situated 1·2 km northwest of New Grange. The mound, composed systematically of alternating layers of turves and stones, is 90 m in diameter and 11·9 m high, and was limited by a retaining kerb of stone slabs, mostly decorated, and indeed in the aggregate providing one of the most notable known assemblages of passage-grave art. Between the kerb and the present edge of the mound is a ditch of much later date and connected with the site's adaptation for a defended seat probably of Irish Iron Age or early medieval kings.

In July 1967, on the west side of the mound an entrance was found leading to a passage *c.* 32 m long, which after a short turn to the right ends in a small rectangular chamber only a little wider than the passage. Megalithic art occurs on most of the wall-slabs of the passage where it approaches the chamber, as well as in the chamber itself, and on three roof slabs. In the passage is a stone basin not in its original position (Eogan 1967).

In August 1968, on the east side of the mound an entrance was found leading to a passage *c.* 34 m long ending in a chamber with a pair of side recesses and an end recess comprising the usual cruciform plan. The chamber has a fine corbelled roof 5·7 m high. For the last 10 m before reaching the chamber, most of the wall slabs and capstones of the passage carry megalithic art. In the north recess is a stone basin decorated both inside and out, with a decorated wall slab behind it (Eogan 1969).

Within the mound are souterrains of much later date. Those inhabiting them may have been responsible for scratching visitors' inscriptions in Ogham in various parts of the passage-grave.

Around the mound are at least sixteen 'satellite' passage-graves, several with decoration (Eogan 1974).

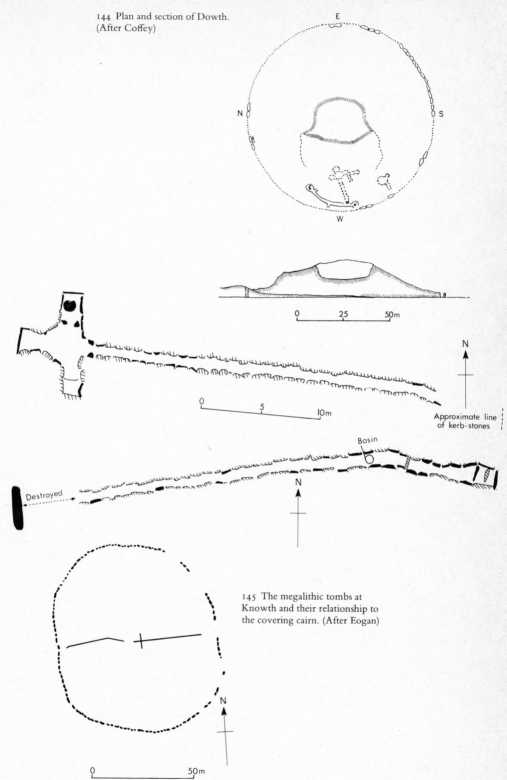

144 Plan and section of Dowth.
(After Coffey)

Approximate line
of kerb-stones

Basin

Destroyed

145 The megalithic tombs at
Knowth and their relationship to
the covering cairn. (After Eogan)

THE DELVIN VALLEY (Co. Meath)

Fourknocks is *c.* 14 km southeast of New Grange, between the Bend of the Boyne and Dublin, and a short distance north of the Delvin river. The passage-grave is in an elliptical mound 20 m maximum diameter and *c.* 3·5 m high, limited by a low wall of rubble broken only at the entrance. From the entrance at the NNE, a passage 5·18 m long proceeds to a large pear-shaped chamber 6·4 m × 5·5 m, with three recesses, the whole presenting the usual cruciform plan. The main chamber is too large to have had an entirely corbelled roof. Corbelling sprang from the walls but a central post-hole implies a post supporting a timber framework above which was probably a roofing of turves or thatch. The passage was either unroofed, roofed with flimsy materials, or despoiled of its roofing soon after being built, as none of its wall-slabs was inclined inwards from the pressure which stone roofing would have imposed. At least twenty-four interments were found in the three recesses and twenty-eight in the passage but none at all in the main chamber; twenty-six were inhumations and twenty-six were cremations. Grave-goods included stone beads and pendants, bone pins and bodkins, and 'marbles'. Of the many decorated slabs, two call for special mention. The first wall-slab on the left as the chamber is entered from the passage is decorated with a crude human face with a body belt well beneath it, and falls clearly into the category of the 'statue-menhir' as found in Brittany. The general impression is that it represents an adult male. Another slab, whose original position is uncertain, is decorated with an evidently female figure, the head and body being shown by a small and large spiral, and the legs by a suitable convention within a frame. The lintels of two of the three recesses are decorated with a motif of lozenges within zig-zags. The passage was blocked after the final burials had been made, but the mound was later re-used for Bronze Age interments in stone cists (Hartnett 1957).

ANGLESEY contains two notable passage-graves – Barclodiad y Gawres and Bryn Celli Ddu. *Barclodiad y Gawres* is sited on the cliff edge on the west coast. Its name is Welsh for 'The Giantess's Apronful'. The mound, which is roughly circular, is 27 m in diameter and had no retaining kerb. The highest cover slab is 2 m high, but the mound, at the time of excavation, nowhere exceeded 1 m in height. The entrance had been on the north side but was destroyed together with the outer part of the passage. The surviving length of passage is *c.* 7 m, and it leads to a chamber directly beneath the centre of the mound. This chamber has the usual pair of side-chambers or recesses and an end chamber, the whole presenting a cruciform plan. The western side-chamber has an annexe, and yielded the cremated remains of two individuals, probably young male adults, with two bone pins most likely used for fastening the clothing. The entrance to this side-chamber had been blocked. The wall-slab at the rear end of each side-chamber, and three wall-slabs where the passage meets the main chamber, bear 'megalithic art', comprising lozenges, concentric circles, spirals, chevrons, and zig-zags (Powell and Daniel 1956).

Bryn Celli Ddu is near the southeast coast and within a mile of
Plas Newydd. The name is Welsh for 'The Hill of the Dark
Grove'. A circular mound – originally 27 m in diameter but now
restored to only half its size to enable the fourteen standing
stones to be seen – is limited by a double retaining kerb, best seen
around the entrance. This kerb is set in a ditch now believed to
belong to an earlier henge monument of which the circle of
fourteen stones was the central feature (O'Kelly 1969; Lynch
1970, 55–61).

From the entrance at the NE, a passage proceeds for 7 m to a
polygonal chamber 2·4 m across. In this chamber is a carefully
dressed standing stone projecting 1·7 m above the floor. Its top is
clear of the roof of the chamber and it should therefore be a
ritual object, perhaps with the function of the continental baetyl.
There are two shorter 'baetyls' on the south side of the passage
opposite a low bench. The chamber contained little except a few
human bones both burnt and unburnt. A *petit tranchet derivative*
flint implement came from the chamber or passage and another
was found in the mound.

Behind the polygonal chamber, in the centre of the mound, is a
pit 1·2 m in diameter and 1·4 m deep, which contained a burnt
human ear-bone, and was covered by a slab. Beside this pit is a
slab bearing on both sides megalithic art in the form of meanders
(the slab, now in the National Museum of Wales at Cardiff, is
replaced on the site by a concrete replica). In front of the entrance
to the mound was a small three-sided structure in which an ox
had been sacrificed.

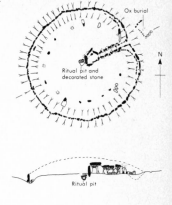

146 Plan of Bryn Celli Ddu,
Anglesey. (After Hemp)

147 Bryn Celli Ddu passage-
grave, Anglesey, a monument
with a complex history.

ORKNEY. *Maes Howe*, the finest of all the chamber tombs in Britain, is just north of the road between Kirkwall and Stromness, *c.* 14·5 km west of Kirkwall. The mound is roughly circular and is 35 m in diameter and 7·4 m high, and contains within it two revetment walls 3·3 m apart, which have added to its stability. It is placed eccentrically on an artificially levelled berm 14–21 m wide, bounded by a flat-bottomed ditch 7·5–18 m wide and *c.* 1 m deep. The present outer bank is modern but may replace an original feature.

From the southwest, the present entrance leads after 2 m to the original door-jambs. A step downwards leads to a slightly wider passage which continues for 9 m to the main chamber. On the left just inside the doorway is a recess to contain the closing slab (still in this recess) when the tomb was in use. At the far end of the passage, beyond another pair of door-jambs, is the main chamber, nearly 5 m square, with walls that are vertical for *c.* 1·4 m and above that are corbelled, converging towards the roof. The original masonry survives for a height of 4 m, and is covered by a modern concrete imitation of corbelling, as the top of the original corbelled roof was destroyed in antiquity or perhaps by the Vikings. In each corner of the main chamber is a square buttress. Leading from the main chamber are two side cells and an end cell, forming with the other elements a cruciform plan. Each cell is raised nearly 1 m above the floor of the main chamber, and on the floor beneath the entrance to each is still the original

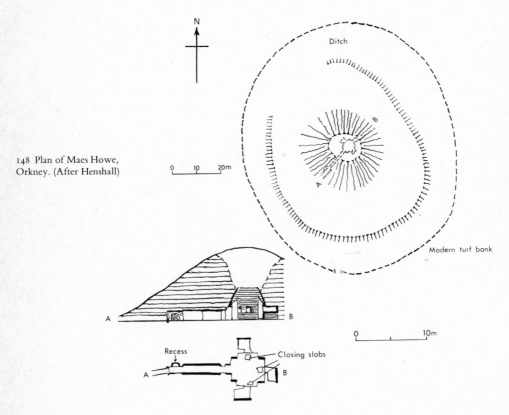

148 Plan of Maes Howe, Orkney. (After Henshall)

149 Interior of Maes Howe, Orkney. Drawing by A. Gibb (1861)

blocking slab. The architectural magnificence of this tomb is due largely to the availability in the region of thinly laminated flagstone and the facility with which it could be worked. Recorded finds were limited to a few fragments of human skull and some bones and teeth of a horse (Henshall 1963, 219–22).

The tomb is of added interest by reason of the walls being incised with twenty-four Viking inscriptions in Runic, some purporting to describe finds of treasure in the tomb (Dickins 1930). There are also Viking engravings of a dragon-like figure or lion, a serpent-knot, and a seal or walrus on the right buttress at the far end (Mackenzie 1937). It is believed that all these Viking scribings are mid-twelfth century.

The Kilmartin cairn cemetery, Argyllshire

The Kilmartin Burn flows southward through a fertile valley between lofty hills to the head of Loch Crinan. In this valley, especially between Kilmartin and Crinan Moss, is an extensive and mainly linear cemetery of later prehistoric cairns. Several contain grooved stone cists clearly derived from wooden originals, and some of their slabs are decorated (Scott 1966 and lecture to Prehistoric Society 1973).

The earliest element is probably *Nether Largie South cairn* (NR 828979), *c.* 40 m in diameter, now roughly circular but probably originally long or trapezoid. Most of the cairn material was removed before Greenwell explored the site in 1864. Slightly southwest of centre is a Clyde-type chamber of four compartments. Within the limits of the cairn on the north and south-southwest are stone cists in line with the axis of the main cemetery and evidently Early Bronze Age insertions into the original Neolithic Clyde-type long cairn. From the northern cist (no longer exposed) Greenwell recovered a food vessel now in the British Museum.

Nether Largie Mid cairn (NR 830983), *c.* 30 m in diameter, was formerly 3 m high but removal of many of the stones for road repairing exposed the two cists now visible, both well off centre; the northern cist has the side slabs grooved to receive the end slabs. Just within the east margin of the cairn was a slab bearing five cupmarks, face downwards when found. *Nether Largie North cairn* (NR 830984), 21 m in diameter and formerly *c.* 2·7 m high, contains slightly north of centre a stone cist with cover slab bearing carvings of ten copper or bronze axe-heads and forty-one cup-marks some of which seem to be earlier than the axe-carvings as those within the latter are shallower. The northern end slab bears carvings of two axe-heads, cutting edge upwards. In 1930, nearly three hundred cartloads of stones were removed from this cairn to provide materials for the protecting wall now surrounding it.

North of the last and west of Kilmartin church is the *Glebe cairn* (NR 833989), *c.* 33·5 m in diameter and still 4 m high. From the central stone cist Greenwell obtained an inhumation with a food vessel of Irish type and a jet necklace. The cairn was enlarged to receive a second stone cist which likewise contained a food

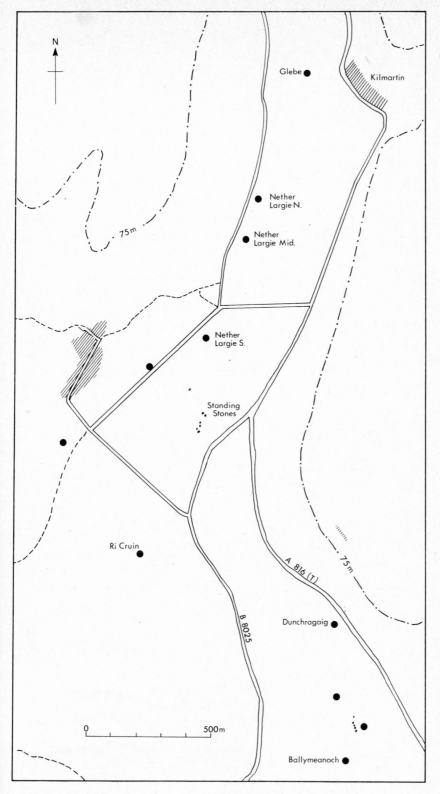

150 The Kilmartin cairn cemetery, Argyllshire. (After Scott)

N

Glebe

Kilmartin

Nether Largie N.

Nether Largie Mid.

75m

Nether Largie S.

Standing Stones

Ri Cruin

A 816 (T)

75m

B 8025

Dunchragaig

Ballymeanoch

0   500m

vessel of Irish type, most likely with an inhumation.

About 1 km south-southwest of Nether Largie South cairn is the *Ri Cruin cairn* (NR 825971), *c.* 20 m in diameter. Most of the cairn material has been plundered, exposing three stone cists, all off centre. The west end slab of the southern cist bears carvings of seven axe-heads, cutting edge sideways. This cist formerly contained a slab incised with a rake-like symbol of uncertain meaning, now destroyed but a cast of it is in the National Museum of Antiquities at Edinburgh. The side slabs of these cists are grooved to receive the end slabs.

To the southeast are the *Dunchragaig cairn* (NR 833968) containing three stone cists, and the *Ballymeanoch mound* (NR 833962). The latter is a round barrow surrounded by a ditch and outer bank and with a causeway at the north-northeast and possibly another at the south – southwest, resembling a henge monument. It contained a stone cist near the centre, and a smaller cist to the northeast yielded a beaker (D. L. Clarke's Northern British type) to Greenwell. About 8 km to the south-southeast at *Badden* (NR 858890) is the find-spot of a grooved cist-slab decorated with lozenge pattern, now in Glasgow Art Gallery and Museum. Other cairns in this area contain grooved stone cists. This is the only area in Scotland where they occur, and they seem to be related to those in the Scilly Isles and in Brittany. The orientation of these cists follows no rule, in this respect differing from that of the Dartmoor stone cists which are nearly all SE–NW.

Practical information

Members of the museum profession, university lecturers, and certain other people engaged in serious study, may obtain a *Cultural Identity Card of the Council of Europe*, which enables the person to whom it is issued to get free admission to most museums and many archaeological sites in Europe (except those in the country of issue). Application should be made to the Central Bureau for Educational Visits and Exchanges, 43 Dorset Street, London, W1.

Tourist excursions are run from Cairo to the pyramids of Giza and Sakkara; from Luxor to the Valley of the Kings; from Athens to Mycenae; from Rome to Cerveteri and Tarquinia; from Dublin to New Grange and the Bend of the Boyne; and from Kirkwall to Maes Howe and other prehistoric sites. These are all useful for a first visit but do not normally leave enough time at any of the sites for the needs of the serious student.

Details of buses given below vary with the season and should be verified locally.

EGYPTIAN PYRAMIDS. The Giza group can be reached by the no. 8 bus from Liberation Square, Cairo, to the Mena House Hotel. The Sakkara group can be approached by taking a bus from Giza village to Badrashein and then walking for about 3 km, but the service is rather erratic and there is much to be said for hiring a car, preferably from Giza or the bus terminus near the Mena House Hotel. The average tourist tends to be pestered at Giza by dragomans, but they can be kind to a serious student who has taken the trouble to learn a little colloquial Arabic.

THE VALLEY OF THE KINGS. First of all it is essential to obtain an Antiquities Ticket from the Service of Antiquities office in Cairo (next to the Egyptian Museum) or Luxor. To cross the Nile from one's hotel in Luxor may entail prolonged bargaining with boatmen unless one goes across with one's own party under a recognized guide. On reaching the west side of the river, one is confronted by an assemblage of cars, donkeys, and donkey-boys desiring custom. The cost of hiring a donkey with boy is about a quarter that of a chauffeur-driven car. The car drivers and donkey-boys know the location of all the most visited tombs and their custodians; the latter are usually well informed on any other tombs which a serious student may wish to visit, and if they do not know the answer they can always refer to the Inspectorate of Antiquities at Qurneh.

The tombs of Tuthmosis III, Amenophis II, Tutankhamun, Ay, Horemheb, Ramesses I, Sety I, Merneptah, and Ramesses

III, V–VI, and IX are electrically lit, but those of Horemheb and Merneptah were closed for repairs in 1972.

MYCENAEAN THOLOS TOMBS. By joining a tourist excursion from Athens to Mycenae and missing the guided visit to the citadel, it is possible to visit the tholos tombs of Aegisthus and Clytemnestra and the Lion Tomb as well as the Treasury of Atreus which is included in the normal tour. By staying for a night or two in a hotel in Nauplia it is possible to catch a morning bus to Argos which links with one from Argos to Mycenae, reaching Mycenae about 11 am. The nine tholos tombs can then be visited on foot and lunch taken (by the historically minded at the Belle Hélène Hotel where Schliemann, Wace, and others stayed while doing their researches). A torch should be taken for inspecting interiors such as the side-chamber in the Treasury of Atreus. Buses leave Mycenae about 3 pm and 6 pm for the return via Argos to Nauplia. Tiryns and its tholos tomb are within walking distance (about 3 km) of Nauplia. There are archaeological museums at Argos and Nauplia. The other tholos tombs, especially those in Messenia, are difficult to reach without a reliable guide, except that near the Palace of Nestor at Pylos.

THE NECROPOLIS OF SALAMIS (CYPRUS). From the Municipal Market in Famagusta there is a morning bus which stops at the custodian's office at the entrance to Salamis (about 7 km). The most important tombs are south of the road between here and the Monastery of St Barnabas (1·5 km), and they should be visited in the morning, which affords the best light for photographs as their entrances mostly face eastwards. Pack lunch (brought from hotel) can be taken at the Monastery of St Barnabas where mineral waters are on sale. A path southwards from the monastery leads (1·5 km) to the village of Enkomi, just east of which is Tomb 77 (the cenotaph of Nicocreon). There are buses from Enkomi back to Famagusta. The area of the tombs tends to be muddy in winter.

ETRUSCAN CEMETERIES. From Civitavecchia, where there are good hotels including the Sunbay Park Hotel just outside the town, buses go from outside the Cathedral to Tarquinia. A ticket for both museum and tombs has to be obtained from the museum, but the painted tombs, which are all on the Monterozzi, must be visited in the morning as they are closed in the afternoon. Lunch can be taken in Tarquinia, and the museum (among the finest for Etruscan material) visited in the afternoon.

From Rome there are buses to Cerveteri, and the Banditaccia Etruscan cemetery is about twenty minutes' walk from the town. Admission to the Monumental Enclosure is by ticket obtainable at the entrance. The tombs are open both morning and afternoon. It is good policy to visit a selection of tombs in the Monumental Enclosure in the morning, and to arrange with the custodian to visit other tombs in the afternoon, if possible including the Regolini-Galassi tomb (only five minutes' walk from the town, and easy to locate as it is approached by a path through iron gates and is covered by a modern hut). The excellent museum, established in the Castle in 1968, should be included in the tour.

SARDINIA AND CORSICA. Alghero is an excellent centre for visiting the prehistoric tombs and cemeteries of northwestern Sardinia. Anghelu Ruju can be reached by the bus from Alghero to S. Marco; there is a bus stop by the site, not quite so far as the terminus. The tombs at Sant Andria Priu have to be approached by car along a road to a spot 6 km east of Bonorva. Elephant Rock is included in the normal tourist excursion from Alghero to Castelsardo. Other practical advice is given in Guido (1963), 212–13.

Many of the prehistoric sites in Corsica can be reached from Propriano where there are good hotels. Tourist excursions are run from Propriano to Filitosa, but a car is essential for visiting other sites.

THE BALEARIC ISLANDS. The most accessible group of rock tombs in Majorca is at Cala San Vicente, where Hemp's tombs 6–9 are in a public garden in the housing estate of Los Encinares, 1·5 km south of the Hotel Molins. The rock tombs at Son Sunyer, Son Toni Amer and elsewhere are difficult to find without well-informed local guidance. The cemetery of Son Real is east of the road midway between Arta and Puerto de Alcudia. Nearly all the best prehistoric sites in Minorca are near or south of the road between Mahon and Ciudadela and may be visited by either bus or car. The best naveta is Els Tudons, 4 km east of Ciudadela, and perhaps the next best are the two at Rafal Rubi, 7 km west of Mahon. The beautifully sited group of sepulchral caves at Cales Coves can be reached by a footpath (1·5 km) from Cala'n Porter.

THE CHANNEL ISLANDS. Both Guernsey and Jersey are well served by local buses and none of the prehistoric tombs here described is more than a few minutes' walk from a bus route. There are museums at St Peter Port and St Helier.

THE BRITISH ISLES: WESSEX AND THE SOUTHWEST. Details of access to almost all the sites described are given in Dyer (1973). The Normanton and Winterbourne Stoke cross-roads groups are within 2 km of Stonehenge. Several of the sites mentioned on Dartmoor involve a good deal of walking.

THE BRITISH ISLES: IRELAND, WALES, AND SCOTLAND. Perhaps the ideal way to explore the tombs in the Bend of the Boyne is on foot and there is a Youth Hostel in the area at Mellifont. In Anglesey the remotest tomb here described is Barclodiad y Gawres for which a car is necessary, and the key has to be obtained from the Department of the Environment, Caernarvon. Bryn Celli Ddu is about 3 km from the tubular bridge across Menai Strait, and the cairns of Plas Newydd and Bryn yr Hen Bobl are in the vicinity. In Orkney, the buses between Kirkwall and Stromness pass the entrance to Maes Howe and go within a short distance of the Onstan chambered cairn, the Ring of Brodgar, and the Stones of Stenness. The Kilmartin cairn cemetery lies nearly all within 1 km of the A816(T) between Cairnbaan and Kilmartin.

References and Bibliography

Abbreviations for titles of periodicals

(Only those quoted more than once are abbreviated)

ActaA	*Acta Archaeologica*
AJA	*American Journal of Archaeology*
AntiqJ	*Antiquaries Journal*
BSA	*Papers of the British School at Athens*
BSR	*Papers of the British School at Rome*
BIALU	*Bulletin of the Institute of Archaeology, London University*
JEA	*Journal of Egyptian Archaeology*
JHS	*Journal of Hellenic Studies*
JPOS	*Journal of the Palestine Oriental Society*
JRS	*Journal of Roman Studies*
MDIO	*Mitteilungen des Instituts Orientforschung*
MonAnt	*Monumenti Antichi*
ProcDorsetAS	*Proceedings Dorset Natural History and Archaeological Society*
PPS	*Proceedings of the Prehistoric Society*
RSP	*Rivista di Scienze Preistorichi*
WAM	*Wiltshire Archaeological and Natural History Magazine*
ZAS	*Zeitschrift für Ägyptische Sprache*

Numbers in the first column indicate the chapters for which these items are particularly relevant. These numbers are in **bold** face for items of special importance. General works are shown in the same column by the letter G. Where nothing appears in this column the item usually refers to points of detail sometimes in three or more chapters.

ABDUL-QADER, M.M. (1966). *Development of the Funerary Beliefs and Practices . . . in the Private Tombs of the New Kingdom at Thebes.* Cairo.

5 ABERCROMBY, J. (1912). *Bronze Age Pottery of Great Britain and Ireland.* Oxford.

1 ADDY, S.O. (1918–20). 'House Burial'. *J. Derbyshire Archaeol. Soc.,* 40–2.

ÅKERSTROM, A. (1970). 'The tomb of the Olimpiadi . . .', in Vanoni, L.C. and Ponzanelli, S. *Scritti di Archaeologia ed Arte in onore di Carlo Maurilio Lerici.* Milan.

6 ALMAGRO, M. (1966). *Las Estelas Decoradas del Suroeste Peninsular.* Biblioteca Praehistorica Hispana. VIII. Madrid.

ANATI, E. (1963). *Palestine before the Hebrews.* London and New York.

ARRIBAS, A. (1964). *The Iberians.* London.

21 ASHBEE, P. (1956). 'The excavation of a round barrow on Canford Heath'. *ProcDorsetAS* 76, 39–50.

G — (1960). *The Bronze Age Round Barrow in Britain.* London.

8 — (1963). 'The Wilsford shaft'. *Antiquity* 37, 116–20.

8 — (1966). 'The dating of the Wilsford Shaft'. *Antiquity* 40, 227–8.

G — (1970). *The Earthen Long Barrow in Britain.* London.

21 ATKINSON, R.J.C. (1954). *Excursion Guide, Prehistoric Society Scottish Meeting 1954.* Edinburgh.

2 — (1956). *Stonehenge.* London and Toronto.

21 — (1965). 'Wayland's Smithy'. *Antiquity* 39, 126–33.

2, 3 ATKINSON, R.J.C. et al. (1951). *Excavations at Dorchester, Oxon.* Oxford.

AUBREY, J. (1881). *Remaines of Gentilism and Judaisme.* Edited by J. Britton. London.

11 BADAWY, A. (1954a). 'Dispositifs architecturaux contre le viol des tombes égyptiennes', in *Bull. Faculty of Arts,* Cairo Univ. XVI/i. Cairo. 69–102.

13 — (1954b). *History of Egyptian Architecture.* I. To the end of the Old Kingdom. Cairo.

13 — (1964). 'The stellar destiny of pharaoh and the so-called air-shafts of Cheops' pyramid'. *MDIO* 10, 189–206.

— (1966). *History of Egyptian Architecture.* II. The first to second intermediate period. Berkeley and Los Angeles.

14 — (1968). *History of Egyptian Architecture.* III. The New Kingdom. Berkeley and Los Angeles.

13 BAER, K. (1960). *Rank and Title in the Old Kingdom.* Chicago.

14 BAIKIE, J. (1932). *Egyptian Antiquities in the Nile Valley.* London.

BEAN, G.E. (1966). *Aegean Turkey.* London and New York.

— (1968). *Turkey's Southern Shore.* London.

— (1971). *Turkey beyond the Maeander.* London.

1 BEHN, F. (1924). *Hausurnen.* Berlin.

BERCIU, D. (1967). *Romania.* London and New York.

BLEGEN, C.W. (1954). 'Excavations at Pylos 1953'. *AJA* 58, 27–32.

— (1963). *Troy.* London and New York.

BLOCH, R. (1960). *The Origins of Rome.* London and New York.

7 BOASE, T.S.R. (1972). *Death in the Middle Ages.* London and New York.

1, 17 BOETHIUS, A. and WARD PERKINS, J.B. (1970). *Etruscan and Roman Architecture.* Harmondsworth.

BOGNAR-KUTZIAN, I. (1963). *The Copper Age Cemetery of Tiszapolgar-Basatanya.* Archaeologia Hungaria 42, N.S. Budapest.

9 BONNER, C. (1941). 'The ship of the soul on a group of grave stelae from Terenuthis' [Lower Egypt]. *Proc. American Philosophical Soc.* 85, 84–91.

17 BRADFORD, J.S.P. (1957). *Ancient Landscapes.* London and Toronto.

G BRANIGAN, K. (1970). *The Tombs of Mesara.* London.

18 Bray, W. (1963). 'The Ozieri culture of Sardinia'. *RSP* 18, 155–90.

Brea, L. Bernabo (1957). *Sicily*. London and New York.

2, 3 Breuil, H. and Lantier, R. (1965). *The Men of the Old Stone Age*. London.

6 Briard, J. (1968). 'Un tumulus du Bronze ancien à Lescongar-en-Plouhinec (Finistère)'. *Gallia Préhistoire* XI, Fasc. i, 247–59.

5 — (1970). 'Un tumulus du Bronze Ancien: Kernonen en Plouvorn (Finistère)'. *L'Anthropologie* 74, 5–56.

3 Broholm, H.C. and Hald, M. (1940). *Bronze Age Costume of Denmark*. Copenhagen.

3 — (1948). *Bronze Age Fashion*. Copenhagen.

4 Brøndsted, J. (1960). *The Vikings*. Harmondsworth.

4 Brothwell, D.R. (1961). 'Cannibalism in Early Britain'. *Antiquity* 35, 304–7.

4 — (1971). 'Forensic aspects of the so-called Neolithic skeleton Q1 from Maiden Castle, Dorset'. *World Archaeology* 3(2), 233–41.

— (1972). *Digging up Bones*. Second edition. London.

12 Brown, F.E. (1931). 'Violation of sepulture in Palestine'. *Amer. J. Philology*, 1–29.

Bruce-Mitford, R.L.S. (1972). *The Sutton Hoo Ship Burial: A Handbook*. London.

G Brunton, G. (1946). 'Burial customs', in Engelbach, R. (editor). *Introduction to Egyptian Archaeology*. Cairo, 199–244.

1 Bryan, W.R. (1925). *Italic Hut Urns and Hut Urn Cemeteries*. Rome.

6 Burgess, C. (1962). 'Two grooved ogival daggers of the Early Bronze Age from South Wales'. *Bull. Board of Celtic Studies* 20(1), 75–94.

12 Burnard, R. (1902). 'The disappearing stone monuments of Dartmoor'. *Trans. Devon Assoc.* 34, 166–7.

3 Butler, J.J. (1963). *Bronze Age Connections across the North Sea*. Palaeohistoria. IX. Groningen.

10 Cadogan, G. (1967). 'Late Minoan IIIC pottery from the Kephala tholos tomb'. *BSA* 62, 257–65.

21 Case, H.J. (1952). 'The excavation of two round barrows at Poole, Dorset'. *PPS* 18, 148–59.

21 (1957). 'The Lambourn Seven Barrows'. *Berkshire Archaeol. J.* 55, 15–31.

7 Castaldi, E. (1965). 'La Frammentazione rituale in etnologia e in preistoria'. *RSP* XX(i), 247–77.

— (1969). *Tombe di Giganti nel Sassarese*. Rome.

2 Charles, R.P. (1965). *Anthropologie Archéologique de la Crète*. Athens.

G Childe, V.G. (1945). 'Directional changes in funerary practices during 50,000 years'. *Man* 45, article 4.

G — (1947). *Prehistoric Communities of the British Isles*. Second edition. London.

G — (1957). *The Dawn of European Civilisation*. Sixth edition. London.

Clark, J.G.D. (1952). *Prehistoric Europe: the Economic Basis*. London and New York.

G — (1969). *World Prehistory, a New Outline*. Cambridge.

Clarke, D.L. (1970). *Beaker Pottery of Great Britain and Ireland*. Cambridge.

3 Clifford, E.M. (1950). 'The Cotswold megalithic culture', in *Early Cultures of North-West Europe*, edited by C. Fox and B. Dickins. Cambridge. 23–40.

21 Clifford, E.M. and Daniel, G.E. (1940). 'The Rodmarton and Avening Portholes'. *PPS* 6, 133–65.

9, 22 Coffey, G. (1912). *New Grange*. Dublin and London.

20 Collum, V.C.C. (1935). *The re-excavation of the Déhus chambered mound . . . Guernsey*. Guernsey.

12 Cook, S.A. (1932). 'A Nazareth inscription on the violation of tombs'. *Palestine Exploration Fund Quarterly*, 85–7.

21 Corcoran, J.X.W.P. (1969). 'The Cotswold-Severn Group', in *Megalithic Enquiries in the West of Britain*, edited by T.G.E. Powell. Liverpool. 13–106.

10 — (1972). 'Multi-period construction and the . . . long cairn . . .', in *Prehistoric Man in Wales and the West*, edited by F. Lynch and C. Burgess. Bath. 31–64.

16 Courtois, J.C. (1969). 'Enkomi-Alasia . . .', in *Archaeologia Viva* II(3), 93–112.

9 Cumont, F. (1922). *The After Life in Roman Paganism*. Yale. Chapter VI. The journey to the Beyond.

21 Daniel, G.E. (1937). 'The chambered barrow in Parc le Breos Cwm . . .'. *PPS* 3, 71–86.

21, 22 — (1950). *The Prehistoric Chamber Tombs of England and Wales*. Cambridge.

20 — (1960). *The Prehistoric Chamber Tombs of France*. London.

— (1963). 'The Personality of Wales', in *Culture and Environment: Essays in honour of Sir Cyril Fox*, edited by I.L. Foster and L. Alcock. London. 7–24.

10 — (1972). *Megaliths in History*. London.

9 Davidson, H.R.E. (1967). *Pagan Scandinavia*. London and New York.

De Laet, S.J. (1958). *The Low Countries*. London and New York.

17 Dennis, G. (1883). *Cities and Cemeteries of Etruria*. Third edition. London.

6, 14 Desroches-Noblecourt, C. (1963). *Tutankhamen*. London.

11, 12 De Zulueta, F. (1932). 'Violation of sepulture in Palestine'. *JRS* 22, 184–97.

12 Dickins, B. (1930). 'The Runic inscriptions of Maeshowe'. *Proc. Orkney Ant. Soc.* 8, 27–30.

Dikaios, P. (1953). *Khirokitia*. Oxford.

Dyer, J. (1973). *Southern England: An Archaeological Guide*. London.

13 Edwards, I.E.S. (1972). *The Pyramids of Egypt*. London.

9 Elgee, H.W. and F. (1949). 'An Early Bronze Age burial in a boat-shaped wooden coffin from northeast Yorkshire'. *PPS* 15, 87–106.

10 ELLIS, H.R.E. (1943). *The Road to Hel.* Cambridge.

4 EMERY, W.B. (1961). *Archaic Egypt.* Harmondsworth.

5 — (1962). *A Funerary Repast in an Egyptian Tomb of the Archaic Period.* Leiden.

22 EOGAN, G. (1968). 'Excavations at Knowth, Co. Meath, 1962–65'. *Proc. Royal Irish Acad.* 66(C), 299–400.

22 — (1967, 1969). 'Excavations at Knowth, Co. Meath . . .'. *Antiquity* 41, 302–4; 43, 8–14.

22 — (1974). Report on . . . Knowth . . .'. *Proc. Royal Irish Acad.* 74 (C), 11–112.

10 ETTLINGER, E. (1952). 'The association of burials with popular assemblies, fairs and races in Ancient Ireland'. *Etudes Celtiques* (Paris) 6, 30–61.

9 EVANS, A.J. (1906). *Prehistoric Tombs of Knossos.* London.

22 EVANS, E.E. (1966). *Prehistoric and Early Christian Ireland: A Guide.* London and New York.

EVANS, J.D. (1956). 'The "Dolmens" of Malta and the origins of the Tarxien Cemetery culture'. *PPS* 22, 85–101.

2, 6 — (1959). *Malta.* London and New York.

5 — (1971). *The Prehistoric Antiquities of the Maltese Islands: a Survey.* London.

13 FAKHRY, A. (1969). *The Pyramids.* Second edition. Chicago.

13 FAULKNER, R.O. (1969). *The Ancient Egyptian Pyramid Texts.* Oxford.

G FILIP, J. (1962). *Celtic Civilisation and its Heritage.* Prague.

— (1966), editor. *Investigations Archéologiques en Tchécoslovaquie.* Prague.

2 FORRER, R. (1922). 'Rites funéraires néolithiques en Alsace: pour que le mort ne revienne plus'. *Bull. Soc. Préhist. Fr.* 19, 138–156.

G FOX, Sir Cyril (1959). *Life and Death in the Bronze Age.* London.

2 FRAZER, Sir J.G. (1933–6). *The Fear of the Dead in Primitive Religion.* London.

4 GADD, C.J. (1960). 'The spirit of living sacrifices in tombs'. *Iraq* 22, 51–8.

1 GALLAY, A. (1972). 'Recherches préhistoriques au Petit-Chasseur à Sion', in *Helvetia Archaeologica.* 10/11, 35–89.

GARROD, D.A.E. and BATE, D.M.A. (1937). *The Stone Age of Mount Carmel.* I. London.

2 GARSTANG, J. (1907). *Burial Customs of Ancient Egypt.* London.

2 GEJVALL, N.G. (1969). 'Cremations', in *Science in Archaeology*, edited by D.R. Brothwell and E.S. Higgs. Second edition. London. 468–79.

8 GELLING, P.S. and DAVIDSON, H.R.E. (1969). *The Chariot of the Sun.* London and New York.

6 GIMBUTAS, M. (1953). 'Battle axe or cult axe?'. *Man* 53, article 73.

G — (1956). *The Prehistory of Eastern Europe.* Part I. Cambridge, Mass.

GIOT, P.R. (1958). 'The chambered barrow of Barnenez in Finistère'. *Antiquity* 32, 149–53.

20 — (1960). *Brittany.* London and New York.

8 GORBEA M.J.A. (1968). *Los 'Idolos Betilos del Bronce 1 Hispano: sas tipos y cronologia,* Trabajos de Prehistoria 25. Madrid.

6 GRACE, V.R. (1940). 'A Cypriote tomb and Minoan evidence for its date'. *AJA* 44, 10–52.

12 GREEN, C. (1963). *Sutton Hoo: the Excavation of a Royal Ship Burial.* London.

4 GREENAWAY, R.D. (1958). 'The Tinkinswood Cat'. *Trans. Cardiff Naturalists' Soc.* 85, 16–20.

2 GRESHAM, C.A. (1972). 'Burials in megalithic chambered tombs', in *Prehistoric Man in Wales and the West: Essays in honour of Lily F. Chitty*, edited by F. Lynch and C. Burgess. 65–6. Bath.

9 GRIERSON, P. (1970). 'The purpose of the Sutton Hoo coins'. *Antiquity* 44, 14–18.

9 GRIFFITHS, J.G. (1966). 'The celestial ladder and the gate of heaven in Egyptian ritual'. *The Expository Times* (Edinburgh) 78, 54–5.

9 GRINSELL, L.V. (1941). 'The boat of the dead in the Bronze Age'. *Antiquity* 15, 360–70.

8 — (1942). 'The Kivik Cairn, Scania'. *Antiquity* 16, 160–74.

9 — (1943). 'The boat of the dead in Ancient Egypt'. *Antiquity* 17, 47–50.

13 — (1947). *Egyptian Pyramids.* Gloucester.

8 — (1951). 'Shaving the eyebrows as a funeral custom'. *Man* 50, article 231.

G — (1953a). *Ancient Burial-Mounds of England.* Second edition. London.

— (1953b). 'Early funerary superstitions in Britain'. *Folklore* 64, 271–81.

— (1957a). 'Archaeological Gazetteer', in *Victoria County History of Wiltshire.* I, (1), 21–279.

9 — (1957b). 'The ferryman and his fee'. *Folklore* 68, 257–69.

21 — (1957c). *The Stoney Littleton Long Barrow.* H.M.S.O. Official Guide. London.

21 — (1958). *The Archaeology of Wessex.* London.

— (1959). *Dorset Barrows.* Dorchester.

7 — (1962). 'The breaking of objects as a funerary rite'. *Folklore* 72, 475–91.

21 — (1966). *Belas Knap long barrow.* H.M.S.O. Official Guide. London.

12 — (1967). 'Barrow treasure . . .'. *Folklore* 78, 1–38.

21 — (1970). *Hetty Pegler's Tump, Uley.* H.M.S.O. Official Guide. London.

— (1972). 'Somerset Barrows. Part II'. *Somerset Archaeol. Nat. Hist.* 115. Supplement.

7 — (1973a). 'The breaking of objects as a funerary rite: Supplement'. *Folklore* 84, 111–14.

10 — (1973b). 'Witchcraft at some prehistoric sites', in *The Witch Figure*, edited by Venetia Newall. London. 72–9.

18 GROSJEAN, R. (1966a). *La Corse avant l'Histoire.* Paris.

18 — (1966b). 'Recent work in Corsica'. *Antiquity* 40, 190–8.

18 — (1972). *Filitosa: haut lieu de la Corse préhistorique.* Seventh edition. Centre de Préhistoire Corse.

10 GUENIN, M.G. (1934). 'Le culte des pierres en Gaule et en France d'après les textes contem-

porains du Vᵉ au Xᵉ siècle', in *Corpus du Folklore Préhistorique* I, edited by P. Saintyves. Paris. 193–201.

18 GUIDO, M. (1963). *Sardinia*. London and New York.

10 — (1967). *Sicily: an Archaeological Guide.* London and New York.

— (1972). *Southern Italy: an Archaeological Guide.* London.

G HABENSTEIN, R. W. and LAMERS, W. M. (1960). *Funeral Customs the World Over*. Milwaukee.

HARDEN, D. B. (1962). *The Phoenicians*. London and New York.

22 HARTNETT, P. J. (1957). 'Excavation of a passage-grave at Fourknocks, County Meath'. *Proc. Royal Irish Acad.* 58(C), 197–277.

2 HASEK, I. (1959). *The Early Únětician Cemetery at Dolní Počernice near Prague. Fontes Archaeologici Pragenses* 2. Prague.

9 HASSAN, S. (1946). *Excavations at Giza*. VI (i). The Solar Boats of Khafra. Cairo.

5 HATT, J. J. (1951). *La Tombe Gallo-Romaine.* Paris.

20 HAWKES, J. (1937). *The Archaeology of the Channel Islands. II. The Bailiwick of Jersey.* St Helier, Jersey.

G HAYES, W. C. (1953). *The Scepter of Egypt.* I. New York.

G — (1959). *The Scepter of Egypt.* II. Cambridge, Mass.

5 HEIDEL, A. (1946). *The Gilgamesh Epic and Old Testament Parallels.* Chicago.

19 HEMP, W. J. (1927). 'Some rock-cut tombs . . . in Mallorca'. *Archaeologia* 76, 121–60.

22 — (1930). 'The chambered cairn of Bryn Celli Ddu'. *Archaeologia* 80, 179–214.

19 — (1932). 'The navetas of Menorca'. *AntiqJ.* 12, 127–35.

6 HENCKEN, H. O'N. (1968). *Tarquinia and Etruscan Origins.* London and New York.

2 HENSCHEN, F. (1965). *The Human Skull: a Cultural History.* London.

3 HENSHALL, A. S. (1950). 'Textiles and weaving appliances in prehistoric Britain'. *PPS* 16, 130–62.

22 — (1963). *Chamber Tombs of Scotland.* I. Edinburgh.

22 — (1972). *Chamber Tombs of Scotland.* II. Edinburgh.

10 HICKMANN, H. (1957). 'Un zikr dans le mastaba de Debhen, Guizah'. *Jour. Internat. Folk Music Council* (Cambridge) 9, 59–62.

15 HIGGINS, R. A. and others (1968). 'The façade of the Treasury of Atreus at Mycenae'. *BSA* 63, 331–6.

12 HILL, Sir G. F. (1936). *Treasure Trove in Law and Practice.* Oxford.

10 HOLDEN, E. W. (1972). 'A Bronze Age cemetery-barrow on Itford Hill, Beddingham, Sussex'. *Sussex Archaeol. Collections* 110, 70–117.

15 HOOD, M. S. F. (1960). 'Tholos tombs of the Aegean'. *Antiquity* 34, 166–76.

— (1971). *The Minoans.* London and New York.

2 HOWELL, F. C. (1970). *Early Man*. Amsterdam.

8 IAKOVIDIS, Sp. E. (1966). 'A Mycenaean mourning custom'. *AJA* 70, 43–50.

6 IMMERWAHR, S. A. (1966). 'The use of tin on Mycenaean vases'. *Hesperia* 35, 381–96.

2 JAMES, E. O. (1957). *Prehistoric Religion*. London and New York.

JAZDZEWSKI, K. (1965). *Poland*. London and New York.

JIDEJIAN, N. (1968). *Byblos through the Ages.* Beirut.

11 — (1971). *Sidon through the Ages.* Beirut.

3 JOFFROY, R. (1954). *Le Trésor de Vix.* Paris.

— (1958). *Les Sépultures à Char du Premier Age du Fer en France.* Paris.

8 JONES, Gwyn (1968). *A History of the Vikings.* London.

12 KAMEL, A. (1907). *Le Livre des Perles Enfouies.* Cairo. (A translation of Arab treasure seekers' guides from the fifteenth to the seventeenth century, dealing partly with the pyramids and other tombs.)

14 KAMIL, J. (1973). *Luxor: a Guide to Ancient Thebes.* London.

8 KAPOSHINA, S. I. (1963). 'A Sarmatian royal burial at Novocherkassk'. *Antiquity* 37, 256–8.

16 KARAGEORGHIS, V. (1962). 'Mycenaean survivals in Cyprus . . .', in *Kadmos* I (i).

16 — (1967; 1970). *Excavations in the Necropolis of Salamis* I, II. Nicosia.

16 — (1969). *Salamis in Cyprus.* London.

KARO, G. (1943). *An Attic Cemetery.* Philadelphia.

20 KENDRICK, T. D. (1928). *The Archaeology of the Channel Islands. I. The Bailiwick of Guernsey.* London.

21 — (1937). 'The Hameldon Down Pommel'. *AntiqJ.* 17, 313.

KENYON, K. M. (1957). *Digging up Jericho.* London and New York.

5 — (1960, 1965). *Excavations at Jericho.* I, II. London.

2 KIVIKOSKI, E. (1967). *Finland.* London and New York.

KLINDT-JENSEN, O. (1957). *Denmark.* London and New York.

G KURTZ, D. C. and BOARDMAN, J. (1971). *Greek Burial Customs.* London.

11 LACAU, P. (1914). 'Suppressions et modifications des signes dans les textes funéraires'. *ZAS* 51, 1–64.

2 LAMBRECHTS, P. (1954). *L'Exaltation de la Tête dans' la Pensée et dans l'Art des Celtes.* Bruges.

8 LATTIMORE, R. (1942). *Themes in Greek and Latin Epitaphs.* Urbana.

13 LAUER, J. P. (1962). *L'Histoire Monumentale des Pyramides d'Egypte.* Cairo.

2 LEEDS, E. T. and HARDEN, D. B. (1936). *The Anglo-Saxon Cemetery at Abingdon, Berkshire.* Oxford.

17 LERICI, C. M. (1960). *Nuove Testimonianze dell'Arte e della Civiltà Etrusca.* Milan.

17 LERICI, C. M. (1962). *Italia Sepolta.* Milan.

12 LE ROUZIC, Z. (1939). 'Les monuments mégalithiques du Morbihan: cause de leur ruine . . .'. *Bull. Soc. Préhist. Fr.* 234.

18 LEVI, D. (1952). 'La Necropoli di Anghelu Ruju . . .' *Studi Sardi.* 10–11, 5–51. (Tombs A–D).

8 — (1956). 'The sarcophagus of Hagia Triada restored'. *Archaeology* 9, 192–9.

L'HELGOUACH, J. (1965). *Les Sépultures Mégalithiques en Armorique.* Rennes.

18 LILLIU, G. and SCHUBART, H. (1968). *Civiltà Mediterranée.* Milan.

15 LÖLLING, H.G. (1880). *Das Kuppelgrab bei Menidi.* Athens.

22 LYNCH, F. (1970). *Prehistoric Anglesey.* Llangefni.

18 MACKENZIE, D. (1910). 'The dolmens, tombs of the giants . . . of Sardinia'. *BSR* 5, 89–137.

18 — (1913). 'Dolmens . . . of Sardinia'. *BSR* 6, 127–70.

22 MACKENZIE, W.M. (1937). 'The dragonesque figure in Maeshowe, Orkney'. *Proc. Soc. Antiq. Scot.* 71, 157–73.

1 MALINOWSKI, T. (1963). 'Funeral customs of the Bronze Age and Iron Age in Poland'. *Archaeology* 16, 183–6.

6 MANNING, W.H. (1966). 'A group of bronze models from Sussex . . .'. *AntiqJ.* 46, 50–9.

13 MARAGIOGLIO, V. and RINALDI, C.A. (1964, 1965). *L'Architettura della Piramidi Menfite.* III, Maidum and Dahshur pyramids; IV, Kheops pyramid. Turin and Rapallo. Text in Italian and English.

8 MARINATOS, S. (1957). 'Excavations near Pylos, 1956'. *Antiquity* 31, 97–100.

10 MASCARÓ PASARIUS, J. (1968). *Preistoria de las Balears.* Palma.

MEANEY, A. (1964). *A Gazetteer of Early Anglo-Saxon Burial Sites.* London.

MELLAART, J. (1967). *Çatal Hüyük.* London and New York.

9 MERCER, S.A.B. (1952). *The Pyramid Texts.* IV. Excursus i. 'Heaven and how to get there'. 1–6. New York.

8 MOBERG, C.A. (1963). *Kiviks graven* (The Kivik Tomb). Stockholm.

2 MODDERMAN, P.J.R. (1964). 'The Neolithic burial vault at Stein'. *Analecta Praehistorica Leidensia.* I. Leiden.

11 MONNET, J. (1951). 'Les briques magiques du Musée du Louvre'. *Révue d'Egyptologie* 8, 151–62.

1 MONTET, P. (1925). *Les Scènes de la Vie Privée dans les Tombeaux Egyptiennes de l'Ancien Empire.* Strasbourg.

17 MORETTI, M. (1970). *New Monuments of Etruscan Painting.* Pennsylvania. Reproductions of thirty-seven recently discovered painted tombs at Tarquinia.

10 MORTILLET, A. de (1897). 'Les Monuments mégalithiques christianisés'. *Révue de l'Ecole d'Anthropologie* 7, 321–38.

G MORTIMER, J.R. (1905). *Forty Years' Researches in the British and Saxon Burial Mounds of East Yorkshire.* London.

2, 3 MURRAY, M.A. (1956). 'Burial customs and beliefs in the hereafter in predynastic Egypt'. *JEA* 42, 86–96.

10 MYLONAS, G.E. (1951). 'The cult of the dead in Helladic times'. *Studies presented to D.M. Robinson* I, edited by G.E. Mylonas. St Louis. 64–105.

15 — (1966). *Mycenae and the Mycenaean Age.* Princeton.

15 — (1967). *Mycenae: a Guide to its Ruins and its History.* Athens.

9 NAUERT, J.P. (1965). 'The Hagia Triadha sarcophagus: an Iconographical study'. *Antike Kunst* (Basel) 8, 91–8.

NEUSTUPNY, E. and J. (1961). *Czechoslovakia.* London and New York.

5, 9 NILSSON, M.P. (1950). *Minoan-Mycenaean Religion.* Second edition. Lund.

9 NOUR, Z. and others (1960). *The Cheops Boat.* I. Cairo.

2 OAKLEY, K.P. (1955). 'The earliest evidence of disposal of the dead'. *Nature* 176, 809.

2 — (1969). *Frameworks for Dating Fossil Man.* London.

22 O'KELLY, C. (1967). *Illustrated Guide to New Grange.* Wexford.

22 — (1969). 'Bryn Celli Ddu, Anglesey: a reinterpretation'. *Archaeol. Cambrensis* 118, 17–48.

10 O'NEIL, H.E. and GRINSELL, L.V. (1961). 'Gloucestershire Barrows'. *Trans. Bristol and Gloucestershire Archaeol. Soc.* 79, 1–15.

1 ONIANS, R.B. (1954). *Origins of European Thought.* 2nd edition. Cambridge.

22 Ó RÍORDÁIN, S.P. and DANIEL, G.E. (1964). *New Grange.* London and New York.

17 PALLOTTINO, M. (1957). *The Necropolis of Cerveteri.* Rome.

17 PARETI, L. (1947). *La Tomba Regolini-Galassi.* Vatican City.

11, 12 PARROT, A. (1939). *Malédictions et Violations des Tombes.* Paris.

PÄTZOLD, J. (1960). 'Rituelles Pflügen beim vorgeschichtlichen Totenkult . . .'. *Prähist. Zeitschrift* 38, 189–239.

10 PEET, T.E. (1916). 'A mortuary contract of XI Egyptian dynasty'. *Liverpool Annals of Archaeol. and Anth.* 7, 81–8.

12 — (1930). *The Great Tomb Robberies of the Twentieth Egyptian Dynasty.* Oxford.

9 PÉQUART, M. and LE ROUZIC, Z. (1927). *Corpus des Signes gravés des Monuments Mégalithiques du Morbihan.* Paris.

2 PÉQUART, M. and S.J. (1937). *Téviec.* Paris.

2 — (1954). *Hoëdic.* Antwerp.

18 PERETTI, G. (1966). 'Une sépulture campaniforme en rapport avec l'alignement des menhirs de Palaggiu'. *Congrès Préhist. de France* (Ajaccio), 230–42.

19 PERICOT GARCIA, L. (1972). *The Balearic Islands.* London and New York.

1, 2 PERROT, J. (1960). 'Excavations at 'Eynan ('Ein Mallaha)'. *Israel Exploration Journal* 10, 14–22.

1 — (1961). 'Une tombe à ossuaires du IV⁰ millénaire à Azor'. *Atiqot* 3, 1–83.

1, 2 — (1968). *La Préhistoire Palestinienne.* Paris. Le Natoufien, 368–84.

4 PERSSON, A.W. (1931). *Royal Tombs at Dendra.* Lund.

13 PETRIE, W.M.F. (1883). *Pyramids and Temples of Gizeh.* London.

— (1907). 'The soul-house in Egypt'. *Man* 7, article 71.

— (1914). 'Egypt in Africa'. *Ancient Egypt* I, 115–27, 159–70.

5 — (1935). *Shabtis.* London.

G — (1937). *The Funeral Furniture of Egypt.* London.

14 PIANKOFF, A. (1954). *The Tomb of Ramesses VI.* New York.

14 — (1962). *The Shrines of Tut-ankh-amun.* New York.

13 — (1968). *The Pyramid of Unas.* Princeton.

21 PIGGOTT, S. (1962a). *The West Kennet Long Barrow.* London.

2 — (1962b). 'From Salisbury Plain to South Siberia'. *WAM* 58, 93–7.

4, 6 — (1962c). 'Heads and Hoofs'. *Antiquity* 36, 110–18.

G — (1965). *Ancient Europe.* Edinburgh and Chicago.

21 —(1973). 'The Wessex culture of the Early Bronze Age', in *Victoria County History of Wiltshire* I(2), 352–75.

2 PIGGOTT, S. and C.M. (1944). 'Excavation of barrows on Crichel and Launceston Downs, Dorset'. *Archaeologia* 90, 47–80.

17 PINCELLI, R. (1943). 'Il Tumulo Vetuloniense della Pietrera', in *Studi Etruschi* 17, 47–113.

PIRENNE, J. (1936). 'Le culte funéraire en Egypte sous l'Ancien Empire', in *Mélanges F. Cumont* II. Brussels, 903–23.

13 POSENER-KRIEGER, P. and DE CENIVAL, J.L. (1968). *The Abu Sir Papyri.* London.

3 POWELL, T.G.E. (1953). 'The gold ornament from Mold, Flintshire, North Wales'. *PPS* 19, 161–79.

1 — (1960). 'Megalithic and other art: centre and west'. *Antiquity* 34, 180–90.

22 POWELL, T.G.E. and DANIEL, G.E. (1956). *Barclodiad y Gawres.* Liverpool.

8 PRESS, L. (1969). 'The location of Minoan displays'. *Man* N.S. 4, 250–5.

9 RADOMERSKY, P. (1955). *The Dead Obolus of the Slavs in Bohemia and Moravia.* Prague. English summary.

19 RAMIS Y RAMIS, J. (1818). *Antiguedades Celticas de la Isla de Menorca.* . . . Mahon.

9 RAMSKOU, T. (1960). 'Lindholm Høje'. Copenhagen.

G RENFREW, C. (1973). *Before Civilization: the Radiocarbon Revolution and Prehistoric Europe.* London.

RICE, T.T. (1957). *The Scythians.* London and New York.

9 RICHARDSON, E. (1964). *The Etruscans.* Chicago.

12 RIEK, G. and HUNDT, H.J. (1962). *Der Hohmi-*

chele. Ein Fürstengrabhugel der Spaten Hallstattzeit. . . . Berlin. Röm.-Germ. Forschungen, 25.

17 ROMANELLI, F. (1959). *Tarquinia: the Necropolis and Museum.* Rome.

1 ROSI, G. (1927). 'Sepulchral architecture as illustrated by the rock façades of Central Etruria'. *JRS* 17, 56–96.

G RUDENKO, S.I. (1970). *Frozen Tombs of Siberia.* London.

20 RYBOT, N.V.L. (1972). *La Hougue Bie, Jersey.* St Helier, Jersey.

5 SACHS, K. (1940). *The History of Musical Instruments.* New York.

4 SAKELLARAKIS, J.A. (1967). 'Minoan cemeteries at Archanes'. *Archaeology* 20, 276–81.

4, 8 SAKELLARAKIS, J.A. and PAPADEMETRIOU, J. (1970). 'Das Kuppelgrab A von Archanes und das kretisch-mykenische Tieropferritual'. *Prähist. Zeitschrift* 45, 135–219.

6 SAVORY, H.N. (1968). *Spain and Portugal.* London and New York.

1 SCHARFF, A. (1947). *Das Grab als Wohnhaus in der Ägyptischen Frühzeit.* Munich.

1 SCHMIDT, H. (1970). 'Vikingernes husformede gravsten', in *National Museets Arbegdsmark* (Copenhagen), 13–28.

22 SCOTT, J.G. (1966). *South-West Scotland.* Regional Archaeologies. London.

19 SERRA BELABRE, M.L. and ROSSELLO-BORDOY, G. (1971). 'Excavacion y restauracion de la naveta meridional de Rafal Rubi (Alayor, Menorca)'. *Noticiario Arqueologica Hispanico* XVI. Madrid.

9 SESTIERI, P.C. (1959). 'A new painted tomb at Paestum'. *Archaeology* 12, 33–7.

4 SHETELIG, H. (1954). 'The Viking Graves', in *Viking Antiquities in Great Britain and Ireland* VI, Oslo. 65–112.

1 SIMPSON, D.D.A. (1971), editor. *Economy and Settlement in Neolithic and Early Bronze Age Britain and Europe.* Leicester.

5 SMITH, I.F. and SIMPSON, D.D.A. (1964). 'A leather worker's grave from North Wiltshire'. *Antiquity* 38, 57–61.

SPAGUE, R. (1968). 'A suggested terminology and classification of burial description'. *American Antiquity* 33(4), 479–85.

SREJOVIC, D. (1972). *Lepenski Vir.* London.

STEAD, I.M. (1965). *The La Tène Cultures of Eastern Yorkshire.* Leeds.

1 STENBERGER, M. (1962). *Sweden.* London and New York.

6 STEWART, E. and J. (1950). *Vounous, 1937–8.* Lund.

2 STONE, J.F.S. (1934). 'A case of Bronze Age cephalotaphy on Easton Down'. *Man* 34, article 51.

8 STUKELEY, W. (1740). *Stonehenge: a Temple Restor'd to the British Druids.* London.

G SULIMIRSKI, T. (1970). *Prehistoric Russia.* London.

18 TARAMELLI, A. (1908). 'Alghero. Nuovi scavi nella . . . Anghelu Ruju'. *MonAnt.* 19, 397–540.

19 TARRADELL, M. (1964). 'La Nécropole de

Son Real'. *Excavs. Arqueolog. en España* 24. Madrid.

TAYLOUR, L.W. (1964). *The Mycenaeans.* London and New York.

14 THOMAS, E. (1966). *The Royal Necropolis of Thebes.* Princeton.

21 THOMAS, N. and APSIMON, A.M. (1966). 'Notes on some Early Bronze Age objects in Devizes Museum'. *WAM* 61, 1–8.

G THURNAM, J. (1870). 'Ancient British Barrows. I. Long Barrows'. *Archaeologia* 42, 161–244.

G — (1871). 'Ancient British Barrows. II. Round Barrows'. *Archaeologia* 43, 285–544.

10 TOWNSEND, E.D. (1955). 'A Mycenaean chamber tomb under the Temple of Ares'. *Hesperia* 24, 187–219.

G TOYNBEE, J.M.C. (1971). *Death and Burial in the Roman World.* London.

13 TRIMBLE, V. (1964). 'Astronomical investigations concerning the so-called air-shafts of Cheops' pyramid'. *MDIO* 10, 183–7.

2 TRINGHAM, R. (1971). *Hunters, Fishers and Farmers of Eastern Europe 6000–3000 B.C.* London.

TRUMP, D. (1966). *Central and Southern Italy.* London and New York.

8 UCKO, P. (1969). 'Ethnography and archaeological interpretation of funerary remains'. *World Archaeology* 2(ii), 262–80.

15 VALMIN, M.N. (1938). *The Swedish Messenia Expedition.* Lund.

19 VENY, C. (1968). *Las Cuevas Sepulcrales del Bronce Antiguo de Mallorca.* Madrid.

19 — (1970). 'Un avance sobre la necropolis de Cales Coves'. *Trabajos de Prehistoria* 27 (N.S.), 97–168.

8 VERMEULE, E. (1964). *Greece in the Bronze Age.* Chicago and London.

VON VACANO, O.W. (1960). *The Etruscans in the Ancient World.* London.

4 VYCICHL, W. (1959). 'The burial of the Sudanese kings in the Middle Ages . . .'. *Kush* 7, 221–2.

15 WACE, A.J.B. (1923). 'Mycenae: the Tholos Tombs'. *BSA* 25, 283–402.

15 — (1949). *Mycenae: an Archaeological History and Guide.* Princeton.

15 WACE, Helen (1966). *Mycenae Guide.* Athens.

1 WALTON, J. (1954). 'Hog-back tombstones and the Anglo-Danish house'. *Antiquity* 28, 68–77.

8 WATANABE, H. (1955). 'Disposal of the dead by the Ainu of Japan'. *Nature* 176, 809–12.

5 WEINBERG, S. (1965). 'Ceramics and the Supernatural: cult and burial evidence in the Aegean world', in MATSON, F.R. (editor), *Ceramics and Man.* Chicago. 187–201.

8 WELLER, M.E. (1970). 'The procession on the sarcophagus of the Mourning Women'. *California Studies in Classical Antiquity* 3, 219–27.

8 WERBROUCK, M. (1938). *Les Pleureuses dans l'Egypte Ancienne.* Brussels.

5 WHEELER, R.E.M. (1929). 'A Roman pipe-burial from Caerleon, Monmouthshire'. *AntiqJ.* 9, 1–7.

WHITEHOUSE, R. (1967). 'The megalithic monuments of south-east Italy'. *Man* N.S. 2, 347–65.

— (1972). 'The rock-cut tombs of the central Mediterranean'. *Antiquity.* 46, 275–81.

17 WILKINSON, J.G. (1856). 'On an Etruscan tomb at Cerveteri' [the Tomb of Reliefs]. *Jour. Brit. Archaeol. Assoc.* 12, 1–34.

5 WILLIAMS, A. (1948). 'Excavations in Barrow Hill Fields, Radley, Berkshire, 1944'. *Oxoniensia* 13, 1–17.

5 WINBOLT, S.E. (1935). 'Romano-British Sussex', in *Victoria County History of Sussex* 3, London. 49, 54, 67.

6 WINLOCK, H.E. (1955). *Models of Daily Life in Ancient Egypt from the Tomb of Meket-re at Thebes.* Harvard and London.

G WOOLEY, C.L. (1934). *Ur Excavations.* II. The Royal Cemetery. London.

G — (1954). *Excavations at Ur.* London.

21 WORTH, R.H. (1953). *Dartmoor.* Plymouth.

9 WRIGHT, R.P. and RICHMOND, I.A. (1955). *Catalogue of the Roman Inscribed and Sculptured Stones in the Grosvenor Museum, Chester.* Chester.

21 WYMER, J. (1966). 'Excavation of Lambourn long barrow'. *Berkshire Archaeol. J.* 62, 1–16.

12 XANTHOUDIDES, S. (1924). *Vaulted Tombs of the Mesara.* London. [Reprinted 1971 with introduction by K. Branigan].

12 ZÜRN, H. (1970). *Hallstattforschungen in Nord-württemberg: die Grabhügel von Asperg.* Stuttgart.

General

Locations of tombs

Sites with little or no structure, including all those of Palaeolithic, Mesolithic and most of early Neolithic period, are excluded.